James Stewart

9 August 2024

THE

SPECTATOR.

Edward Evan's Book

1770.

VOLUME *the* EIGHTH.

The

THE

SPECTATOR.

Edward Evan's Book

1770.

VOLUME *the* EIGHTH.

EDINBURGH:

Printed by A. DONALDSON, and fold at his
Shops in London and Edinburgh.

MDCCLXVI.

IN SEARCH
OF THE LAST BARD

The Life & Legacy of Edward Evan
(1716-1798)

James C. Stewart

Foreword by Mary-Ann Constantine

CYNON VALLEY HISTORY SOCIETY
CYMDEITHAS HANES CWM CYNON

First published in 2024
Cynon Valley History Society § Cymdeithas Hanes Cwm Cynon
www.cvhs.org.uk

ISBN 978-0-9531076-6-7

Front cover illustration by Grace Payne and Lexi Richards,
Ysgol Gyfun Gymraeg Rhydywaun ©Addoldai Cymru
Back cover photograph of the Cynon valley from Ton Coch © James C. Stewart

Printed by Print Evolution, Merthyr Tydfil

I ddisgynyddion Edward Ifan a Pali Ton Coch

To the Descendants of Edward Evan and Pali Ton Coch

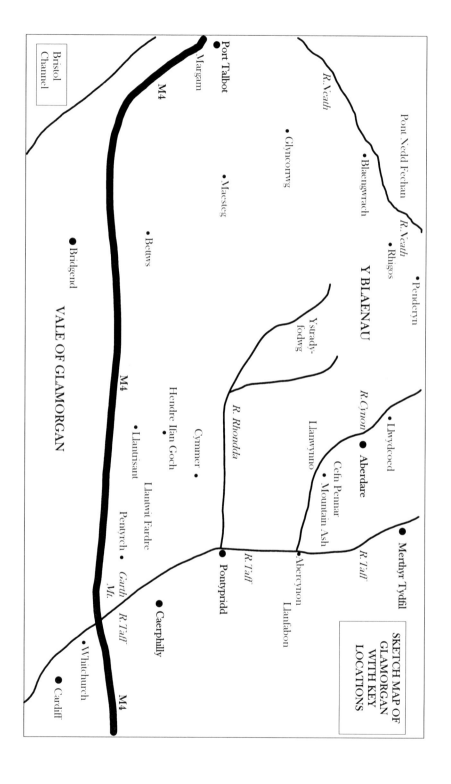

SKETCH MAP OF
GLAMORGAN
WITH KEY
LOCATIONS

Bristol
Channel

VALE OF GLAMORGAN

Y BLAENAU

M4

• Port Talbot

• Margam

R.Neath

Pont Nedd Fechan

R.Neath

• Rhigos

• Blaengwrach

• Glyncorrwg

• Maesteg

• Bridgend

• Betws

• Penderyn

Ystrady-
fodwg

R. Rhondda

R.Cynon

Llanwynno

• Llwydcoed

Cefn Pennar

• Aberdare

• Mountain Ash

• Abercynon

Llanfabon

• Merthyr Tydfil

R. Taff

Cymmer •

Hendre Ifan Goch
•

• Llantrisant

Llantwit Fardre

Pentyrch •

• Pontypridd

R. Taff

Garth
Mt.

R. Taff

• Caerphilly

• Whitchurch

M4

• Cardiff

CONTENTS

APPENDICES

ACKNOWLEDGEMENTS   175

FOREWORD

University of Wales Centre for Advanced Welsh and Celtic Studies

Like many other people, I imagine, I only knew Edward Evan indirectly, through the words of his friend and disciple, Iolo Morganwg, as the only other 'regular Bard in Glamorgan, or in the world'. The work of G.J. Williams and my own colleagues helped to contextualise that bold claim, describing a world of learning and poetic craft in the Glamorgan uplands that shaped Iolo's vision of himself, and this respectable Dissenting Minister, as 'the only legitimate descendants of the so-long-celebrated Ancient British Bards'. But I was busy trying to fathom Iolo himself (I never even got close, of course), and Edward Evan remained a figure in the hinterland – the man who died on the day of the Gorsedd on the Garth in June 1798; a shaper, an influence, and then an absence.

This book, for the first time, brings Edward Evan of Ton Coch fully into view. Poet and minister, farmer, musician, neighbour, husband, father, his long life spanned a period of intellectual and economic change whose impact would come into dizzying effect with the massive industrialization of the valleys in the following century. James Stewart's vivid and sympathetic portrayal of Evan and his world offers multiple windows onto the eighteenth century, not only in the Cynon Valley, but across south Wales. And this is much more than a standard third-person biography. A career in journalism has trained Stewart to quiz his sources, and to seek out experts and practitioners in different fields: what exactly did happen to the manuscript of the Gododdin during Edward Evan's lifetime? How do you string a harp with horsehair, and what are the qualities of its sound? There are many voices in this book beside those of the author and his subject.

Stewart's family connection to Edward Evan provokes reflections on how memories are shaped and become a part of history. He uses Evan's own Welsh-language poems as the starting point for his biographical explorations. First published in 1804 and curated by the poet's son Rhys, the collection was reprinted four times in the century following his death. Extending the story into the lifetime of Rhys Evans reveals how the poems were read and repurposed in radical new contexts, underscoring the importance of the Glamorgan bard's legacy. They certainly evoke a world which in many ways is wholly unlike our own. It is difficult to imagine those sparser landcapes of the pre-industrial Blaenau – the difficult roads, the different possibilities and expectations of community, language, work and worship. But Stewart has a deft way of layering new landscapes over old, and helping the reader to understand how many of the patterns which created eighteenth-century south Wales shaped, and continue to shape, our world today.

§

A NOTE ON TRANSLATION AND SPELLING

All translations are the author's, unless otherwise stated.

I have maintained the spelling and punctuation from original sources – which often differs from modern practice – apart from very rare alterations for clarity (e.g. 'ascent' instead of 'assent' in a poem in English by Iolo Morganwg).

Since I am writing in English I have normally used the English version of place names, so Aberdare (not Aberdâr), but have kept the original when quoting.

People's names can appear in different versions. So Edward Evan can be Edward Ifan, Edward ab (or ap) Ifan (Edward son of Ifan). He was sometimes referred to as Edward Evans (which became the family surname used by his sons). In his bardic guise he was often referred to as Iorwerth (the Welsh version of Edward); Iorwerth ap Ifan, Iorwerth Gwynfardd Morganwg etc. I refer to him as Edward Evan but have kept the original form when quoting.

Quotations from Edward Evan's poems are from the 1874 edition of *Afalau'r Awen* unless otherwise stated.

J.C.S.

TO THE READER

I believe I have obtained what is more precious in my sight than land or belongings – a consciousness of the values cherished by my forefathers and a sense of personal responsibility for their survival.[1]

This book is dedicated to my aunt Mary Green, born Mary Kingsbury, namesake and descendant of Edward Evan's granddaughter. Her research laid the foundations for this exploration of the life and legend of the Bard of Ton Coch.

When my mother and her sister were girls in a Carmarthenshire vicarage in the 1930s, they looked forward to the annual visit of their aunt from the mining valleys of Glamorgan. She would tell the children stories about their father's family in Aberdare, which they never forgot. There was the tale of an ancestor who went to jail after losing a legal battle over the ownership of coal below her farm. Then there was a blind harpist whose harp remained in the family for a hundred years – until it was abandoned in Belgium on the eve of the Second World War. When the aunt had gone home, my grandmother would tell the children to take no notice of these stories told by her husband's sister; they were rubbish – all made up – she said.

Many years later it become clear that there was more than a grain of truth in these legends. There was indeed a blind harpist, or at least a harpist who went blind. And the woman, who was indeed arrested, was the granddaughter of an even more interesting character, the poet and radical minister Edward Evan of Ton Coch, who lived from 1716 to 1798. The harpist was his son, who learned the instrument from his father. Edward Evan's poems were so popular that they were printed four times in the century after his death. Remembered, at least among Welsh speakers, in the first half of the twentieth century, he would be all but forgotten by the twenty-first.

Remarkable stories were told about old Edward Evan after his death. He was revered as 'the last of the ancient bards', a direct descendant of the Celtic druids and the essential link between the distant past and the Gorsedd of Bards created by Iolo Morganwg. And it was said that he had preserved the priceless manuscript of the earliest poem written in Welsh, the *Gododdin* of Aneirin, which had gone missing sometime in the late eighteenth century.

There is a brief biography of the bard in the fourth edition of his poetry published in 1874. This was the starting point for a journey of exploration to uncover more about his life and work – and the lost world in which he lived and flourished.

He is a fascinating figure not only in himself but because he stands at the threshold of the industrial revolution which changed the face of south Wales beyond all recognition. He was one of those whose religious radicalism, rooted in the politics of the seventeenth century, kept the flame of liberty alive for the democratic campaigners of the nineteenth. Morgan Williams, the leading Merthyr Chartist in the 1830s, remembered Edward Evan for his advanced political views. But his poetry appealed equally to radicals, ironmasters and landed gentry in the new industrialised Glamorgan of the century after his death.

The son of a family of tenant farmers, with little or no formal education in Welsh or English, he was a weaver, a harpist, a carpenter and glazier, a farmer, a woodsman, a bard, and a radical minister of religion. He was remembered as 'a poet in a thousand' and 'a true lover of the Welsh language; a wise and learned singer and preacher; a brotherly poet; a man of good works'. It was said that his fame would last 'as long as the River Taff flows to the sea'.

Researching this story has meant exploring many fields – fields of scholarship and fields in the landscape of Glamorgan – to bring the world of Edward Evan alive and to trace the enormous upheavals experienced by his people in the century when his poetry was popular.

If this story has strengths, it is largely thanks to those who have spent long years investigating this world. If it contains errors or misinterpretations, the fault is entirely my own. As Rhys Evans wrote in his preface to the first edition of his late father's poems 220 years ago, 'I ask you to tolerate anything you find wrong or erroneous … I beg you to remember that it is easier to find faults and errors than to correct them, which is the wish of your fellow countryman'. J.C.S. 2024

---

[1] Williams D. J., *Hen Dŷ Ffarm* ('The Old Farmhouse') (1953), translated by Waldo Williams.

CHAPTER 1

1840 – False Gods

Mae pedwar duw ym Mrydain Fawr,	*Four gods there are in Britain now,*
Yn cael eu dirfawr barchu,	*And all respected greatly,*
Yn lle Duw'r nefoedd doeth o hyd,	*Instead of heaven's all-wise God,*
Sy'n dal y byd i fynu. [1]	*Who holds the world in safety.*

In 1840 the twin iron towns of Merthyr Tydfil and Aberdare were 'the heartland' of the campaign for democratic reform and the People's Charter.[2] The previous year as many as twenty Chartists had died when troops opened fire on them in Newport. The leading Chartist, Morgan Williams, printed two poems in September 1840 in his radical Welsh newspaper, *Udgorn Cymru*. The first, by an anonymous poet, attacked the power of Mammon in the land; the second, written in the previous century by Edward Evan of Ton Coch, echoed that theme, condemning the worship of the 'false gods' of anger, avarice, pride and gluttony.[3]

Merthyr was by far the biggest town in Wales, and 'the first Welsh town to be captured by radical dissent'.[4] The papers published there by Morgan Williams and David John – *Udgorn Cymru (The Trumpet of Wales)* and the *Advocate & Merthyr Free Press* – were considered dangerous and seditious by the authorities. The Marquess of Bute, Lord Lieutenant of Glamorgan, was warned by magistrates that the issue in which Edward Evan's poem was printed 'contains a body of instructions for the organisation of the Chartist Association throughout the Kingdom'.[5]

In this time of political ferment and establishment paranoia, poems condemning 'false gods' could be read as a thinly-veiled attack on the wealth, power, and greed of ironmasters, the landed gentry and the Justices of the Peace. Indeed, later in 1840, the magistrates of Merthyr sent the Home Secretary a copy of the *Advocate*, which included an outspoken attack on 'the political corruption of our Rulers, the dishonesty and fraud of Mammon-seeking men'.[6]

The 1830s had been a time of turmoil across Wales. In 1831, ironworkers in Merthyr and Aberdare had staged an armed uprising which ended with the hanging of Dic Penderyn, who had been falsely convicted of killing a soldier. Towards the end of the decade, a rural revolt in the name of Rebecca saw attacks on tollgates by farmers in the west. And the campaign for democratic reform gathered widespread support in the industrial areas of Glamorgan and Monmouthshire. In 1839 gatherings of five thousand or more were held near Aberdare and Merthyr – at Hirwaun, Penyrheolgerrig and Rhymney.[7] And in November that year 'physical force' Chartists had marched on Newport and been met by the armed forces of the state.

This is the context in which an apparently innocuous 'moral' poem by a revered Welsh bard from the previous century was reprinted for the readers of a paper monitored and feared by the British establishment. Many of the leading Chartists and other prominent figures in the iron towns had subscribed to a new edition of Edward Evan's poetry published in 1837.[8] To explain its appeal, its impact, and its relevance, it is necessary to explore the life and legend of a poet who was remembered both as a radical dissenter and as the supposed last of the ancient 'druidic' bards.

---

[1] Edward Evan, 'Mae Pedwar Duw ym Mrydain Fawr', *Afalau'r Awen* (1837 & 1874, p.59).
[2] Gwyn A Williams, 'Dic Penderyn', *Llafur* Vol 2. No.3 (1978), p. 110.
[3] *Udgorn Cymru (Trumpet of Wales)*, (September 1840), p.6.
[4] *Llafur* Vol 2. No.3, p. 110.
[5] Report of the magistrates of Lower Miskin & Caerphilly, 3 Oct. 1840, Cardiff Central Library: CCL Bute XX.161.
[6] *The Advocate & Merthyr Free Press*, 1 Nov 1840; National Archives: HO1840/57. John Bruce Pryce of Dyffryn, was Merthyr's Stipendiary Magistrate and the landlord of of Rhys Evans, son and publisher of the poet, at Ton Coch.
[7] Joe England, Morgan Williams: *Merthyr's Forgotten Leader*, Merthyr Tydfil Historical Society (2014).
[8] See Chapter 19.

CHAPTER 2

2021 – Lives & Legends

Yn iach iti'r hen fwthyn,
Hen gartre'r beirdd dros ronyn,
Lle buont ganwaith wrth y tân
Yn gwneuthur cân ac englyn.

Dros fwy na chant o flwydda'
O fewn i'r breswyl yma,
Bu'r awen yn blaguro'n llon,
Ond darfu hon ei gyrfa. [1]

Farewell to you, old cottage,
Farewell old home of the bards,
Where many times beside the hearth
They made their songs and poems.

For a hundred years and more,
Within this little dwelling,
The muse - the 'awen'- lived and bloomed,
But now her songs are silent.

It was in the spring of 2021, as pandemic restrictions were loosened, that my search began for traces in the landscape of Edward Evan of Ton Coch. I walked with a friend across the golf course at Mountain Ash, on a plateau high above the Cynon Valley, looking for the remains of a farmhouse whose name was once well-known across Wales as the home of the bard. The fairways between tee and green have replaced fields with names like Gwaun Pennar Isaf, Drysiog, Cae Pen y Rhiw and the meadow called Ton Coch, the Red Field, which gave its name to his farm and his home.

It was the first day the course had been open for over a year. We met a pair of veterans, enjoying the spring sunshine, who remembered when the remains of the farmhouse walls were still standing. They knew a club member whose grandmother had lived there until her marriage around the time of the Great War. We followed their directions to a spot near the fourteenth green where a pile of overgrown stones was all that remained of a cottage built in the late seventeenth century, not long before Edward Evan's birth.[2] Below the site, the name survives in Ton Coch Terrace on the steep road that climbs up towards Cefnpennar ridge and the mountain separating the ancient parishes of Aberdare and Merthyr Tydfil.

Though he is all but forgotten now, Edward Evan was remembered and honoured a century ago. On 8 July 1916, the cottage on the golf course was the destination of a group of pilgrims who gathered to mark the bicentenary of his birth. Speeches were made and they heard a poem composed in honour of the poet and his home, including these lines:

Y Ton Coch fu'n tanio cân   *Ton Coch lit the flame of song*
Ar dafod Edward Ifan.[3]   *On Edward Evan's tongue.*

It was after the death of Edward's son that the family's connection with Ton Coch was broken and the verses at the head of this chapter were composed by his grandson. The poem is a tribute not only to a family of poets and musicians, but an elegy for a vanished world. Theirs was a way of life which stretched back hundreds of years in the uplands of Glamorgan, the life of small farmers and craftsmen living among the sparsely populated hills and, in this family, cultivating not only the land but also the musical and poetic traditions whose roots lay deep in the history of Wales.

In Edward Evan's work as a *bardd gwlad*, a people's poet, farming was a constant theme, which is no surprise, considering that it was at the heart of his own life from the time of his birth. In a poignant tribute almost a century after his death a local poet prophesied that his fame would live 'as long as the meadows of Ton Coch bring forth clover and nourishment for man and beast'.[4]

In July 1916 the Great War was in its second year, but the pilgrims on the golf course honoured the memory of the bard.[5] Forty years later still, shortly after the Second World War, an account of the poet and his background ended with a biblical reference from the chapter of Ecclesiasticus which begins 'Let us now praise famous men'.[6]

> Was he not one of those about whom it was said that they were 'leaders of the people by their counsels, and by their knowledge of learning meet for the people, wise and eloquent in their instructions; such as found out musical tunes and recited verses in writing'.[7]

The legends associated with Edward Evan go back to the days of Henry

VIII and an ancestor, a blacksmith called Hywel Gwyn y Gôf. He lived at Pantygerdinen in the parish of Aberdare and owned the iron furnace at the Dyffryn. Hywel became rich, but he feared for his wealth, so he went with his young daughter Gwenllian and buried his gold under one of the cairns on the mountain between Aberdare and Merthyr.

Nothing else is known about Hywel Gwyn or Gwenllian until she married a man by the name of Dociar. She remembered seeing her father hiding money on the mountain, so she and her husband went and found the gold. And that's why the cairn was named after her, Carn Gwenllian Dociar.[8] Another legendary ancestor lived a century later, in the time of Oliver Cromwell. Hywel's great grandson Rhys was renowned for a feat in which he used his team of oxen to clear away many great oaks from the forest on Craig y Bwlch at the top of Hirwaun Common.

This was an old established family and their descendant, a great grandson of Rhys, was Edward Evan of Ton Coch, whose poems were so popular that they were printed four times in the following century, when his own legend flourished.

He was revered as 'the last of the ancient bards', a direct descendant of the Celtic druids, and the essential link between the distant past and the Gorsedd of Bards, created by Iolo Morganwg, and embedded in the revived Eisteddfod. Another legend was that he had preserved the priceless manuscript of the earliest poem written in Welsh, the *Gododdin* of Aneirin, which had been lost sometime in the late eighteenth century.

It was not only as this legendary figure that he was remembered, but as one of those whose religious radicalism, rooted in the politics of the seventeenth century, kept the flame of liberty alive for the Chartists of the nineteenth. He stood at the threshold of the industrial revolution and his poetry resonated in the new age of iron and coal which changed the face of south Wales beyond all recognition.

The son of tenant farmers, with little or no formal education in Welsh or English, he was a weaver, a harpist, a carpenter and glazier, a farmer, a woodsman, a bard, and a radical minister of religion. Iolo called him 'a poet in a thousand'[9] and he was remembered as 'a true lover of the Welsh language; a wise and learned singer and preacher; a brotherly poet; a man of good works'.

Edward Evan was the only person born in the old parish of Aberdare included in the first edition of the Dictionary of National Biography in 1889.[10]

EVANS, EDWARD (1716–1798), Welsh poet, was a 'bard according to the rites and ceremonies of the bards of Britain,' and his pedigree is traced in one unbroken line to the ancient Druids. He was pastor at the Old Meeting House, Aberdare, from 1772 to 1798.[11]

It is noteable that this short entry makes no mention of his radical dissenting views. With its reference to bards and druids, it gives less weight to the facts of his life or the impact of his poetry than to the legends which grew around him after his death on the Summer Solstice in 1798 – though those legends too had a radical edge.

---

[1] Rees Evans, 'Farewell to Ton Coch' (c.1871) included in *Afalau'r Awen* (1874), pp.163-4. 'Awen' ('The Muse') was included in the title given to the second and later editions of Edward Evan's poetic works – *Afalau'r Awen* ('The Fruits of the Muse').

[2] Royal Commission on Ancient & Historic Monuments in Wales, *Inventory of Ancient Monuments in Glamorgan, Vol. IV, Part 2* (1988), p.290.

Geoff Matthews, former chairman of the Golf Club, remembers the ruins of the cottage being demolished to use the stone on another project on the course.

[3] Henry Lloyd ('Ap Hefin'), *Y Darian* (13 July 1916).

[4] 'Mabonwyson' (William Henry Dyer c. 1837-81), *Y Gwladgarwr* (21 January 1881).

[5] This was the end of the first week of the Battle of the Somme, in which more than a million men from both sides eventually became casualties.

[6] R. T. Jenkins, *Bardd a'i Gefndir*, Trans. Hon. Soc. Cymmrodorion (1948), p.144.

[7] *Ecclesiasticus* 44.1.

[8] See *Gardd Aberdâr* (1854), p.42. Carn Gwenllian Dociar is one of several cairns on Aberdare Mountain.

[9] Iolo Morganwg, 'Marwnad Edward Evan', NLW MS21423E.

[10] George Smith, *Dictionary of National Biography* (1885-1900). Henry Austin Bruce, Lord Aberdare, former Home Secretary, born in Dyffryn House below Ton Coch in 1815, was included only in a supplement to the Dictionary published later.

[11] Edward Evan actually retired as Minister at the Old Meeting House in 1796. The entry in the *Dictionary of Welsh Biography*, by R. T. Jenkins (1959), makes no mention of druidic bards.

CHAPTER 3

1798 – Alban Hefin – Midsummer Day

Old Garth in Glamorgan, majestic and bold,
That mountain deemed sacred by Druids of old,
Displays its ascent to the traveller's eye
Like a high turnpike road that leads up to the sky.

Here barrows and cromlecks are scattered around -
By old painted Britons 'twas called holy ground,
And the bards here related the hero's high deeds
and call'd him a God who for liberty bleeds.[1]

The legend of Edward Evan begins with the day he died, 21 June 1798. It was Midsummer Day, when his friend Edward Williams had gathered a group of poets and fellow radicals on top of the hill which dominates the gorge of the River Taff above Cardiff and the Bristol Channel. To mark *Alban Hefin*, as they called the summer solstice, they laid out small stones[2] in a circle around the prehistoric burial mound[3] which stands on the summit. In this sacred space, Williams, in his bardic role as 'Iolo Morganwg',[4] unsheathed a sword and summoned the Bards of Glamorgan to a *gorsedd* in the name of 'God and All Goodness' calling out '*Y Gwir yn erbyn y Byd*' – 'The Truth against the World'.[5]

In the century after his death, as the legend of Edward Evan developed, his absence from that gathering on the Garth Mountain in June 1798 was an essential part of the story. 'He died on the day he had appointed to meet the Bards of the Chair of Glamorgan'[6]. He was 'a bard according to the rites and ceremonies of the Bards of Britain', with a pedigree that could be traced in a direct line from the ancient Druids.[7] And that 'unbroken line' could be followed without any of the 'trickery' a priest would need to establish his supposed 'apostolic succession' from St Peter.[8]

The legend had longevity. It lived on in an obituary for Edward Evan's son, Rhys, who died in 1867, where his father was described as 'at one period the sole living Druidical Bard – a bard according to the rites and ceremonies of the Island of Britain. By him the renowned Iolo Morganwg was ordained and the order preserved'. [9] Forty years later it was again claimed that 'the preservation of this noted bardic cult may be traced mainly to his efforts'.[10]

'The Mountain Shepherd', the poem quoted above, was written by Iolo Morganwg in 1780 and encapsulates all the key elements of his philosophy. First and foremost, the location is Glamorgan, the centre of Iolo's universe. And it is a high point, a mountain 'sacred' to Druids since the days when ancient Britons went about like painted Picts. There are barrows or 'cromlechs' with echoes of the 'Druidic temple' at Stonehenge. And there are bards gathered here – poets to 'praise men of courage' who fought and bled for 'Liberty' in the face of oppression.

The first meeting of the Gorsedd of Bards of the Island of Britain, with its 'druidic' ceremonies was held by Iolo Morganwg on Primrose Hill in London in 1792. In the years that followed he had been marking each solstice and equinox with a bardic meeting, a *gorsedd* or 'eisteddfod', on one of the outlying hills of the Glamorgan uplands. These sound today like the gatherings of a group of poetic eccentrics, but they were seen as something more sinister by the magistrates of Wales at the time, just as the Chartists would be fifty years later. After the outbreak of war between England and revolutionary France in 1793, the authorities kept a close eye on these 'bards', who mixed their ancient Druidism with a dissenting 'Jacobin' radicalism and calls for Liberty and The Rights of Man'.[11]

In exploring the life and times of Edward Evan of Aberdare, the stories told about him after his death have a powerful resonance. And for me, the meeting on the Garth is particularly resonant because I have walked there for forty years and lived at its foot – in the village of Gwaelod y Garth – for fifteen. Now, whenever I pass through the fields below the mountain, or cross its top, I think of the bards of Glamorgan and their *gorsedd* on the day the old poet died. In 2022, more than two hundred years after that midsummer meeting, I witnessed a very different gathering on the mountain as the sun set on the second of June. Hundreds of people trooped up to the barrow, not to honour republicanism or liberty but to see a beacon lit in honour of the Diamond Jubilee of Queen Elizabeth, a direct descendant of George of Hannover who had come to the throne just two years before Edward Evan's birth.[12] From this high point, answering flames could be seen on hilltops across the Bristol Channel. As the crowd sang 'God Save the Queen' that night, I wondered whether any would have known of that meeting long ago, when Iolo Morganwg and his companions came under suspicion of treason for supporting the revolutionary ideas of the French, who had sent their own monarch to the guillotine just three years earlier. Was there, somewhere in the distance, a faint echo of Iolo's *Breiniau Dŷn* ('The Rights of Man'), which they sang to the tune of 'God Save the King' at his republican gatherings?[13]

There seems no doubt that Edward Evan's absence would have been keenly felt. Iolo referred to him as *Iorwerth Gwynfardd Morganwg*, 'Edward the Druid of Glamorgan'.[14] The year before he died one of the bardic fraternity published a poem urging him to attend a forthcoming 'eisteddfod'. Addressed as a 'famous bard, of great talent', he was asked to come to support and teach his fellows, because without him their meetings 'lacked energy and vigour'.

Ni wneuthom yn hwyrol gymdeithas chwarterol,	*We recently held our quarterly meeting,*
	The timing was good,
I gwrddyd yn brydol, anwyfol yw'r nôd,	*but we failed in our aim;*
	Our practice was hopeless without
Ac hefyd aniban heb Iorwerth ap Ioan;	*Edward Evan*
I ddatgan y drefan o'u drafod.[15]	*To show us the rules and to kindle the flame.*

The legend that he had a special, inherited 'druidic' authority can be traced back to the years before Iolo held the first meeting of the Gorsedd of Bards, and to a letter published in 1789 in the *Gentleman's Magazine*, a journal which was read throughout the English-speaking world. The letter stated that 'besides Edward Williams' (Iolo Morganwg), 'there is, I believe, now remaining only one regular Bard in Glamorgan, or in the world: this is the Rev. Mr. Edward Evans, of Aberdare, a Dissenting Minister. These two persons are the only legitimate descendants of the so-long-celebrated Ancient British Bards; at least they will allow no others this honourable title.'[16]

It is generally believed that 'J.D. of Cowbridge' who signed that letter was in fact Iolo Morganwg himself; in any case, its effect was to burnish his bardic credentials. The importance of the story was that if Edward

Evan had at one point been the last surviving Druidic Bard, then Iolo, who was thirty years younger, could inherit from him by 'apostolic succession'. The legend cast an elderly dissenting minister from the remote parish of Aberdare in the role of the last survivor and 'the continuing link between ancient and modern Druidism'.[17] After Edward Evan's death in 1798, Iolo would claim that he alone preserved 'the learning of the ancient bards of the nation'.[18]

Edward Evan was revered not only for his supposed bardic heritage, but because he was reputed to have had a tangible link to one of the earliest and most celebrated of Welsh poets, Aneirin the 'High King of Bards'. In a legend that travelled as far as America, it was said that he had preserved the priceless manuscript of the sixth century poem, the *Gododdin*.

The legends, as much as the facts about his interests, activities and connections, make him a fascinating representative of eighteenth-century Glamorgan. At the time of his death in 1798, there were just 1,400 inhabitants in what was still the largely rural parish of Aberdare, but in the following century industrialisation made the Cynon valley 'the Australia of Glamorgan'.[19] First the ironworks, then the coal mines pulled in workers and their families from all over Wales and beyond. By 1871, the population had reached 40,000. The valley emerged from the squalor of its industrial 'frontier' years and Aberdare became a proud town boasting one of the finest public parks in Britain. Edward Evan's son, born in the old world, witnessed the transformation of the valley from the sparsely populated, traditional, rural society of his father to an urban 'splendour' which inspired comparison with the cities of the Continent. The mountains remained, whitewashed farmhouses like Ton Coch still stood on the hillsides, but the world below had been transformed, as this description of the area in 1871 makes vividly clear.

> If only the old bard, Edward Evan of Ton Coch could look down at the valley, from the dwelling where he spent most of his life ... and behold the magnificent buildings, the numerous businesses, the tall chimneys, the many places of worship, the broad streets, the fine schools, and the thousands of people crowded together and weaving their way around; instead of the deep silence which reigned then, he would hear engines – almost entangled together – whistling, wheezing and puffing. Instead of the splendour of dark winter nights, he would see gaslights, like a host of stars, illuminating all sides. Indeed, if the old bard could

only see these changes, he would turn into a Druid in an instant.
He would believe he had been transformed and transported to
one of the splendid cities of the Continent.[20]

This talk of a bard who might 'turn into a druid' sits strangely in the
hard-edged industrial society which the booming iron and coal industries
had created in the uplands of Glamorgan, where Edward Evan's poetry
resonated with the Chartists campaigning for democracy in the 1830s and
40s. But 'the renowned' Iolo Morganwg, his Gorsedd of 'druidic' Bards,
and the restored Eisteddfod represented another aspect of nineteenth
century Wales, one based on a nostalgic reverence for the language, poetry,
music and ancient roots of the Welsh people. This is the frame into which
the legend of Edward Evan fits.

Facts and legends; it's all about the stories you tell. For Iolo and his
bardic circle it was about their links to the ancient druids. They made
a physical connection to that story at the burial mound, the barrow, on
top of the Garth Mountain where they met. For them it was a holy relic,
concrete evidence that they were following in the footsteps of their 'druidic'
predecessors.

Tales of druids and their remains had roots in the previous century when
John Aubrey was one of the first antiquarians to describe Stonehenge and
other stone circles as 'druidic temples'.[21] There were also stories about
'druidic' relics on the hills above Aberdare, where numerous cairns were
interpreted as ancient burial sites. In a history of the parish published in
1853, there is a clear reference to the legendary Edward Evan.

> There are certainly druidic remains, such as stone burial
> chambers, in Aberdare and it's believed that there were druids
> in this parish more recently than anywhere else in Wales. In
> the last century several burial chambers were discovered on the
> mountain between Merthyr and Aberdare.[22]

In one of these 'the small bones of old druids' were found. Other stone
burial chambers – *cistfeini* – were believed to lie on the same mountain,
beneath cairns like Carn Gwenllian Dociar, with its links to stories about
the earliest known ancestor of the 'Druid' Edward Evan.

Then there's the legend that Edward was the 'old person at Aberdâr'
mentioned in the manuscript of the *Gododdin*, as one of those who had
preserved this treasure of the Welsh nation.

There are different ways one can approach such stories. As a sceptical
journalist, I want to track down the evidence, pin down the facts, discover

more of the context and present a documentary account of Edward Evan's life and legacy. There is strong factual evidence of the popularity of his poetry in the new industrial world of the1830s, among the Chartists and even among their opponents. Legends are more elusive, but they have a life and a validity of their own. Their very existence is a fact, and they can illuminate a different sort of truth. They deserve to be heard, enjoyed, and explored as a rich inheritance and as colourful reminders of how people made sense of their lives and their connections.

The iron and coal industries endured for two hundred years, but heavy industry disappeared from the Cynon valley as quickly as it had arrived. Gone now are the mines, the tall chimneys, the canal, and all but one railway. Who could forget passing at night the flaming Phurnacite Plant, which produced smokeless fuel for the cities of England and pumped out pollution for the people of the valley? A Satanic Mill if ever there was one, it is also gone. The many places of worship are mostly empty, including the successor to the Old Meeting House, where Edward Evan was minister for twenty-five years.[23] And almost lost too is any memory of the life and work of the harpist and bard, whose poetry was so popular in the new, industrialised Glamorgan, who became a legendary link to an imagined, 'druidic' past, and of whom it was said that his fame would last 'as long as the River Taff flows to the sea'.[24]

---

[1] Iolo Morganwg,'The Mountain Shepherd' (1780), quoted in Ffion Mair Jones *The Bard is a Very Singular Character* (2010), pp. 196-7 & 284-5. (Ascent is spelt 'assent' in the original.)

[2] See Cathryn Charnell-White *Bardic Circles* (2007), p.4.

[3] Such a mound is the original meaning of the word *gorsedd* which Iolo used to describe both his bardic meetings and their locations. See *Bardic Circles*, p.119.

4 Iolo (diminutive of Iorwerth - Edward) of Glamorgan.

[5] They may have worn 'druidic' robes or, more likely, simply an armband to denote their bardic status. (See 'Bardism' in William O. Pughe, *Heroic Elegies etc.* 1792).

[6] Josiah Jones, *Geiriadur Bywgraffyddol* (1867).

[7] Smith's *Dictionary of National Biography* (1885-1900).

[8] R. J. Jones, 'Edward Evan, Toncoch', *Y Darian* (5 December 1918).

[9] *Cardiff Times and Newport & South Wales Advertise,* (7 September 1867).

[10] T. R. Roberts, *Eminent Welshmen* (1908), p.99.

[11] See Iolo to Wm. O. Pughe (12 May 1798), *Correspondence of Iolo Morganwg*, Letter no. 472.

[12] As Princess Elizabeth, the Queen had been invested as a member of the Gorsedd, in the woods just below Ton Coch, at the National Eisteddfod held in Mountain Ash in 1946 (see Chapter 23).

[13] See Mary-Ann Constantine, *The Perils of Performance: From Political Songs to National Airs in Romantic-Era Wales (1790–1820)*; Intersections, Volume: 43 (2016), pp.266-286.
  For the words of 'Breiniau Dyn' see Cathryn A. Charnell-White, *Welsh Poetry of the French Revolution 1789-1805* (2012), pp.154-160.

[14] Gwynfardd ('druid') is the highest bardic order in the Gorsedd of Bards, see *Geiriadur Prifysgol Cymru*.

[15] Edward Williams ('Iolo ap Iorwerth Gwilym'), *Cyfaill y Cymru* (1797). 'Iorwerth ab Ioan' is one of the versions of the poet's name in Welsh, more usually as a 'bardic' name. He is also referred to as Edward ab Ifan, Edward Ifan and – in English – Edward Evan or Evans.

[16] *Gentleman's Magazine* (1789), pp 976-977.

[17] *Cardiff Times and Newport & South Wales Advertiser* (7 September 1867).

[18] G. J. Williams, *Iolo Morganwg* (1956), pp.118-9.
  John Jones, *History of Wales* (1824), shows Iolo in a list of the 'presiding bards' of the Glamorgan *gorsedd* stretching back to 1300, as the successor of Edward Evan, who is unique, as the only example of a single named bard at any period. Only Edward is named between 1760 and 1824, while every other period shows a presiding bard and several gorsedd members.

[19] Gareth Williams, in *Cwm Cynon*, ed. Hywel Teifi Edwards (1997), p.160.

[20] 'Shwnad Pacman', *Y Gwladgarwr* (4 November 1871).

[21] G. J. Williams, *Traddodiad Llenyddol Morgannwg* (1948), p.227.

[22] *Gardd Aberdâr* (1854) p.42.

[23] The successor to the original Old Meeting House (Yr Hen Dŷ Cwrdd), built in 1862, is preserved by the Welsh Religious Buildings Trust (Addoldai Cymru): https://welshchapels.wales/hen-dy-cwrdd/

[24] 'Mabonwyson' (William Henry Dyer c. 1837-81), *Y Gwladgarwr* (21 January 1881).

CHAPTER 4

1770 – 'Edward Evan's Book'

Afalau, ffrwythau ffraethlon,	*Apples, abundant fruits*
- yr Awen	*of the Muse,*
Wir rywiog ireiddlon,	*Truly fresh and noble,*
Seigiau da nid soegion,	*Nourishment not nonsense,*
Llyfr iaith braidd fel llefrith bron. [1]	*A book whose language flows like milk.*

Three old books are my most tangible connection to Edward Evan. I have two volumes of his poetry, one printed in 1816, a hundred years after his birth, and the other from 1874. I also have a leather-bound copy of *The Spectator* in which he wrote 'Edward Evan's Book 1770'. The same handwriting can be seen in a letter to his landlord, and in the register of the Old Meeting House in Aberdare, where he entered the names of the people he baptised. It is a remarkable experience to open the varnished leather covers of *The Spectator* and see where he wrote with a quill pen so clearly on the title page. The book has been passed down the generations of Edward's descendants and found its way to me, a solid link in an otherwise tenuous chain stretching back more than two hundred and fifty years.

His poetry was published only after his death, but several works were printed in his lifetime. He and his fellow-poet, Lewis Hopkin, produced a Welsh verse translation of the Book of Ecclesiastes, with its well-known reference to 'a time to live and a time to die'. He translated Samuel Bourn's *Lectures for Children* into Welsh; and the text of a sermon he gave to a meeting of dissenting ministers in Cardiganshire was printed along with two hymns he composed for the occasion.

Edward Evan's greatest legacy are his poems, collected by his son and first published in 1804, six years after his death. Copies of all four editions have been preserved in libraries in Wales and beyond. It was said that, after the Bible, *Llyfr Edwart Evan* ('Edward Evan's book') was the most popular in the Neath Valley in the nineteenth century.[2] G. J. Williams, in his History of the Literary Tradition of Glamorgan,[3] notes that his poetry was said to be as well-loved among the people of the *Blaenau* – the Glamorgan uplands – as *Canwyll y Cymry*, the work of 'the Old Vicar', Rhys Prichard.[4]

The first collection was entitled *Caniadau Moesol a Duwiol* ('Moral and Godly Poems') an off-putting title in these post-religious days, but one which even in 1804 did not reflect the range of its contents. There are, certainly, godly poems as might be expected from the pen of a devout minister of religion, dissenting or otherwise. The best of these convey a Christian message firmly founded in a vision of a loving God. The 'moral' poems explore many aspects of human conduct and society. And both these categories reflect the volume's sub-title: 'Encouragements to live a good life and to behave in a loving way towards all the human race'. The later editions were called *Afalau'r Awen* – 'The Apples of the Muse', though they kept the 'moral and godly' reference as a subtitle.

He wrote many love poems, some to girls as a young and carefree poet, others as a husband to his two wives. There are translations into Welsh of works by well-known English poets, including Alexander Pope, Samuel Butler and Isaac Watts. Then there are many poems which reflect the world in which he lived, and which introduce the reader to people of all classes in the Glamorgan uplands in the eighteenth century. These are perhaps the most appealing, the work of a *bardd gwlad*, a people's poet, reflecting a society which largely vanished in the century after his death when his poems became so popular.

Take these lines, sent along with payment to an old farm labourer called Rhys Wiliam, 'an honest, gifted man', at the request of his employer, Morgan Thomas. The poet celebrates the enduring skill of the old reaper, who could still sharpen a blade and wield a scythe.

Mae'n wych, o edrych ei oedran, - etto,	*He's magnificent, when you think of his age –* *His aim still keen;*
Heb atal ei amcan,	*Everyone who sees him says:*
Yn ddidwyll pawb a dd'wedan',	*If he cuts less, he still cuts clean.*
Os lladd lai mae'n lladd yn lân.[5]	

In Edward Evan's role as a people's poet, farming was a constant theme, which is no surprise since it was at the heart of his own life from his birth to his death.

[1] Gwilym Tew of Llandâf. One of several poetic tributes to Edward Evan's work published in *Afalau'r Awen* (1816).

[2] D. Rhys Phillips, *History of the Vale of Neath* (1925), p.552.

[3] See G. J. Williams, *Traddodiad Llenyddol Morgannwg* (1948), p.246.

[4] 'Yr Hen Ficer', Rhys Prichard (c.1579-1644), Vicar of Llandovery. '*Cannwyll y Cymry* (The Welshman's Candle), published in 1681, was a compiled copy of Pritchard's earlier published works, with some additional verses. None of these editions came into print during Pritchard's lifetime, however once published, they became best-sellers. Many of his poems and verses were of a colloquial tone, and it is no surprise therefore that their content attracted an ordinary and sometimes illiterate audience.' https://www.library.wales/discover-learn/digital-exhibitions/europeana-rise-of-literacy/poetry-volumes/cannwyll-y-cymry

[5] Edward Evan, Afalau'r Awen (1874), p.64.

CHAPTER 5

1716 – The Descendants of Hywel Gwyn y Gôf

I hen Siôn Rhys o Lwydgoed	*Old John Rees of Llwydcoed*
'Roedd chwech o blant 'rwy'n gwybod,	*Was father to six children,*
Fe gymm'rwd dau i'r bywyd hir,	*Two of them passed to another life*
Cyn immi'n wir eu canfod.	*Before I got to know them.*
Mi welais dri o'i feibion,	*Three of his sons - I saw them*
Yn heinif ac yn gryfion,	*As strong men, fit and healthy;*
Ac un o'i ferched hyn fe' wis,	*One of his daughters I recall*
Yn fenyw hoenus ddigon. [1]	*Was lively, blithe and bonny.*

'Old John Rees' was Siôn, son of the Rhys who cut the oaks on Craig y Bwlch. His son was Ifan, a farmer and weaver who lived, like his father, in Llwydcoed. He was known as Ifan Siôn Rhys, after his father and grandfather. Theirs was one of the oldest families in Aberdare parish, with their home in a farmhouse called Penyrallt, below the mountain road, '*y gefn ffordd*', which led from Aberdare to Merthyr Tydfil. By the time Edward Evan (Edward Ifan) was born in 1716, most people called the farm Tir Ifan Siôn Rhys, after his father, the man who farmed it.

The poet's birthplace is long gone. The land was bought, after Edward's time, by Thomas Jenkin Gibbon of Fforchaman and the new houses which he built for iron workers around 1801 were called Tregibbon, after him. The whole straggling hamlet now goes by that name, which is written on the side of the old chapel on the corner of the lane leading down from the Merthyr Road to the site of Penyrallt. Beyond Tregibbon is land scarred by tipping from the ironstone and coal mines which supplied the ironworks. Though there is now no trace of the works, nor of Penyrallt and its fields, the neighbouring farmhouses at Pentre Bach and Gelli Deg, still stand on the north side of the old mountain road.

In 1827 Thomas Jenkin's grandson married Mary Evans, Edward's granddaughter, and, as Mary Kingsbury, she became the owner of the land at Llwydcoed. In a legal document as late as 1856 her grandfather's birthplace was still referred to as 'Tyr Evan John Rees'.

§

Lo! here 'twixt Heaven and Earth I swing,
And whilst the Shuttle swiftly flies,
With cheerful heart I work and sing
And envy none beneath the skies.[2]

The first thing recorded about Edward's life is that when still a boy he worked as a weaver like his father Ifan. The sort of loom on which he made woollen cloth can be seen in the Esgair Moel mill from Llanwrtyd, now at the National Museum of History at St Fagans. Dewi Jones, the weaver there, began as an apprentice in 1988 and had to learn the same skills as did the young Edward in the 1720s. He does everything from spinning the wool to washing and drying the finished cloth. On the day I met him, he was trying to complete a shawl which had been left on the loom during the pandemic lockdown. While the weaver was on furlough, moths had a field day and Dewi needed to repair several of the warp threads which run the length of the loom.

He's a patient man, wearing much-repaired blue overalls. He started weaving thirty-five years ago simply because he needed a job, but he clearly now takes a pride in being one of only a handful of professional weavers still working by hand. 'What gives me pleasure is to see something I have woven, washed and hanging on the line to dry – something I have made from start to finish'.

The wooden loom, about the size of a four-poster bed, might have stood in the farmhouse at Penyrallt.[3] There may have been an outside weaving shed or there's even a possibility that the weaving was done at Llwydcoed Mill. The loom would probably have been made by a local carpenter and in Edward Evan's time would not have had the metal components fitted to the Esgair Moel loom. Nor, until 1733, could it have had the 'flying shuttle' (the 'swallow'[4]) which allows the weaver to whip the weft swiftly through the opened warp; pushing it through by hand would have made the work slower, though otherwise the process was the same.

To make room for the shuttle and its bobbin of thread to mesh, the warp threads are lifted in sequence by treadles, or pedals, under the loom. It's a noisy process; as the weaver moves his feet in a dainty dance, the mechanism lifts and drops, and the shuttle flies back and forth. Dewi pointed out that the young Edward would not have been able to work the loom until his legs were long enough to reach the pedals from the long wooden bench from where he operates.[5]

Weavers like these made cloth or flannel, and almost every parish in Glamorgan had its weavers, as well as fullers who cleaned and compressed the cloth to make a dense, waterproof felt. A water-powered fulling mill was known in Welsh as a *pandy*, which is a common element in place names such as Tonypandy. There was a fulling mill in Aberdare, which Mary Mathew bequeathed to her son Miles in 1694, along with 'all the watercourses thereunto belonging'. The mill was later leased for a yearly rent of £15.[6]

John Bradford of Bettws near Bridgend, one of Edward Evan's fellow Glamorgan poets, was a fuller and dyer of cloth.[7] And in one of his poems celebrating local life Edward urged the weaver Morgan Williams of Penyrheolgerrig, grandfather of the famous Merthyr Chartist, to send a load of woven work to the fulling mill.

Ar daith dyro'r gwaith gwyn,	*Send the rough work off*
– i'r hŷ bannwr,	*– to the valiant fuller,*
I'w bwnnian yn frethyn.[8]	*To pound it into cloth.*

There's a record of a weaver called John Deer of St Athan in the Vale of Glamorgan, who also had a small farm with cattle and sheep. When he died in 1718, he left his grandson 'my looms with all their appurtenances and all other implements belonging to my trade or mystery of weaving'.[9] Weaving could be done, especially in the winter months, at any time when there was no other work on the hill farm.

---

[1] Edward Evan: 'A poem in the measure of a *Triban* written when the last of my grandfather's children was buried', *Afalau'r Awen* (1874), p.31.

[2] James Maxwell ('the Weaver-Poet of Paisley'), *Weaver's Meditations* (1756).

[3] In George Eliot's novel, the weaver Silas Marner's cottage contains only a loom, a

bed, a table and a couple of chairs.

[4] In Welsh, the shuttle which flies back and forth is called 'yr wennol' (the swallow).

[5] In 1980 the Irish broadcaster RTÉ recorded the life and work of a family of traditional Donegal handweavers on their small farm in the north-west of Ireland. The footage of the loom in action shows how young Edward worked in the 1720s, just as Dewi Jones does today. And like the family at Penyrallt three hundred years ago, the McNelis brothers combined their spinning and weaving with work on the farm at Ardara where they raised crops, cattle and sheep.

[6] Moelwyn I. Williams in *Glamorgan County History, Vol. 4* (1974), p.339.

[7] William Thomas's Diary, July 1785; South Wales Records Society (1995).

[8] *Afalau'r Awen* (1874), p.90.

[9] *Glamorgan County History,* Vol. 4. (1974), p.339.

CHAPTER 6

The Scythe

Rhowch o'ch gwaith, eilwaith olwg,	*Sell your good work,*
- am arian,	*well finished,*
I werin Morganwg,	*To the people of Glamorgan,*
Bladuriau, heb droiau drwg,	*Good sharp scythes, without a fault,*
I ymlid gwair yn amlwg.* [1]	*To cut hay in the sun.*

Edward Evan lived all his life on farms and wrote often about the work of farmers. But he left no account of the family's life in the early 1700s, weaving, and farming their land in the *Blaenau* – the uplands of Glamorgan. There are conflicting accounts of what life was like for these small farmers. According to one, they would have had difficulty growing almost any crops; in the middle of the century it was said that, unlike the 'fruitful' Vale of Glamorgan, 'the north of this county is so full of mountains that almost nothing is to be had.'[2] They would have earned their living 'mainly by rearing livestock, and in producing cheese, butter, and wool for market.'[3]

On the other hand, about the time that Edward was born it was reported that farmers in Aberdare grew some oats and barley, though only a small proportion of the land was classed as arable.[4] In 1771, however, it was said that wheat was grown in the parish, where 'the land is naturally very good'.[5] At Hendre Ifan Goch, near Cymmer, where Edward Evan lived for several years as an apprentice to Lewis Hopkin, they harvested both wheat and oats.[6]

In 1785 a correspondent to the *Gentleman's Magazine* in London reported on agriculture in the uplands:

> The northern parts of Glamorgan swell into high mountains,

21

covered over with sheep and small black cattle, that, in winter as well as summer, depend alone for food on the heathy and grassy surface of the mountains; these mountains, where a little cultivation has with difficulty penetrated, produce good corn, and exhibit proofs of sufficient fertility, were the natives sensible of the advantages accruing from proper cultivation; one obstacle to this, it must be owned, is their steep ascents, which make it difficult for teams and carriages to pass and work.[7]

Most small farms were less than sixty acres, some freehold, but many rented from larger landowners. There's no way of knowing the size of Penyrallt, but Ton Coch, where Edward farmed from 1749, was seventy-nine acres.[8] Aside from any grain, farmers and their families raised sheep and cattle. Sheep were often sheared for their fleeces twice a year and were also milked. While farmers in the *Blaenau* kept many more sheep than cattle, a cow was a much bigger investment, even though, grazing the hills, it was worth only a third as much as one kept in the Vale.[9]

Life for Edward Evan and his family may have been hard. According to one account the standard of living of upland smallholders was often little better than that of labourers and their homes were described as 'the habitations of wretchedness'.

> Several of the lower kind of farmers, and their dependants, have their tables as scantily supplied with the luxuries of salted bacon, butter and cheese, as even those of the paupers they are forced to relieve.[10]

The demands of the landlord and the uncertainties of the weather put pressures on tenant farmers, which is what Edward Evan always was. 'A late harvest, a single crop failure, or an outbreak of disease among the livestock were all factors which affected adversely the economic and social welfare of individual farmers (especially small farmers) for several years afterwards.'[11] On top of all this were the risk of illness, rent arrears and tithes due to the Church even from non-conformists. But one historian issued a warning:

> It is easy to rush to the conclusion that because their implements were old and cumbersome and their system of husbandry contrary to more enlightened ideas, the peasantry of Glamorgan farmed on a subsistence level, but this would be far from the truth.[12]

However difficult their material condition, Edward Evan painted a positive picture of family life in the poem about his grandfather's six children, described as decent, loving and happy people. In another poem, he praised the life of the farmer.

Er maint eu trafferthion, 'dwy'n gweled neb dynion	*In spite of their troubles there isn't a person*
Mor esmwyth a'r hwsmon, a'i galon ddi gûr;	*More carefree than farmers whose minds are at peace;*
'Nôl gweithio'i ddiwrnod, fe gwsg dan ei gysgod,	*When labour is over, sleep comes to them easy,*
Heb syndod trwy ddefod yn ddifyr. [13]	*No worries disturb their just slumber.*

They had to be flexible though. While diversification has become a necessity for many Welsh hill farmers in the twenty-first century, it is nothing new.[14] 'The peasant farmer and his family strained every muscle, and exploited every subsidiary or supplementary occupation, in order to help balance the household budget.'[15] Spinning, weaving and knitting were traditional activities alongside outdoor labour.

As a young man, Edward Evan travelled to work on farms across the *Blaenau*, mowing hay in the summer, and sometimes falling out with the farmer, as in this case when he had a bad experience with Gryffydd Jenkin of Corwgfychan, Glyncorwg.

Cyn lladdo'i wair i Gryffydd,	*Before I'll mow for Griffith*
Tyf gwair ar ben y mynydd;	*Hay will grow on the mountain*
A'r creigydd cras yn tyfu'n ŷd	*And oats grow on the rugged crags*
A gwenith hyd y gwaunydd. [16]	*And wheat up on the moorland.*

Well into his old age, Edward Evan continued to work on the farm, though he lamented the loss of strength which meant that he could no longer cut hay as he had as a young man.

Lladd gwair, di anair er daioni, – dwys	*Mowing is a good job – but it's heavy;*
Nid oes ynwyf egni,	*I haven't got the strength.*
Ni ddigwydd i mi ddiogi;	*Never was I lazy, but now*
Hen egwan faban wyf fi. [17]	*I'm feeble like a baby.*

§

There is no way of knowing what the cottage in Llwydcoed was like. It may have been similar to Ton Coch, the remains of which were surveyed in the 1960s. There the original building was a large single room or 'hall', divided by a partition at one end to create a small inner room, probably a bedroom. The cow house was built onto the structure later and the living space was enlarged later still to create another room beyond the great fireplace. A winding stone staircase built into the side of the chimney breast led to an upper floor under the roof.[18]

A picture of the inside of a Glamorgan cottage was painted in 1792 by Julius Caesar Ibbetson, who produced a series of watercolours depicting the life of ordinary people in Wales at that period.[19] It shows a large room with a huge fireplace and a flagged stone floor. It is thought to be in the Vale and is probably bigger than the upland cottages. The family are sitting around, and in, the great fireplace, with a pile of wood on the floor ready to burn. Through an open doorway a cow can be seen in the connected cowhouse.

Ton Coch and Penyrallt may have resembled the Cilewent farmhouse from Radnorshire, which can be seen at the National Museum in St Fagans. It's a long house, with a living room at the front and a dairy at the back. There is one doorway through which people and animals entered, a feature which can still be seen at Fforchaman, where Edward Evan's granddaughter lived after her marriage. There was sleeping accommodation in the warm hay loft above the animals' quarters. This is a type of farmhouse once common in mid and south Wales and the flagged floor and fireplace are reminiscent of Ibbetson's painting.[20]

From the outside, there's no doubt the farmhouse and any other buildings at Penyrallt would have looked spick and span, with a regular coat of white. The correspondent to the *Gentleman's Magazine* quoted above reported that 'Glamorgan people whitewash their handsome stone built cottages without as well as within, three or four times a year'.[21] Matthew Williams of Bath said that 'the taste of the Welsh peasantry in the adorning of their cottages, is perhaps almost peculiar to themselves. They wash and paint the whole of them white, tiles and all, from top to bottom.'[22]

Travellers were less complimentary about conditions indoors, though it should be remembered that they may have brought their prejudices with them. John Byng complained in 1787 that 'however they may make an outside show of neatness by the whitewashing of their houses it would [be] well they should apply to a tub of water for the cleanliness of the inside of their houses which, like their persons are ever in filth and nastiness.'

In *Hen Dŷ Ffarm* ('The Old Farmhouse'), his memoir of rural life in Carmarthenshire, D. J. Williams describes the 'hilly and remote' location of the farm to which his grandfather moved in 1840, at the age of thirty.

> Penrhiw was a long, low straw-thatched house like the old houses generally ... My grandfather ... made it into a long one by adding a parlour to it. The kitchen was large, and the heavy oak beams under the cross rafters were low. To these hung an abundance of the usual farmhouse commodities, hams and thick sides of bacon, a few pieces of beef, salted black, nets of shallots and ropes of French onions, baskets of various sizes and shapes, a couple of pigs' bladders full of lard.

There were bedrooms upstairs and down, but Jaci Penrhiw died at the age of seventy-seven in a heavy oak cupboard bed in the parlour, where he had been nursed for almost a year, while his baby grandson (the young D. J.) lay in a crib by the fireplace nearby. Perhaps old Siôn Rhys of Llwydcoed in the *Blaenau*, had died in such a bed downstairs at Penyrallt, surrounded by his family, two hundred years earlier.

---

[1] Edward Evan, 'Verses sent by the poet to the blacksmiths of Llanonn to order new scythe blades for himself and his neighbours', *Afalau'r Awen* (1874), p.119.

[2] Moelwyn I. Williams in *Glamorgan County History, Vol. 4* (1974), p.322.

[3] Ditto.

[4] See *Gardd Aberdâr* (1853).

[5] Dr Josiah Tucker, Dean of Gloucester (June 1771), quoted in Geoffrey Evans, *History of St John's Church Aberdare* (1982), p.34.

[6] Lewis Hopkin, Letter 12 August 1765 in Lemuel James, *Hopkiniaid Morganwg* (1909), p.120.

[7] *Gentleman's Magazine* (1785), pp.604; quoted by G. J. Williams in *Iolo Morganwg* (1956). This smacks a little of Iolo's own authorship.

[8] Tithe map of Aberdare 1844 (51-2/49), National Archives, via National Library of Wales: https://places.library.wales

[9] *Glamorgan County History, Vol. 4*, p.325.

[10] W. Davies, quoted in David Jones, *Before Rebecca* (1973), p.3.

[11] *Glamorgan County History, Vol. 4*, p.338.

[12] Ditto, p.337.

[13] *Afalau'r Awen* (1874), p.62.

[14] At Hendre Ifan Goch, where Edward Evan lived for many years as an apprentice to Lewis Hopkin, the present farmers run a camping site alongside the sheep farm.

[15] *Glamorgan County History, Vol. 4*, p.338.

[16] *Afalau'r Awen* (1874), p.175.

[17] Ditto, p. 121.

[18] RCAHM Wales *Inventory of Ancient Monuments in Glamorgan*, Vol. IV, Part 2 (1988), p.290.

[19] Donald Moore, *The Earliest Views of Glamorgan* (1974), p.21.

[20] https://museum.wales/stfagans/buildings/cilewent/

[21] *Gentleman's Magazine* (1785), p.603.

[22] https://sublimewales.wordpress.com/material-culture/whitewash/

[23] Ditto.

[24] It was near Glyn Cothi from which Edward Evan's radical Unitarian successor at the Old Meeting House in Aberdare, Thomas Evans, took his bardic name, 'Tomos Glyn Cothi'.

[25] D. J. Williams, *Hen Dŷ Ffarm* (1953). Translated by Waldo Williams. (Bilingual edition 1996), p.178.

CHAPTER 7

'The native rudeness of the country'

> Blaenau, *which in English we call mountains,*
> *being three times double as much and more in*
> *quantity as the low country, is divided from the*
> *same by almost a continual direct ridge or hill, in*
> *length from the east to the west.*[1]

> *Clearly the Almighty had never intended 200,000*
> *human beings to live at those valley heads. The*
> *ironmasters corrected Him on the point.*[2]

There is little accurate information about the population of the *Blaenau*, the hill country of Glamorgan, in Edward Evan's lifetime. It was in the second half of his life, from 1757 onwards, that the small and scattered ironworks, 'eking out a tenuous existence based on local supplies of timber'[3], were overtaken by investment and technological change and the population began to grow. Based on the 1670 Hearth Tax, it is estimated that the population of the whole county of Glamorgan in the half century before Edward Evan's birth was around 40,000.[4] The first census, in 1801, revealed that around that number lived in the part of the county consisting of the port of Cardiff and its mountainous hinterland; a quarter of these were in what, by then, were 'the industrial districts' of Merthyr and Aberdare.

The bulk of the population outside of these small townships lived in hamlets and villages dotted over the vale of Glamorgan and in scattered hill farms. Though the iron industry was well established in Merthyr and to a smaller extent in Aberdare, the demand for iron had not yet reached the dimensions of future years when machine tools made the manufacture of iron goods easier, and steam-engines, iron bridges, and railway lines caused a wave of intense industrial activity in iron-making districts.[5]

Edward Evan was a man of the hills. He was born, lived, farmed, and died in what was a remote and mountainous country, a long way from the centres of commercial life in the Britain of his day. His birthplace in Llwydcoed was 700 feet above sea level; the cottage at Ton Coch was considerably higher at an elevation of almost 900 feet.[6] Scattered hill farms are common in upland Wales, but it is very difficult now to appreciate the remoteness of Aberdare parish in pre-industrial times.

The Garth Mountain, where Iolo and his *gorsedd* met in 1798, marks the beginning of the *Blaenau* north of Cardiff and the coast. It is the highest point on the long ridge which Rhys Merrick (quoted above in 1578) described running from east to west across the county, dividing the lower-lying Vale of Glamorgan from the mountains and valleys to the north. If you travel west along the M4 motorway from Cardiff to Swansea, the Vale is to the south, with an average elevation of 200 feet above sea level. The ridge and the *Blaenau* lie to the north, where the average height of the modern county borough of Rhondda Cynon Taff is 825 feet. Like the Garth, many of the high points of the *Blaenau* are known as mountain, *mynyddau*, in Welsh.

The *mynyddau* of Glamorgan can certainly feel like real mountains in bad weather. Thirty years ago, when winters were colder, I have been on the Garth after heavy snow and strong winds had carved great overhanging cornices. It is often an inhospitable environment in winter, but in summer the cuckoo can be heard in the woods and larks fly high overhead, distracting walkers from their nests in the bracken. The open mountain top is common land and still grazed by farmers with the right to put sheep or cattle on it. The views from the summit on a clear day are unequalled; to the south and west the hills of Exmoor; to the east the mouth of the Severn and the bridges; to the north the high peaks of the Brecknock Beacons; and almost vertically below the eastern outcrop, the river Taff in its glaciated valley.

Before industrialisation, the small, scattered, whitewashed farmhouses of Glamorgan, like Ton Coch, were often located on the hillsides, where many can still be seen, high above the later terraces of houses which snake along the valley bottoms and the lower slopes. The old village of Aberdare itself, with its mediaeval church built around 1200, lay in a wide, open valley surrounded by hills. A drawing by one of the Bacon sisters from 1828 shows how it must have been for hundreds of years, a cluster of cottages with the mountains behind.[7] Travellers from Merthyr in 1799 looked down on it from their horses:

> At length, entering further in the vale, we perceived at the distance of two miles the village of Aberdare, plentifully and rather beautifully intermixed with wood: a luxuriant spot encroaching on the fruitless waste … Aberdare consists of near an hundred homes remarkable for their neat appearance; not a cot but it was as white as milk.[8]

The trip to Aberdare to find the ruins of Ton Coch took me through the heart of what are now known as 'the Valleys', but in Edward Evan's day, it was not the valleys but the hills – the *Blaenau* – which gave the area its name. To reach Mountain Ash golf course for the first time, I took the dual carriageway which goes north from Cardiff and the coast, heading for Merthyr Tydfil and Brecon. The A470 passes through the Taff gorge with the Garth Mountain to the west and for much of the way follows the course of the former Glamorgan Canal which was built in the 1790s and 'brought through mountainous scenery with wonderful ingenuity'.[9] At Abercynon, the road to Aberdare forks to the north-west and again follows the course of an old and vanished canal, above the river Cynon. By car or train, the journey is easy, but it was not so in Edward Evan's time. Although the later canals, railways and roads were constructed close to the valley bottoms, these were often impassable in the old days and the ancient trackways wound around and over the hills, which may explain Iolo's reference to the Garth as like 'a high turnpike road'.

John Bruce Pryce, father of the first Lord Aberdare, and owner of the Dyffryn Estate in the days of Edward Evan's son, remembered the challenge of travelling there around the year 1799, just after the poet's death.

> If someone wanted to visit Aberdare from the east in the late eighteenth century, wheeled vehicles had to be left at Abercynon and if the occupants were disinclined to walk, the only means of transport further up the valley was a sledge cart. Though the road was bad, it finished altogether at Duffryn, since no thoroughfare had been left between the enclosed lands of Duffryn and Aberaman. The traveller then had to make his way through Craig Isha and Abercwmboi woods, thence to

Aberaman Mill then through the bed of a brook by Abergwawr and Ynyslwyd, entering the village where the Black Lion now stands. Another track from Duffryn ran up to Cefnpennar and down into Cwmbach, and thence to Aberdare.[10]

At much the same time, travellers from Merthyr Tydfil recalled riding to Aberdare on horseback over the high ridge between the two parishes.

> Before us was a valley and, above, mountains characterising the native rudeness of the country. The ground below is barren and morassy, and the mountains themselves afford not even fern or heath. Their form is wild, irregularly projecting or retreating, and the collective rains have trenched their sides with furrows.[11]

But beauty is in the eye of the beholder. A correspondent to the *Gentleman's Magazine* in 1785, who was probably Iolo, was at pains to paint a positive picture:

> These valleys are generally very beautiful, and together with their fortifying hills, exhibit some of the finest landscapes in the world; the bottoms fine meadows, traced by clear rivers or brooks; the sides a diversified scene of sloping lawns, ascending woods, and hanging rocks, from whence trinkles many a clear and cascading rill, whilst from their upper regions are heard the songs and whistlings of genuine shepherds.[12]

Writing fifty years later, by which time the iron works were 'conducted on a very extensive scale', Samuel Lewis still agreed with the previous description, describing 'the delightful mountain vale of Cynon, which is remarkable for picturesque and romantic scenery, and is equally characterised by features of beauty and grandeur'. Both he and Iolo appear to have seen the landscape with the eyes of those influenced by the new perspectives of the romantic movement.

> Its majestic groves of oak and fir, alternating with fruitful corn-fields and luxuriant meadows, are finely contrasted with precipitous and barren rocks, and enlivened by the bold sweep of the river, which in some of its windings appears to be hemmed in on every side by lofty and sterile mountains.[13]

In 1749 Edward Evan would almost certainly have heard 'the great Methodist Divine' John Wesley preach at Aberdare after riding 'sixteen Welsh miles' from Cardiff 'over the mountains'.[14] This was his second visit that year and his journal describes an isolated Welsh-speaking community:

> About noon we came to Aberdare just as the bell was ringing for

a burial. This had brought a great number together, to whom, after the burial, I preached in the church. Few could understand me so Henry Lloyd when I had done interpreted the substance of my sermon in Welsh.[15] We had almost continual rains from Aberdare to the great rough mountain that hangs over the vale of Brecon.[16]

Edward Evan travelled widely and knew the lie of the land. When the poet Rhys Morgan of Pencraig-nedd composed lines in praise of a new turnpike road in the Neath Valley in 1770, Edward responded with a poem of his own complaining that the higher section which led to Hirwaun and on to his home in Aberdare was unfinished and almost impassable.

Mae'n llawn o ddiffeithwch,	*It's a path of desolation,*
Gan bob rhyw serth anferthwch	*Dangerous slopes to walk on,*
Gerrig yn lleithig y llwch.[17]	*Nothing but mud, dust and stone.*

A painting by Ibbetson from 1792 shows just such a rough track north of Cardiff between Llandaff and Pontypridd, running between rocky outcrops. Three girls are seen riding on a pony close to the ruins of the mediaeval Castell Coch.[18] In the following century, Edward Evan's son Rhys was inspector of roads for Aberdare and wrote a poem asking Thomas Wayne, treasurer of the Turnpike Trust, to supply stone for repairs.[19]

There were some early improvements for travellers, most notably the famous bridge – Pont-y-tŷ-pridd – built in 1756, one of few substantial river crossings at that time. It was the work of Edward Williams, a stone mason (like his namesake Iolo Morganwg) who succeeded in bridging the Taff at the fourth attempt, with a revolutionary design in which holes built into the high arched structure reduced the weight of the stonework.[20] It is still an impressive construction, standing alongside a modern and uninspiring road bridge. At the time it was the longest single-span arch in the world. Edward Evan praised the bridge in a poem as an achievement unequalled in Wales, or anywhere in Europe.

Bwa mewn sylfaen sailfawr,	*A bow of stone on strong foundations*
- nid gwrthrudd,	*- no bad intention,*
Ond gwrthddrych dych'mygfawr ...	*But an object of great invention …*

'E saif hon yn llon, uwch ben lli',
- dirfawr,
I dyrfa fyn'd drosti.[21]

It stands proud above the flood
- a great path
For crowds to pass on.

The town of Pontypridd eventually grew up around the new bridge, just as Llwydcoed expanded when the ironworks opened and Thomas Jenkin Gibbon began the building of new houses. But in Edward Evan's boyhood there were only twenty scattered farms and cottages in his native hamlet, including Tir Ifan Siôn Rhys where the young lad learned to weave and to play the harp.

---

[1] Rhys (Rice) Merrick, Morganiae Archaiographia (1578) in D. L. Davies & Geoffrey Evans (editors), The Land Your Fathers Possessed, Cynon Valley History Soc. (2011) p.18.

[2] Gwyn A. Williams, The Merthyr Rising (1998), p.22.

3 W. E. Minchinton, Industrial South Wales 1750-1914, (1969), p.xi.

[4] Glamorgan County History, Vol. 4, p.311.

[5] T. M. Hodges, 'Peopling of the Hinterland and the Port of Cardiff (1801-1914)', Economic History Review XVII (1947), p.4.

[6] 100ft = 30 metres.

[7] Geoffrey Evans, A History of St John's Church, Aberdare (1982), p.18.

[8] Robert Clutterbuck (1799) in The Land Your Fathers Possessed, pp.30-31.

[9] John Bird, Cardiff Directory and Guide (1796).

[10] John Mear, Hanes No.13, Cynon Valley History Soc., 1997, based on the account of John Bruce Pryce, father of Lord Aberdare (See The Land Your Fathers Possessed, p. 26).

[11] Robert Clutterbuck (1799) in The Land Your Fathers Possessed, pp.30-31.

[12] Gentleman's Magazine (1785), p.604.

[13] Samuel Lewis, Topographical Dictionary of Wales, Vol. 1 (1833).

[14] The Land Your Fathers Possessed, p.25.

[15] This was the Vicar of Rudry, who accompanied Wesley on his trip.

[16] John Wesley, 6 April 1749, quoted in A History of St John's Church, Aberdare, pp.42-43.

[17] Edward Evan in Trysorfa Gwybodaeth neu Eurgrawn Cymraeg (1770) pp.46-47 in the poetry section.

[18] Donald Moore, The Earliest Views of Glamorgan (1978), p.16.

[19] See Afalau'r Awen (1874), p.175 and Old Aberdare Vol.2, Cynon Valley History Soc. (1997), p.77.

[20] See 'Edwards, William (1719 - 1789)', Dictionary of Welsh Biography.

[21] Afalau'r Awen (1874), p.51

CHAPTER 8

The Harp

Tydi gai gariad hafaidd hefyd,
A llawer carol fy'm dyn fywiol,
yn dy fywyd;
A llais y delyn ymhob dolydd,
I'm dyn hoyw gael ei llanw
mewn llawenydd. [1]

You shall have love in the months of summer,
And my girl will have music,
wherever she goes;
The voice of the harp in every meadow
To fill my sweetheart with nothing but joy.

For one week every summer for several recent years, harps could be heard throughout the village of Gwaelod y Garth, at the foot of the mountain where Iolo's *gorsedd* met. Young players were guests in many houses as they took part in an international summer school organised by Catrin Finch and Elinor Bennett. Two of Wales's most famous harpists, they taught in the chapel and village hall, but their pupils could be heard through open windows practising in the houses where they stayed. A promising young harpist from the Netherlands played in my own home. Now a professional, Michelle Verheggen had won a scholarship to study with Catrin Finch. The former Royal harpist was our neighbour at the time, so we would occasionally hear her playing across the way. But there is nothing to compare with live harp music in your own home.

It was once common for great houses in Wales to employ a harpist who would play at meals and on special occasions. But according to the historian Robert Griffith there was a time when almost every house in Wales had a harp[2]. There's no evidence that harping was an inherited calling in Edward Evan's family, but they were certainly musical. Iolo Morganwg described Ifan, Edward's father, as 'something of a poet and a good singer'. In the poem in which he remembered his father's brothers

33

and sisters, Edward recalled their liveliness and love of music.

Rhai chwannog iawn i ganu,   *They were all keen on singing*
A chellwair a difyrru,   *And fun and entertainment;*
A thuedd crŷf mewn llan a llys,   *No matter where they found themselves*
I'r dymmer hoenus hyny.[3]   *They showed a joyful spirit.*

R T Jenkins described this picture as typical of 'the old way of life of the *gwerin* of Wales – the small cottager, happy and droll, rhyming and singing'.[4] Edward became a musician, from the age of thirteen playing the harp and no doubt singing at weddings and local festivals. When he joined the Glamorgan bards at their eisteddfod in Cymmer on St Davids Day in 1735, Rhys Morgan saluted the nineteen-year-old newcomer as *Ned lân, lais organ*, 'honest Ned with the musical voice'. Dafydd Nicolas also paid him a handsome tribute:

Iorwerdd, brydferdd ei bryd,   *Welcome, handsome Edward,*
Delynor da Wyl Ynyd,   *Fine harpist for a feast day,*
Fab Ifan, gyngan ei gerdd,   *Son of Evan, sweet in song,*
Difawr ing, dofwr angerdd.[5]   *Slayer of sorrow and discord.*

According to the biography published with his poems in 1874, he was taught by a local shoemaker who was said to be somewhat mean and hard to please. But Iolo (who was much closer in time) named Edward's teacher as Tomas ab Owain of Aberdare, 'a harpist by calling'.[6] Whoever taught him did a good job. As with weaving, winter was the season when there was time for something other than work on the farm and during his first winter of practising Edward learned to play sixty tunes and became a master of 'the Welsh harp'.

The modern concert harp stands up to six feet tall, has three rows of strings, with pedals to alter the pitch. The instrument which became famous as the 'Welsh harp' was the triple harp, which had three rows of strings but no pedals. It became popular in the eighteenth and nineteenth centuries, although it was difficult to string and hard to play. But the instrument played in Wales before that had just one row of strings; this was the harp that Edward Evan played and what the biography meant when it referred to his mastery of the 'Welsh harp' as a boy. In his musical survey, Thomas Price ('Carnhuanwc') was clear: 'Edward Evan, of Aberdâr was a performer on the single harp'.[7]

Price was one of the last people to see and hear the single-stringed instrument. He remembered a harpist who performed on it in the late eighteenth century, in the last years of Edward Evan's life:

> The earliest recollection I have of the harp is that of Old Sam the harper, who lived at Builth, and whom I have often seen, previous to the year 1800, going towards Llanafan feast and other places, to play for dancing, carrying his harp slung at his back. His name was Samuel Davies, and he might have been about 50 years of age at that time. I have also seen him, on the club feast at Builth, play before the club whilst they walked in procession to church. He carried his harp slung about his shoulders, so as to be able to play as he marched along. His harp was a single string harp, and formed like the other single stringed harps of the time. It was between 3 and 4 feet high or thereabouts. When he sat down to play, he crossed his feet, so that the back of one foot touched that of the other, and let the bottom of the harp rest on the calves of his legs. Old Sam the harper sometimes played for dancing on the green and in the open air.

As the single harp was portable, young Edward would have had no trouble taking it with him as he travelled around to play at weddings, dances and the traditional festivals. The most popular of these were the *gwyliau mabsant*, 'wakes' or revels, originally held to mark the saint's day of a parish patron saint. People from surrounding areas stopped work and gathered to dance, sing and watch games like *bando* and football – even bull-baiting and cock-fighting. But these celebrations had lost their religious connection and the name *mabsant* was also used for dances, *taplasau haf*, held on Saturdays throughout the summer. In Aberdare celebrations took place in different parts of the parish on Easter Monday, Whit Monday and old St John's Day (24 June).[8]

> Every lad and lass danced on holidays and highdays, at fairs and weddings, and especially at the village festival, the Glamorgan Revel, or 'Gwyl a Gwledd Mabsant' … When sunset approached the sound of violin or harp, or sometimes both together, would be heard proceeding from the public rooms of the inns. It was a remarkable fact that these minstrels invariably came down from the hilly regions, from Gellygaer or Llanwonno, or some distant place.[9]

Young Edward Evan was just such a travelling musician from the *Blaenau* playing the harp in the churchyard, a field, a barn or an inn, accompanying or singing love songs, surrounded by revellers enjoying themselves, perhaps to excess. It was 'a pleasant, carefree life in his early years, wandering from one parish to another, with plenty of drink and chatter'.[10]

> The dancing in the Mabsant was excellent. Wales was renowned for good dancers in those days. Originally the Mabsant was a pleasant gathering of old and young, when mirth and melody were at their best, and the dancing would have done justice to any mansion … Musicians went from Mabsant to Mabsant regularly every year, and were in great repute for their skill. My father and many others remembered an old Glamorgan harpist who for sixty years had made the same circuit. He began his itinerary at the age of twenty-three, and continued it until he was over eighty-three.[11]

Some of the music of the old days survived into the twentieth century. It was sixty years ago that a young Roy Saer began his travels around Wales collecting and preserving the tunes of the country. When I met him at his home in Cardiff, he told me how he visited elderly people who knew the old songs. He would stay in a caravan which he towed behind a Land Rover in order to access the most remote farms. He had with him a heavy reel-to-reel tape machine to record the music and took photographs of the old singers. Roy became an expert on many aspects of traditional Welsh culture including *mabsantau* and *taplasau haf*. [12]

When Methodists began to take a grip on Wales, the 'revels' were in their sights. On a visit to Llanfaes near Brecon in 1741 John Wesley observed what he called 'innocent diversions', but he dissuaded the people from taking part, quoting the words of St Peter to condemn 'lasciviousness, lusts, excess of wine, revellings, banquetings, and abominable idolatries'. At Whitchurch, near Cardiff, where the revels were attended by 'the gentry and clergy' and lasted a week, he called: 'Awake thou that sleepest, and arise from the dead, and Christ shall give thee light'.[13]

Thomas Price ('Carnhuanwc'), who was an Anglican clergyman, heard from his father how the preaching of the Methodists had impacted popular culture:

> The introduction of Methodism made a great change in the habits of the people. Dancing was altogether discouraged as profane. My father told me that he remembered an old man

... who play'd the harp, but who joined the Methodists or Dissenters and then gave up the harp and threw it under the bed, where it lay till it got mildewed and worm-eaten and fell to pieces.[14]

Thomas Charles of Bala, an Anglican clergyman who had become a Methodist – and a killjoy – rejoiced in 1791:

This revival of religion has put an end to all the merry meetings for dancing, singing with the harp, and every kind of sinful mirth, which used to be so prevalent amongst young people here. And at a large fair, kept here a few days ago, the usual revelling, the sound of music, and vain singing, was not to be heard in any part of the town; a decency in the conduct, and sobriety in the countenances, of our country people, appeared the whole of that fair, which I never observed before; and by the united desire of hundreds, we assembled at the chapel that night, and enjoyed a most happy opportunity.[15]

Roy Saer believes that Thomas Charles's particular loathing for the harp was because, throughout Wales, it was the main instrument played to accompany dancing. He referred to the harpist Edward Jones ('The King's Bard'), who commented in 1802 on the profound effect of these changes.

The sudden decline of the national Minstrelsy, and Customs of Wales, is in a great degree to be attributed to the fanatick impostors, or illiterate plebeian preachers, who have too often been suffered to over-run the country, misleading the greater part of the common people from their lawful Church; and dissuading them from their innocent amusements, such as Singing, Dancing, and other rural Sports, and Games, which heretofore they had been accustomed to delight in, from the earliest time. In the course of my excursions through the Principality, I have met with several Harpers and Songsters, who actually had been prevailed upon by those erratic strollers to relinquish their profession, from the idea that it was sinful. The consequence is, Wales, which was formerly one of the merriest, and happiest countries in the World, is now become one of the dullest.[16]

Despite the efforts of the Methodists, the *mabsantau* and *taplasau haf* continued in some areas into the nineteenth century. Edward Evan's first wife came from Penderyn, not far from Aberdare, where the *mabsant* was said to have been held as late as 1866. Among those who led the dancing there were three generations of harpers from Pont Nedd Fechan – Hywel Lewis, his son Thomas, and his granddaughter Jennet.[17] It's more than possible that Hywel was the harpist at a 'Welsh ball' held at a tavern in their village in 1798, when the Rev. Richard Warner from Bath was impressed by the dancing and the playing.

> On a sudden the dance ceased, and the harper, running his finger rapidly down the chords of his instrument, gave the accustomed signal, on which every gentleman saluted his partner three or four times with considerable ardour. The dancing then re-commenced with such spirit, as convinced us that this interlude had added to the energies of all the parties concerned.[18]

Edward Evan would have known about the last *taplas haf* dance in Aberdare, which took place in Cefnpennar, close to his home at Ton Coch.

> In 1789, they met as usual but the weather was very bad, with wind and rain, so they went into the barn of a man called Dafydd Edward Shon. When the old man heard the harp and the dancing in his barn, he lost his temper and refused to let them stay in the place. So they all had to leave and that was how the *taplas haf* ended in this parish.[19]

Edward had given up playing in public long before that final *taplas* in Aberdare. The last harpist to play at such dances in the parish was said to be Siôn Siams (John James) who may well have been the son of Siams Siôn (James Jones).[20] According to Iolo Morganwg, Edward Evan's last performance had been 'at the wedding of Siams Jones of Aberdare, on a Friday; he himself married the following Monday … he never played the harp afterwards, except at home for the entertainment of family and friends'.[21] That would make him twenty-seven when he stopped playing in public. According to the biography published in *Afalau'r Awen* in 1874, he 'hung his harp on the willow' because 'he saw he was slipping down into a foul swamp of drunkenness'.

Though he became a dissenter and later a minister, Edward Evan was no Methodist and no killjoy. The poem about his father's family celebrated their love of fun and entertainment. When his colleague Dafydd Nicolas wrote a poem condemning public houses as dwellings of the devil, Edward responded with a defence of drink in moderation.

Glân yw'r dw'r, a rhwydd y rhed	*Water's clean and easily*
I dorri syched gwannwr,	*Refreshes one who's thirsty;*
Os cawn ni beth o'r cwrw a'r bir,	*If we take a drop of beer,*
Rhown ddiolch i'r Creawdwr.	*Give thanks to our Creator.*

Fe all y Cristion cywir farn	*Any Christian strong in faith*
Mewn tafarn dderbyn swccwr,	*Is welcome in a tavern,*
A d'od oddiyno'n lân,	*And can leave without a taint*
Er gwaeth'r hen wrth'nebwr. [22]	*In spite of Satan's tempting.*

But Edward must have feared he would end up like William John of Abergavenny, who died in 1792: 'A skillfull harper, of about 55 years of age, and a man by Report that killed himself by Drinking'.[23] So he turned his back on the revels and played no more in public.

§

> David did not have, flourishing of faith,
> A single string made from dead sheep;
> The virtuous prophet David
> Never made, swift magic of minstrels,
> Any harp, entertaining skill,
> Except of horsehair, proper song.
> Wise is the easy lively expression
> Of the harp of shining black horsehair.[24]

There is a fascinating twist to the tale of Edward's harping, which is another connection to the mediaeval bards. Several of them composed poems asking – or thanking – their patrons for a harp strung with horsehair, not with brass strings like the Irish, nor 'inferior' gut like other harps. Iolo Goch was one of them, calling King David as his witness in the poem quoted above.

'The last druidic bard' may also have been the last person on record who had seen a harp strung with 'shining black horsehair'. In one of his numerous notebooks, Iolo Morganwg records what he had learned about the *delyn rawn* (the horsehair harp) which had disappeared by the time he wrote in 1802. Edward Evan was his source and he told Iolo about a harpist called Gruffudd Evan from Llanwynno who lived around 1730. The *delyn rawn* was his instrument and he knew how to wind the horsehair into strings long enough for the harp – a skill which Iolo said had now been lost.

> These old harps are no longer to be found in the *Blaenau* of Glamorgan, with the frame skillfully made of wood covered with the skin of a horse or calf. It is said that the whole effect was more melodious and softer than that from wooden frames, but not high-pitched nor so loud. (From the memory of Edwd. Evan of Aberdare). [25]

Earlier accounts of Welsh horsehair harps emphasise the difference in their sound compared to the Irish harp with its brass strings. The harpist Rhodri Davies described the evidence Iolo had gleaned about the *delyn rawn* as very significant. 'It means Edward Evan would be the last person as far as anyone knows to have had contact with this type of harp'.

After several years of researching the literature on this ancient instrument, Rhodri Davies had one made by Alun Thomas, a harp maker in Fishguard, and Gaynor Howell of Narberth, an expert in the use of animal skins. The wood was scooped out to make the back of the frame, with leather stretched and sewn across to complete the sound box. It's a small instrument and cost around £3,000. The strings are horsehair with bone pins to tighten them. It stays in tune but is vulnerable to damp and the strings can break or buzz. This *delyn rawn* is another tantalising link to the lost world of pre-industrial Wales.

Rhodri's interest is, above all, in the unique sound of the instrument. It is very gentle, which confirms what Edward Evan told Iolo. Unlike modern harps, the strings are plucked with the nails and there is no ability to sustain a note. As he demonstrated, the effect – the resonance – is very different from the modern folk harp or the renaissance harp in his collection. Rhodri has recorded an album called *Y Delyn Rawn* on which he experiments with the range of sound this ancient harp can make.[26] 'Sometimes, when I'm improvising, playing the horsehair strings, it feels as though the spirit of the horse comes out in the sound and rhythm,' he told me.

Though Edward Evan hung his harp on the willow, he may have written music for the instrument. Thomas Price, who referred to his playing the single harp, said he also composed some pieces 'which are in the possession of Mr Morris, of Newport'.[27] Robert Griffith refers to 'Evans, Edward of Aberdare', reporting that he was said to be the author of several pieces of music.[28] But as Griffith adds that this harpist flourished around the year

1830, he must be referring to the poet's son, who was also Edward and a well-known harpist.

According to the biography, Edward Evan turned his mind from harping to the rules of Welsh poetry. But he kept a close connection with music. Traditionally, all poems were composed to a metre, a rhythm or measure related to music and dance and almost all in *Afalau'r Awen* are called a '*cân*' – a song.[29] The titles of several mention a harp tune to which they could be sung. Many of these are poems on the theme of love, set to tunes popular in eighteenth century Wales: '*Calon Drom*' ('Heavy Heart'), 'Draw Cupid' ('*Serch Hudol*'), 'Guinea Windsor', '*Gwêl yr Adeilad*', 'Lovely Peggy' and 'Sweet Richard'. As the names suggest, many of the popular tunes of the day were imports from England.

It's not only the poems with a tune named in the printed edition that might have been sung. One copy of *Afalau'r Awen*, now in the National Library of Wales, belonged to John Jenkins, vicar of Kerry in Montgomeryshire from 1807 to 1829. Jenkins is a fascinating character, who kept open house at his vicarage in the first week of January, welcoming all comers 'provided only that they could compose an *englyn*, sing a song, or play the harp'. Along with the Bishop of St David's he set out to 'rekindle the bardic skill and ingenuity of the principality … by holding eisteddfodau in different places in the four provinces'.[30] The first of these was held at the Ivy Bush in Carmarthen in 1819.[31]

Pasted into the vicar's copy of *Afalau'r Awen* is a cutting from the *Gentleman's Magazine* of July 1798, recording the recent death in Aberdare of Edward Evan, 'the much esteemed Minister of a Society of Protestant Dissenters in that place; one of the most eminent of the Order of Ancient British Bards, and no mean performer on the harp'.

It is said that Jenkins's main interest was the collection of old airs and melodies, so it's no surprise that he took a close look at the poems of a harpist. He made a note, against many of the poems, of the harp tune to which they could be sung. These include '*Ymadawiad y Brenin*', '*Y Forwyn Las*', '*Bryniau Iwerddon*', 'Limbo', 'Nutmeg & Ginger', '*Anhawdd Ymadael*', '*Y Dôn Fechan*' and '*Sally Blodau'r Ffair*'.[32]

Two of Edward Evan's compositions were included in the only volume of Welsh folk songs with both music and words published before the twentieth century, *Ancient National Airs of Gwent and Morganwg*.[33] Both appear as poems in *Afalau'r Awen*, but in Maria Jane Williams's publication (dedicated to Queen Victoria 'by special permission') they are presented as songs she collected 'in their wild and original state'. She was awarded the prize at the Abergavenny Eisteddfod of 1837 'for the best collection of original unpublished Welsh airs, with the words as sung by the peasantry of Wales'. The forty-three songs are arranged for voice accompanied by harp or piano.

'*Mab Addfwyn*' (translated here as 'The Gentle Swain') is sub-titled in *Afalau'r Awen* 'a song in the form of a boy's complaint after being rejected by his love', a theme with which Edward was well acquainted. Jane Williams writes that it was 'learned in the valley of Tawy' (the Swansea Valley) and in a handwritten note in the manuscript names her source as 'Griffith'. The score is marked 'plaintive', and Daniel Huws, who edited a modern edition of the book, describes the tune as a common one, often associated with the words by Edward Evan, which 'undoubtedly went into oral circulation'.[34]

Huws is less convinced about Jane Williams's assertion that the other song, '*Y Ferch Fedydd*' ('The Goddaughter') was 'commonly sung in several districts', because the words of the two verses she prints are so close to those of the poem published in *Afalau'r Awen*; but he doesn't rule it out. In the book it is entitled 'advice to my goddaughter to avoid a foolish marriage', but the poem had been known for many years, since it was first printed in Edward Evan's lifetime in a journal, *Trysorfa Gwybodaeth*.[35] It may be relevant that Jane Williams lived in the Neath Valley, where Edward's poems were said to have been very popular.

Evidence that his verses continued to be sung comes from an article in *Y Gweladgarwr* from 1881 in which the writer recalls a recent meeting with a prominent tenor, William Hopkin of Aberdare, who sang many songs composed by 'the beloved old bard of Ton Coch'.[36]

[1] Edward Evan, *Afalau'r Awen* (1874), p.10

[2] Robert Griffith, *Llyfr Cerdd Dannau* (1913), p.163.

[3] *Afalau'r Awen* (1874), p.31.

[4] R. T. Jenkins, *Bardd a'i Gefndir*, Trans. Hon. Soc. Cymmrodorion (1948), p.100.

[5] Ditto, p.110.

[6] G. J. Williams, *Traddodiad Llenyddol Morgannwg* (1948), p.247.

[7] Thomas Price ('Carnhuanawc'), *Literary Remains* (1855), p.408.

[8] *Gardd Aberdâr* (1853), p. 41

[9] Howells, John, 'The Glamorgan Revel (Gwŷl a Gwledd Mabsant)', *Red Dragon* V, (Jan-June 1884), pp. 131 & 134.

[10] *Traddodiad Llenyddol Morgannwg*, p.247.

[11] Mary Trevelyan, *Folk-Lore and Folk-Stories of* Wales (London, 1909), p. 258 (in Allan James, *Diwylliant Gwerin Morgannwg* (2002), pp.170-171.

[12] Roy Saer's research for a lecture he gave to the Welsh Folk Dance Society in 1984 has been an invaluable resource for this chapter: *Traditional Dance in Wales During the 18th Century* https://www.welshfolkdance.org.uk/dawnsiau/roy_saer.htm.

[13] Quoted by Roy Saer (op. cit.).

[14] Thomas Price ('Carnhuanawc') in Ann Rosser, *Telyn a Thelynor* (1981), p.44.

[15] D. E. Jenkins, *The Life of the Reverend Thomas Charles of Bala* (1910), quoted by Roy Saer (op. cit.).

[16] Edward Jones, *The Bardic Museum*, p. xvi, quoted by Roy Saer (op. cit.).

[17] D. Rhys Phillips, *History of the Vale of Neath* (1925), p.585.

[18] Ditto, p.588

[19] *Gardd Aberdâr*, pp.41-2.

[20] Iolo says Siams Jones lived 1710-1785, which fits – and *Gardd Aberdâr* has Siams Sion Gregory of Llwydcoed, born about 1712, said to be a bard and father of a bard.

[21] Quoted in *Bardd a'i Gefndir*, p. 102.

[22] *Afalau'r Awen* (1874), p.106, 'Complaint to Dafydd Nicolas about the tavern'.

[23] R. T. W. Denning (ed.) *Diary of William Thomas 1762-1795* (1995), p.406.

[24] Iolo Goch (c.1325–c.1398), 'Praise of the Horsehair Harp'; English translation by Dafydd Johnston, *Gwaith Iolo Goch* (1993), p.130.

[25] Iolo Morganwg, National Library of Wales MS13146A, pp.417-9.

[26] Rhodri Davies, 'Y Delyn Rawn': https://rhodridavies.bandcamp.com/album/telyn-rawn

[27] *Literary Remains*, p.409.

[28] *Llyfr Cerdd Dannau*, p.196.

[29] In Welsh the same word can be used for a song or a poem and *cerdd*, meaning music or song, can also refer to poetry. From the earliest days the art forms of the poet and the harpist in Wales were closely related and a harpist could be known as a *bardd telyn* (a 'bard of the harp').

[30] 'John Jenkins ('Ifor Ceri', 1770-1829)', *Dictionary of Welsh Biography*.

[31] John Jenkins's copy of *Afalau'r Awen* is bound with five poems composed by Tomas ap Gwilym for the Carmarthen eisteddfod of 1819, including a tribute to General Thomas Picton, now infamous for his involvement with slavery, but hailed as a hero after his death at Waterloo in that year. The 1819 Eisteddfod was where Iolo Morganwg succeeded in combining his *gorsedd* ceremonies with the festival.

[32] This last is usually known as 'Fanny Blooming Fair'. For many of these tunes see Phyllis Kinney, *Welsh Traditional Music* (2011).

[33] Maria Jane Williams, *Ancient National Airs of Gwent and Morganwg*, (1844). Facsimile edition, Welsh Folk Song Society (1988), with an introduction and notes by Daniel Huws. The collection includes five songs attributed to Edward Evan's friend and colleague Dafydd Nicolas, who was closely associated with the Williams's home at Aberpergwm.

[34] In one of the Ceri manuscripts, John Jenkins links 'Mab Addfwyn' to the tune *Cainge Glyn Cynon* (The Glyn Cynon Air), which is apt considering Edward Evan's

lifelong association with the Cynon Valley. See *Journal of the Welsh Folk Song Society*, no. 2, p.100.

[35] *Trysorfa Gwybodaeth neu Eurgrawn Cymraeg* (1770), poetry section, pp.5-6. In Maria Jane Williams's collection, the tune to which the poem is set is close to that known as '*Mi fildiais dŷ newydd*'.

[36] *Y Gweladgarwr* (21 January 1881).

CHAPTER 9

The Hat of Willow

Fi sy'n fachgen ieuanc ffôl,   *A young and foolish lad am I,*
Yn byw yn ôl fy ffansi.[1]   *I go where fancy leads me.*

'Watching the White Wheat' (*'Bugeilio'r Gwenith Gwyn'*) is one of the most popular of Welsh traditional songs, in which the 'young and foolish lad' is employed to guard the crop 'which someone else will reap'. He sings of his love for a girl named Ann and swears his undying devotion, as long as the sea is salt and the heart beats in his breast. 'Tell me truly', he asks, 'is it me or another who is dearest to you'?

As a travelling harpist, a hired farmhand, or an apprentice carpenter and glazier, handsome Edward Evan[2] travelled widely across the *Blaenau*, working in seventeen parishes[3]. He was, by his own account 'a young and foolish lad':

> When I was around seventeen or eighteen years of age I was too frivolous and flighty to grasp anything of value or significance.[4]

Many of his earliest poems tell stories of love, often unrequited. In view of the popularity and 'morality' of *Afalau'r Awen*, it's noteworthy that love poems are the first six in the collection published by his son. [5]

Young Edward began to study the strict rules of traditional Welsh poetry after he had hung up his harp, when he mastered the art as an apprentice to Lewis Hopkin. His father was said to be 'something of a poet' and may have taught him the basics, but it is not known whether he had any formal schooling as a boy.[6] According to Iolo Morganwg he loved making poetry from his childhood. The first poem he wrote, as a boy known as Nedi, mentions a weaver called Tabitha who worked at the mill in Llwydcoed. It is in the form of a *triban*, particularly popular in Glamorgan.

45

Dwy Gallyn, Twm a Siencyn,	*Two Catrins, Tom and Jenkin*
A Rosser, clywch fy englyn	*And Rosser – hear me singing;*
Ac hefyd Nedi bach yn wir,	*And there's little Neddy too,*
Tabitha hir dy bwthyn.[7]	*Tabitha in her cabin.*

The earliest evidence of a school of any sort in Aberdare comes from a report dated seventeen years before Edward Evan's birth. What became the parish of Aberdare was for centuries a subsidiary part of the extensive parish of Llantrisant, and St John's church was officially a 'parochial chapel'. In 1699, The Society for the Propagation of Christian Knowledge recorded that the Vicar of Llantrisant, Rev. James Harris, 'saith he hath begun catechetical lectures in ye severall chapells of his great Parish, and hoped to be able to carry them on together with the schooling of poor children'. In 1724, when Edward was eight, Harris informed the Society that 'a charity school for 20 boys' was being set up at Llanwynno, about six miles from Aberdare.[8]

According to Iolo, the absence of formal schooling was no obstacle to literacy in the Glamorgan of his youth:

> We need no regular schools for one Neighbour gives another
> a few lesson[s] two or three times a week for half an hour at a
> time, and the pupil is soon able to read his native language. It
> is an usual thing in Wales for a few young, and sometimes older
> persons, of both Sexes to attend for an hour twice or thrice a
> week at a place where a goodnatured neighbour, and such may
> always be found, will give them some instruction in reading
> Welsh, and often in writing. A month of such instructions gener-
> ally enables the pupil to proceed in his own strength.[9]

Iolo says Siams Siôn[10] taught Edward reading, writing, and poetry before his apprenticeship, but claims he could read only as far as the end of Matthew's gospel![11] The *Dictionary of National Biography* refers to the same teacher: 'He received very little education in his early, formative years, but he was later taught by James John, a hooper and farmer from Aberdâr, who was well read in both Welsh and English and a fairly good poet'.[12] Lewis Hopkin wrote a tribute to James John, after his death, describing him as a true friend of Iorwerth (Edward) and praising his poetry.[13]

Edward's early poems were in the metre of the Glamorgan *triban*, 'one of the main glories of the popular literature of the Welsh nation',[14] but he soon moved onto more ambitious poetic forms.[15] At the age of seventeen or eighteen, the 'frivolous and flighty' youth began the apprenticeship which would change his life.[16] He went to live and learn at Hendre Ifan Goch, some twenty miles from home, with the poet Lewis Hopkin who taught him carpentry, glazing and poetry – and undoubtedly influenced his religious thinking. Hopkin had moved to Hendre Ifan Goch[17] in the parish of Ystradfodwg in 1734. Eight years older than Edward, he was an important figure in the group of Glamorgan poets who met at the eisteddfod in Cymmer in 1735. That was where Edward's attendance was recorded in verses by Rhys Morgan and Dafydd Nicolas, not long after he had come under Lewis Hopkin's wing.

The set subject for the poetic gathering at Cymmer was 'Death' and several of the compositions were included in the collection of Lewis Hopkin's work published in 1813.[18] Two by Edward Evan show that he had begun to write in the strict metre *englyn* form which Hopkin had taught him, mastering the traditional art of alliteration and internal rhyme known as *cynghanedd*.

Another young poet who turned up at this eisteddfod was Wil Hopcyn, whose name and legend became attached to the song *Bugeilio'r Gwenith Gwyn*. He seems to have been a disruptive influence on the gathering, reciting a poem insulting to the bards. In a poetic riposte, Hopkin Lewis described him as bad-tempered and rude and accused him of shamefully coming to spoil their enjoyment.[19]

Apart from this apparent insult to the bards at Cymmer, nothing certain is known about Wil Hopcyn, although his name became famous in the following century through its association with the song, which was attributed to him and in which he was said to be the 'young and foolish lad'. The story – though not the song – tells tells how Ann Thomas, the Maid of Sker, died of a broken heart because her wealthy family did not approve of Wil, the poor boy who loved her.[20] This situation echoes that in the first of Edward Evan's poems in *Afalau'r Awen*, where the poet bemoans the fact that his beloved's family care nothing for his talents. All they are interested in is material wealth, but he lacks land and does not have 'sheep bleating on the hillside'. 'The bard Myrddin and Taliesin the magician, with all their insight, could never have predicted how the world would come to love riches above all else,' he moans.[21]

Edward Evan learned to write poetry in a range of strict bardic measures. But many of his love poems are in a form of free verse which includes elements of *cynghanedd*. These and other pieces he wrote have been compared to the much-loved poems of Huw Morys ('Eos Ceiriog'), who died a few years before Edward's birth and is believed to have originated this style.[22] Their similar approach may partly explain the popularity of *Afalau'r Awen* in the nineteenth century.[23]

When I met Wyn James, an expert on the literature of this period, to discuss Edward Evan's poetry, he was struck by the effectiveness of another style in which he wrote. It's known as *Tri Thrawiad*, after the three strong beats in the last line of each verse. This is the form of the second poem in *Afalau'r Awen*, cast as a dialogue between the poet and Ann Henry of Margam 'when he was an apprentice'. Ann, like the Maid of Sker, was probably the daughter of a wealthy farmer, but in this case it is she who has second thoughts about the idea of marrying a boy like 'Nedi'. The poem is an amusing and effective ding-dong in which the poet protests against Ann's change of heart, reminding her how loving she used to be and how he hoped they would wed. But she comes back at him:

Aros y glanddyn a gwrando di ronyn,	*Hang on there, handsome, and listen a moment,*
Ti 'mrwymaist dros gettyn ryw ffortun rhy ffest;	*You promised a maiden a fortune in haste;*
Mursendod afrifaid yw clywed prentisiaid	*It's a great irritation to hear an apprentice*
Yn cymmell at ferched siwt orchest.[24]	*Approach a young girl with such nonsense.*

He reminds her how she used to enjoy his harping, good music and a fitting song.

Aros, 'rwy'n cofio bûm gynt yn dy bleso,	*Wait, I remember that once I could please you,*
A'r delyn â'm dwylo trwy deimlo mor dêg,	*The harp in my hands often made you feel fine,*
Ti gerit yn hollol ryw fiwsig iawn foesol,	*You delighted to hear harmonious music,*
A charol barodol ber adeg.	*And dance tunes amused you at one time.*

Ann is having none of it and advises him to try elsewhere.

Dod heibio'th gerdd fedrus, y peth oedd yn felus	*Forget your sweet music, for that which was pleasing*
Sy'n awr yn wrth'nebus oer warthus ei wedd;	*Is now quite distasteful and shameful to me;*

| 'Rwyn clywed dy dafod fel ynfyd ddiflasdod, | *The sound of your singing is foolish and tasteless,* |
| Diffrwythdod nau hynod anhunedd. | *Quite boring and frankly unpleasant.* |

It was not the last scathing reference to his harping and singing, nor the last sharp answer from a girl to his musical charms.

Pwy lawenydd difudd dafod,	*Where's the pleasure, worthless talker,*
Ddaw o'r delyn erfyn arfod?	*From the twanging of your strings?*
Holl ferched cerddi goleu gwelwch,	*For the girls who hear your love songs,*
Aent yn farwol a'u difyrwch,	*Fun and music will be over*
Pan 'ddel baban anian inni,	*When a baby's in the picture.*
Pob gwag ddifyrwch gwn nas gellwch ond ei golli,	*You'll forget your empty pastimes, And you'll know the choice you're stuck with,*
A thyma ddaw o ddewis cydmar,	
Yn lle telyn 'fe gair gwedyn	*When your hand is on the cradle*
siglo'r gadar.[25]	*not a harp string.*

There's no way of knowing whether all the love songs were autobiographical, whether several references to 'Gwen' relate to another real girl, or whether some were poetic exercises on a traditional theme. Whichever it was, young Edward doesn't seem to have had much luck with the ladies, even though fellow poet Rhys Morgan thought he had what it takes.

Tau genni fi siwt ddoniau,	*If I had skill like you have*
I ganu'n dynn ar dannau,	*To play upon the harp strings,*
Mi fynnwn ferch i dorri'm chwant,	*I'd get the girl I'm longing for,*
A dale gan o bunnau. [26]	*And she would make me wealthy.*

Ann Henry of Margam took her affection and her money elsewhere. She appears again in a series of englynion written when the poet heard that his former love had married another man. For the rest of the summer, everyone would know his dreams were over.

| Pawb a'm gwel mewn het helig, | *All will see my willow hat,* |
| Isel o fraint yn salw frig.[27] | *Humiliation on my head.* |

There's a traditional English song which goes 'All around my hat I will wear the green willow'.[28] Evidence of the willow hat in Wales comes from

D. J. Williams in *Hen Dŷ Ffarm*, where he recalls his uncle Jâms's adventures in courting, a hundred and fifty years after Edward Evan's humiliation.

> I have some recollection … of the mirth in the house when one of the maids put a willow cap on his head the day Elen the We-nallt was married, she being one of his old sweethearts, and of my puzzlement over the term 'willow cap'. I many times afterwards heard of this practice, but this is the only instance I know of its presentation to the disappointed lover in accordance with the custom of a past age.[29]

There's no way of knowing how far young Edward and his girlfriends went in their 'light-hearted meetings in the green fields'.[30] Much has been written about the tradition of 'bundling' – courting in bed – but that seems to have been, in most cases, a deliberate prelude to a wedding.[31] In Edward Evan's love poems, he almost always talks in terms of marriage and a partnership for life as the goal of his courtship. But in a later poem he gives advice to young men and women from 'one who knows from experience' what it is to be 'carried away' by uncontrollable affections so powerful they give a young lover no peace. He warns the boys to stay away from 'dens of iniquity' and condemns those who exploit a maiden and leave her in the lurch. The girls are warned not to be tempted by flattery to go into dark places and advised to give their 'pearls' only to their husbands. It's what you'd expect from a minister of religion, but there's no suggestion that sex is shameful, and his preaching carries more weight when prefaced with his confession that he knows the power of sexual desire. He makes the point again in the poem advising his goddaughter not to marry unwisely, the song included in *Ancient and National Airs*.

Mae'r iengctyd yn hoywon a'u nwydau sydd gryfion,	*Young people are lively, their passions are burning*
Y rhai'n fel olwynion yn rhwyddion a rêd.[32]	*And carry them on like a wheel running free.*

But it's not only the young that get carried away!

'Rwi'n gweled yr wythnos c'yd a phythefnos	*The length of a week seems as long as a fortnight*
Yn hir i'w ei haros ar f'einioes ifi.[33]	*Waiting so long feels a lifetime to me.*

That's Edward Evan, aged sixty in 1776, eagerly anticipating his second wedding, to Mary Llewelyn, and still taking pride in his appearance.

> Er myn'd yn oedrannus w'i   *Though not a young man, I'm still*
> etto'n gysurus   *feeling lively,*
> Nad wyf yn amharchus anafus   *And handsome enough to be seen*
> dan nenn.   *in the world.*

He had married his first wife, Margaret Thomas in 1744, when he was twenty-eight and no doubt was equally excited about that wedding. There's no love poem addressed to her, but he bade farewell to the life of a bachelor, and the wooing of other girls, because he had found a 'wise and loving' companion. Someone else would have to compose the love songs now and Cupid must take aim at other men.[34]

Margaret was the daughter of Thomas Hywel Thomas of Clun-perfedd farm in Penderyn, not far from Llwydcoed, and according to Iolo Morganwg she brought money with her.[35] They were married by licence, with a marriage bond,[36] signed with Edward Evan's distinctive signature and witnessed, surprisingly, by Theophilus Evans, the Vicar of St David's, Llanfaes, Brecon.[37] The contract binds the poet, along with the vicar, to see the marriage through or forfeit the considerable sum of £100 'of good and lawful money of great Britain'.[38] Such penalties were set very high in order to deter 'irregular marriages', but there was no way Edward could possibly have paid it if any legal obstacle had been discovered. The licence itself cost five shillings – fifty pounds in today's money.

Only Anglican clergy could conduct marriages until 1836, when non-conformists were allowed to marry in their own places of worship. When a new Marriage Act came into force in 1754, only a marriage conducted by the Established Church could guarantee the legitimacy of children and this may have been a consideration even ten years earlier.[39] Marriage bonds were used when the Established Church approved a marriage by licence rather than by the usual 'calling of banns' in the parish of each of the parties.[40] In this case Edward Evan was a non-conformist, and did not attend a parish church. The same was probably true of Margaret. If that was the case it could explain why a landless carpenter and glazier might be an acceptable husband for the daughter of a well-to-do farmer, who was prepared to put money behind the couple. The connection may well have been the Old Meeting House at Blaengwrach, one of the early dissenting congregations in Glamorgan. It served a wide area, including Penderyn, and its minister Henry Davies had started an offshoot at Cymmer, near

Porth where Lewis Hopkin was a deacon.[41] It was almost certainly Hopkin's influence which brought Edward Evan to active dissent and it was at Blaengwrach, years later, that he was ordained before becoming minister at the Old Meeting House in Aberdare.

The wedding went ahead without a hitch in Penderyn church and the young couple took a tenancy at Cefnpennar, no doubt with the help of the money Margaret brought to the marriage. They lived and farmed there for five years before becoming tenants of the Dyffryn Estate at nearby Ton Coch in 1749. Unfortunately, nothing more is known of Margaret. They were married for thirty years but had no children and she died in 1774. The poem Edward wrote after her death contains some of his most moving lines.

Hi oedd fy ngherdd, hi oedd fy nghân	*She was my music, she my song,*
Ddyn dirion lân ei dwyrudd;	*A happy, fair-faced woman;*
'Rwi'n awr fel deryn gwael ei gwŷn	*I'm now a bird of plaintive tune,*
Dan gysgod llwyn yn llonydd.[42]	*Lost in a shaded woodland.*

After two years alone, in 1776 he married Mary Llewelyn, a widow from Rhigos who was seventeen years younger. She became well known as 'Pali Ton Coch' after the farm where she lived until her death at the age of ninety-one in 1823. Mary (Mali, Pali) was said to be a descendant of the poet Dafydd Benwyn, 'the most prolific of the Glamorgan bards' of the sixteenth century.[43]

The story of Edward Evan takes us back to his meeting with the Glamorgan bards of the eighteenth century, who were said to gather occasionally at Pont Nedd Fechan, where Dafydd Benwyn and his circle had held their eisteddfodau two centuries earlier.[44] The central figure in this circle, and the most important in Edward's development, was Lewis Hopkin to whom he was apprenticed both as a poet and a carpenter.

---

[1] *Bugeilio'r Gwenith Gwyn* ('Watching the White Wheat'), traditional.
[2] Iolo agreed with Dafydd Nicolas that Edward Ifan was 'dyn prydferth' ('a handsome man'); R. T. Jenkins, *Bardd a'i Gefndir*, Trans. Hon. Soc. Cymmrodorion (1948), p.110.
[3] *Afalu'r Awen* (1874), p.166.
[4] Edward Evan: 'To the Reader', *Llyfr y Pregethwr*, Bristol (1767), p.3.
5 R. T. Jenkins: 'There's no sort of order of the poems in the book and very few

references, internal or external, to help with dating. As a rule, it is guesswork, but it is quite certain that the love poems date from before 1744.' *Bardd a'i Gefndir*, p.111.

[6] It is possible that Edward Evan attended the Dissenting College in Carmarthen before his ordination in 1772. See chapter 15.

[7] *Gardd Aberdâr* (1854), p.81. The name Callyn occurs in a traditional Glamorgan tune *Callyn Serchus* and in a poem of that name by Dafydd Nicolas, friend of Edward Evan and reputed author of the popular song *Y 'Deryn Pur*.

[8] See Geoffrey Evans, *History of St John's Church Aberdare* (1982), p.41. He notes that from 1739 to 1773 one of the Welsh circulating charity schools established by the Rev Griffith Jones, Vicar of Llanddowror, was located at various places in Aberdare, including the Parish Church.

[9] G. J. Williams, *Iolo Morganwg* (1956), p.111.

[10] This may be the same Siams Siôn (James Jones) at whose wedding Edward played in public for the last time. See G. J. Williams, *Traddodiad Llenyddiaeth Morgannwg*, p.312 and note 53, p.248. 'James Jones was a friend of Edward Evan, a poet, harpist and an associate of the Glamorgan bards.' See also NLW MS21311A – Iolo's notebook with the name, signature and poems of James Jones of Aberdare.

[11] R. T. Jenkins, *Bardd a'i Gefndir* (1948), pp.105-6.

[12] 'Evan [Evans], Edward (1716–1798)', *Dictionary of National Biography*.

[13] Lewis Hopkin: 'i James Jones', *Y Fêl Gafod* (1813), p.47.

[14] *Iolo Morganwg*, p.59.

[15] There are only three *triban* included in *Afalau'r Awen*; numbers XIV, XXI and XXII, all of which have a direct sense of local life.

[16] There is some disagreement about his age when he began his apprenticeship. The biography in *Afalau'r Awen* (1874) says he became a carpenter and glazier when he was 23 and G. J. Williams (*Traddodiad Llenyddol Morgannwg*) takes this as his age when he began to learn; but R. T. Jenkins (*Bardd a'i Gefndir*), very reasonably interprets this to mean that he became a qualified craftsman at the age of 23, having spent six or seven years as an apprentice.

[17] Hendre Ifan Goch: https://mapcarta.com/W1033522005 https://www.facebook.com/hendreifangochfarm/

[18] Lewis Hopkin, *Y Fêl Gafod* (1813).

[19] G. J. Williams, *Traddodiad Llenyddol Morgannwg* (1948), p.251.

[20] 'The history of the Welsh text of this song is very complicated. It is probably a medley of folk stanzas from a number of sources, "improved" by Taliesin Williams (1787-1847) and wed to a verse composed by his father, "Iolo Morganwg".' E. Wyn James, 'Watching the White Wheat and That Hole Below the Nose: The English Ballads of a Late-Nineteenth Century Welsh Jobbing-Printer', in Sigrid Rieuwerts & Helga Stein (eds), *Bridging the Cultural Divide: Our Common Ballad Heritage* (2000), pp. 178-94.

[21] *Afalau'r Awen* (1874), p.7 (sung to the tune 'Sally Blodau'r Ffair' according to note in the copy belonging to Rev. John Jenkins).

[22] 'Morys, Huw ('Eos Ceiriog', 1622 - 1709)', *Dictionary of Welsh Biography*.

[23] *Traddodiad Llenyddol Morgannwg*, p.290. Williams gives as an example Poem XLVIII,

set to 'Y Galon Drom'.

24 Edward Evan, *Afalau'r Awen* (1874), p.10, 'An amusing poem in the form of a dialogue between the author and Ann Henry of Margam, when he was an apprentice'.

25 Ditto, p.84, 'Debate between a boy and girl, set to Y Galon Drom'.

26 Ditto, p.41, 'Advice from three friends on marriage' (triban).

27 Ditto, p.89, 'Verses the author wrote when he heard his old sweetheart had married another'.

28 Made famous in a version by the band Steeleye Span. https://en.wikipedia.org/wiki/All_Around_My_Hat_(song)

29 Williams D. J., *Hen Dŷ Ffarm* ('The Old Farmhouse') (1953), Bilingual edition, translated by Waldo Williams (1996), p.184.

30 'Farewell to the bachelor's life', *Afalau'r Awen* (1874), p.16.

31 There is evidence of sexual activity that did not go 'all the way', but also that during the eighteenth century there was a new condemnation of masturbation – mutual or otherwise. A resulting emphasis on penetrative sex may partly explain an increase in the rate of illegitimate births. See Angela Joy Muir (2018), 'Courtship, sex and poverty: illegitimacy in eighteenth-century Wales', *Social History*, 43:1, pp. 56-80.

32 'Advice and warning to young people', *Afalau'r Awen* (1874), p.23.

33 Ditto, 'A Poem composed when I was marrying Mary Llewelyn', p.36.

34 Ditto, 'Farewell to the bachelor's life', p.16.

35 Clun-perfedd was later known as Clyn Perfedd and now as Glyn Perfedd.

36 National Library of Wales MS: *Brecon B89/165.*

37 It is a mystery why Theophilus Evans, a scourge of non-conformity, would have have underwritten the marriage bond, particulary as Penderyn, where the wedding was to be held, had no connection to his several parishes. See Roberts, E. P. (1959), 'Evans, Theophilus (1693 - 1767)', *Dictionary of Welsh Biography*. An advertisement for a new printing of Theophilus Evans's most celebrated work, *Drych y Prif Oesoedd*, appears in the 1804 edition of Edward Evan's poetry (*Caneuon Duwiol a Moesol*), published by the same printer, W. Williams of Merthyr Tydfil.

38 The equivalent of £20,000 today https://www.bankofengland.co.uk/monetary-policy/inflation/inflation-calculator.

39 I am grateful to D. L. Davies for this insight. See Belinda Meteyard, 'Illegitimacy and Marriage in Eighteenth-Century England.' *The Journal of Interdisciplinary History*, vol. 10, no. 3, (1980), pp. 479–489.

40 Anthony Camp: The history and value of genealogical records: marriage by license, in *Practical Family History* (UK), no. 53 (May 2002) pp 34-36. See also: https://www.familysearch.org/en/wiki/Marriage_Allegations,_Bonds_and_Licences_in_England_and_Wales

41 Thomas Rees & John Thomas, 'Cymar [Cymmer], Llantrisant [Parish]', *History of the Welsh Independent Churches*, Vol 2, p.345. https://www.genuki.org.uk/big/wal/GLA/Hanes5

42 'Farewell to my life companion', *Afalau'r Awen* (1874), p.33.

43 *Cymru*,Vol. 43 (1908), pp.225-6. If this is the case, then all of Edward Evan's descendants, including the author of this book, are also descended from Dafydd

Benwyn. See also reference in Chapter 11 to Edward Evan's connection with the MS of Dafydd Benwyn's poetry now in the Bodleian Library, Oxford.

[44] D. Rhys Phillips, *History of the Vale of Neath* (1925), pp. 540-541.

CHAPTER 10

1751 – 'The Wonderful and Surprising Little Welchman'

> **H**ail little child, great is thy grief and pain;
> **O**ld in thy youth, small things doth thee sustain;
> **P**ast hope of thriving, both in limbs and sense;
> **K**ept in a narrow sphere by Providence.
> **I**nnocent life hast thou, not knowing health,
> **N**igh to partake of an eternal wealth.[1]

Lewis Hopkin's 'acrostic' verse expresses his compassion for his son, who was born, with a rare and incurable condition, around the time that Edward Evan came, as an apprentice, to live with the family at Hendre Ifan Goch. The story of Hopkin Hopkin's 'innocent life' reveals how very different from today were attitudes in eighteenth century Britain. It also shows how even the remote and sparsely populated uplands of Glamorgan were connected to the great metropolis of London with its more than half a million inhabitants.

Lewis Hopkin was a remarkable man in many ways, as his eldest son, Lewis junior, recalled:

> He was apprenticed to a joiner and carpenter, which trades he followed till several years after he was married, together with that of a glazier, stone-cutter, and wire-worker; but in the latter part of his life took a farm, and added to that a largish country shop. He was a man of universal genius both for literature and mechanics. He was employed by many in surveying, planning, measuring, calculating, writing all sorts of law instruments, and doing inummerable little ingenious jobs mostly gratis, for he

never coveted money. He could exercise any trade that he had seen better than most of its professors; he could and did build a house, finish and furnish it himself.[2]

He was said to be a great reader in Welsh and English. According to Iolo Morganwg he knew Latin. He collected books and possibly manuscripts and had copies of the *Spectator*, which may be how Edward Evan came by the book now in my possession.[3] He was a descendant of Hopcyn Thomas Phylip, a *cwndidwr* – a composer of songs or carols. And he was a religious dissenter.

Lewis Hopkin's wife, Margaret Bevan, was from a well-known family of Quakers and he left the Church of England, becoming a non-conformist. But his devout Christian faith did not prevent him from exhibiting his disabled son in what can only be called 'freak shows'.

In London, a broadsheet was issued to advertise the appearance at a cafe in Fleet Street of 'the Wonderful and Surprising Little Welchman',

> Who has given general Satisfaction to all the Curious that have seen him, insomuch that they all agree that he is the greatest Prodigy in the known World ... being far beyond the expectation of all those that come to see him ... Servants and common people may see him for 6d. [sixpence] each.[4]

Two of of the Hopkins' eight children suffered from a condition which meant they did not grow normally and aged prematurely. *Hopcyn Bach*, Little Hopkin, was taken to London in 1751 and put on public show. He never grew taller than two feet seven inches and died aged only seventeen, looking like an old man. A suit made for him can still be seen in the National Museum of Wales.[5]

It is remarkable to think that a family from the remote uplands of Glamorgan would have made the necessary connections to exhibit their child in London, where 'many of the nobility and gentry took great delight to see him and bestowed many favours on him and his parents'.[6]

If Lewis Hopkin 'never coveted money' as his son Lewis claimed, it is difficult to understand the motivation for putting the disabled child on show. Such was the fame of little Hopkin that he was presented to the Prince of Wales (later George III), who gave him a gold watch, an annual pension and a promise of ten guineas each time he appeared at court.

This royal connection has echoes of the tradition of the 'court dwarves' employed by monarchs across Europe in the seventeenth and eighteenth centuries. They were traded between royal families or even presented as a gift from one ruler to another.[7] The last official court dwarf was said to be Josef Boruwlaski, a Pole born in 1739 and known as 'Count Jozef', who toured around the palaces of Europe and ended his life in the city of Durham at the age of ninety-seven.[8]

'Giants' were just as popular as unusually small people. Henry Blacker, born in Sussex in 1724, grew to be seven feet four inches tall and was known as the 'Living Colossus' or the 'British Giant'. He was on show at Charing Cross in London in 1751, the same year as Hopkin Hopkin was in the capital. The following year one newspaper advertised that he could be seen 'by any number of persons' at Ludgate from nine in the morning until nine at night'.[9]

Any deformity could attract an audience. Around 1770 a handbill was produced 'to acquaint the Nobility, Gentry, and Curious in General' of the arrival in London of 'a most astonishing Phaenomenon in Nature which is allowed to be the greatest Curiosity that was ever seen in Europe'.

> A young man, Six Feet High, Born with small Hands, which grows out of his Body about three inches below his Shoulders, on Arms whose Length do not exceed *Four Inches*, without any Fore-arm or Elbow, and has only *Three Fingers*, without any *Thumb*, on either Hand ... He may be seen at any Time, from Ten o'Clock in the Morning until Nine at Night. Admittance – Ladies and Gentlemen 6d. Tradesmen 3d. [10]

In 1751 Little Hopkin was also shown in Bristol, where John Browning saw him.

> I went myself to view and examine this extraordinary, and surprising but melancholy subject; a lad entering the 15th year of his age, whose stature is no more than 2 feet and 7 inches, and weight 13 pound, labouring under all the miserable and calamities of old age, being weak and emaciated, his eyes dim, his hearing very bad, his countenance fallen, his voice very low and hollow; his head hanging down before, so that his chin touches his breast, consequently his shoulders are raised and his back rounded not unlike a hump-back, he is weak that he cannot stand without support.[11]

The boy's death was announced in the *Gentleman's Magazine* in 1754.

> March 19. In Glamorganshire in Wales, of mere old age and a gradual decay of nature, at seventeen years and two months, Hopkins Hopkins, the little Welchman, lately shewn in Lon-

don. He never weighed more than seventeen pounds, but for three years past no more than twelve. The parents have still six children left; all of whom no way differ from other children, except one girl of twelve years of age, who weighs only eighteen pounds, and bears upon her most of the marks of old age, and in all respects resembles her brother when at that age.[12]

His father's poem suggests that Hopcyn Bach was limited not only in size but in 'sense', which would make the exhibiting of him seem even more abusive to a modern observer. However, the detailed account of his life in the history of the family reports that both Little Hopkin and his sister Joan were 'perfect in their intellects'. What's more the book quotes a *triban* said to have been composed spontaneously by the boy when he was asked to help with the harvest.

Peth bidyr a di-natur
Yw tyny yn ôl y blatur
I'r bachgen bach 'naeth ddim erioed
Ond chwarae a bod yn segur. [13]

The scythe with its long handle
Is dirty and unnatural
For the little boy who's only ever
Played around and rested.

The boy's poetic ability is attributed by the author to 'the *awen barod* of his race', the 'ready muse' which made his father the pre-eminent member of the eighteenth century bardic circle in the *Blaenau*.

---

[1] Lewis Hopkin, 'To his Son', *Y Fêl Gafod* (1813), p.68.

[2] Rev. Lewis Hopkin Jnr., in Lemuel James, *Hopkinaid Morganwg* (1909), p. 115.

[3] R. T. Jenkins, *Bardd a'i Gefndir*, Trans. Hon. Soc. Cymmrodorion (1948), p. 109.

[4] Wellcome Collection, 'Hopkin Hopkins: the wonderful and surpising little Welchman'. https://wellcomecollection.org/works/p9qs4yv4

[5] https://museum.wales/blog/1486/UK-Disability-History-Month---The-wonderful-and-surprising-Little-Welchman/

[6] *Hopkiniaid Morganwg*, p.109.

[7] https://www.throughouthistory.com/?p=4417

[8] https://en.wikipedia.org/wiki/Józef_Boruwłaski

[9] https://www.bl.uk/collection-items/poster-advertising-mr-henry-blacker-the-british-giant

[10] https://digital.bodleian.ox.ac.uk/objects/d3ac6f81-bc70-4767-894d-800328501949/

[11] Letter from John Browning to Henry Baker (12 September 1751), quoted in Sem

Phillips, *The History of the Borough of Llantrisant* (1866).

[12] *Gentleman's Magazine* (1754) p.191. The sister, Joan, died of smallpox at the age of 13.

[13] *Hopkiniaid Morganwg*, p.111.

CHAPTER 11

1735 – Master Singers in every Measure

Tryssor maith o waith hen wyr	*The work of the old men*
– naturiol,	*– great treasure,*
Gantorion pob messur;	*Singers in every measure;*
Personau parod synwyr,	*Quick-witted people for sure,*
Eithaf ban, a'r iaith yn bur. [1]	*None better, and the language pure.*

Sometime around the year 1727 Dafydd Thomas, a young man from Cardiganshire, moved to Glamorgan where he met and worked with John Bradford the weaver, fuller and dyer who kept the fulling mill or *pandy* at Bettws near Bridgend. Bradford (1706-85), was said to be 'a great disbuter and a Nominated Deist or free thinker'.[2] He was also a poet and one of the members of the bardic circle which Edward Evan joined in the 1730s.

Edward met Dafydd Thomas at a turning point in his life and their meeting was to have a significant influence on his later poetic output. It happened about the time that he left home in Llwydcoed and moved to Hendre Ifan Goch in the parish of Ystradfodwg to begin his apprenticeship with Lewis Hopkin. Thirty years later he remembered Dafydd.

> He was a man of strong natural qualities and well educated ...
> He had a talent for the muse and a fluency of speech. Around
> the year 1730, he set himself to learn the rules of grammar and
> correct composition, and he became very able and inventive in
> Welsh poetry. [3]

He also recalled Dafydd's connection with Rees Price, who had taken over the dissenting academy at Brynllywarch not far from Bettws and ran a school at Ty'n Ton in the same area until his death in 1739. Price was an important figure in the world of Glamorgan dissent, both as a minister and teacher. It seems likely that both Dafydd Thomas and John Bradford studied with him. His son Richard Price, born in 1723, is one of the most interesting and significant Welshmen of the eighteenth century – a leading Unitarian and champion of liberty in America, France and Britain.[4] This connection between the Glamorgan poets and the family of a prominent political radical like Richard Price is highly significant. Edward Evan lived long enough to see Price pilloried for his support of the French Revolution.[5]

Dafydd Thomas's mastery of the rules of traditional Welsh poetry was the result of the help which he, like Edward, received from the 'Glamorgan Grammarians', the group of poets who studied recently-published grammars setting out the rules of traditional strict-metre composition, and held *eisteddfodau*, like the one at Cymmer in 1735.[6] Edward and Dafydd met in 1733 or 1734, some time before Edward attended that St David's Day meeting. The date is significant in view of uncertainty about when he began his apprenticeship with Lewis Hopkin and when the latter moved to Hendre Ifan Goch.

In the brief biography included with the 1874 edition of *Afalau'r Awen*, Edward is said to have begun to learn the crafts of carpentry and glazing from Lewis Hopkin at the age of twenty-three, which would have been in 1739. But since there is no doubt that it was Hopkin who taught him poetry as well as woodwork, that date does not explain how he had sufficiently mastered the rules of traditional composition to be able to submit a poem in the strict metre at the 1735 eisteddfod. R. T. Jenkins believes it is likely he left home at the age of seventeen or eighteen to begin his apprenticeship with Lewis Hopkin who had moved to Hendre Ifan Goch in 1734.[7] This was presumably after Hopkin's marriage and before the birth of his eldest son that December.[8] Edward probably joined him there that year, which would mean he was twenty-three not when he began, but when he finished his apprenticeship five years later.

By 1734, Dafydd Thomas's own brief marriage had ended unhappily and he had moved to the fulling mill at what is now Tonypandy, in the parish of Ystradfodwg where Edward lived with Lewis Hopkin. Dates and locations explain their meeting, their mastery of Welsh poetry, and the fact that they were both included in the list of seven Grammarians named by John Bradford. These were Dafydd Hopcyn of Coity, Rhys Morgan of Pencraig-nedd, Lewis Hopkin, Edward Evan, Dafydd Nicolas of Aberpergwm, Dafydd Thomas, and Bradford himself.[9] Dafydd Thomas died in 1735, so it is not known whether he attended the eisteddfod held at Cymmer, not far from the *pandy* and Hendre Ifan Goch.

After Dafydd's death, Edward found among his papers a translation into Welsh verse of the first chapter of the Book of Ecclesiastes. Thirty years later he and Lewis Hopkin completed and published the work left unfinished by the untimely death of their friend and colleague. It was in the preface that Edward described himself as 'young and foolish' at the time, which suggests it was only later that he realised the potential value of the composition Dafydd Thomas had begun. It was his apprenticeship as a poet among the Glamorgan Grammarians and his growing interest in religion which equipped him to complete the work.

Edward had mastered the form of the popular Glamorgan *triban* as a boy, but it was Lewis Hopkin who taught him the more complex metres of traditional Welsh verse. The master was eight years older than his pupil and was a truly remarkable man. There seems no doubt that he and the other nonconformist Grammarians had a strong influence on Edward Evan's religious beliefs and, perhaps, on his decision to turn his back on *mabsantau* and 'hang his harp on the willow'.

Lewis Hopkin is believed to have joined one of the dissenting congregations led by Henry Davies, minister at the old meeting house at Blaengwrach whose history stretched back to the previous century. Between 1730 and 1734 Davies had established a meeting at Garth in the parish of Llanharan, not far from Cae'r Lan where Lewis was almost certainly living before his move to Ystradfodwg.[10] The meeting at Cymmer, which he certainly joined, was founded by Davies in 1739 and Lewis is said to have become a deacon there. In later life he had a pulpit from which he preached in the barn at Hendre Ifan Goch.

> He was esteemed by all that knew him for his wisdom, integrity, ingenuity, and piety, in which he was so zealous in his latter years, that he kept meetings on Sabbath-day evenings from house to house to expound the scriptures to the edification of many.[11]

Lewis was by no means the only dissenter among the Grammarians. John Bradford was described as a 'Deist' and free-thinker. Iolo, apparently quoting Bradford, reported that Rhys Morgan was a dissenting preacher, and he was probably a member of the meeting house at Blaengwrach.[12] Dafydd Thomas, like Bradford, was a member of Rees Price's congregation at Bettws and Dafydd Nicolas may also have been there, at Ty'n Ton. G.

J. Williams concludes: 'It's clear there was a close connection between Old Dissent and the literary revival in Glamorgan.'

Many years later, and after Lewis Hopkin's death, a meeting was organised in Llantrisant, of which Edward would surely have known. It was advertised 'to the Welsh' as a meeting of bards, poets and writers 'in order to preserve and maintain the old Welsh language, which was once respected by our fathers but is now neglected by the foolish people of Wales, who do not recognise their folly'.[13] Siencyn Morgan, who had studied with the 'Grammarians', wrote to Iolo, complaining that he had not attended the meeting in 1771, and urging him to support another gathering in the new year.

> We can only expect the Llantrisant meeting to die out unless
> you make your best effort to send to Edward Evan of Aberdare,
> together with Wiliam Dafydd of Glynogwr,[14] to come and see
> you once or twice to make firm arrangements. It could be very
> beneficial and constructive for the old Welsh language, and
> could bring other advantages, and build bridges between fellow
> countrymen and sustain the muse a little amongst us and enable
> us to interpret many of the notions within our society for the
> benefit and advantage of each other.[15]

§

In Richard Wagner's opera *Die Meistersinger* ('The Mastersingers of Nuremberg') the central character, Hans Sachs, is based on a famous historical poet and musician who lived in the sixteenth century. Though it may seem unlikely, there are some striking resemblances between him and Edward Evan, the eighteenth century harpist and bard of Glamorgan. They shared not only a love of music and poetry; both were skilled craftsmen, Hans a shoemaker, Edward a carpenter and glazier. They were protestants by religion, Sachs a well-known follower of the reformer Luther, Edward Evan a renowned non-conformist. Each married for a second time, not long after the death of his first wife, Edward aged sixty, Hans at sixty-six. And most importantly they were both prominent members of groups who preserved the old poetic traditions of their nations.

The historian Gwyn A. Williams famously asked 'When was Wales?' The same question might have been asked of Germany. In the time of the Mastersingers of Nuremberg, there was no German state, only lands where a common language was spoken. It was the language which gave people a sense of identity as 'Germans'. At the end of the opera, Sachs pays tribute to the poets who sustained the language and its culture through hard times.

> Our Mastersingers cared for it in the best way that they could, cherishing it and keeping it true according to their lights. It lost its noble pedigree when princes and courts no longer valued it, but still it remained German and true.[16]

There are powerful echoes here of the story told about Wales after the union with England, at exactly the time when the historical Hans Sachs lived. In the nineteenth century, the accusation made against the Welsh ruling class (the *uchelwyr*) was that they turned to English after the 'Acts of Union'. The bards and musicians they had always sponsored fell on their own hard times, and the survival of traditional bardic culture hung by a thread. Change the word 'German' to 'Welsh' in the passage above and one could imagine these words as a tribute to poets like the 'mastersingers' of Glamorgan – Lewis Hopkin, Edward Evan and their companions who rediscovered and revived the tradition.

Wagner's Mastersingers compete to compose songs according to rigid metrical and musical rules, which are satirised in the opera because of the way the art form had become fossilised. Young David, Sachs's apprentice both as a cobbler and a poet, tries to explain the rules of the Masters' songs.

> So many in name and number – the strong and the gentle – so hard to remember! The short, long and overlong tones; the 'writing paper' and 'black ink' melodies; the red, blue and green tones; the hawthorn, straw and fennel tunes; the tender, the sweet and the rose tones, the rosemary and wallflower melodies .....[17]

In *Afalau'r Awen* you can read the verses Edward Evan composed in the twenty-four traditional metres of Welsh poetry, which mirror the twenty-four musical forms mastered by the mediaeval harpists. These are a few of the titles: *unodl union, unodl gyrch, unodl grwcca, prost cyfnewidiog, prost cadwynog, deuair hirion, cywydd llosgyrniog, gorchest y beirdd*. They don't generally have such flowery names as the Mastersingers' measures, but the last one in that list is 'The Bards' Masterpiece' and its definition makes clear the sort of complexity involved in the craft.

> An exceptionally ingenious bardic metre, in which every two syllables of the first twelve rhyme alternately, and every four of the twelve (as well as the seven last syllables) form a '*cynghaneddd*

groes' – an alliterative '*cynghanedd*' – in which the consonants in the first part of the line are repeated in the same order in the second part. [18]

This is not the place to go into any further detail. The poems written in these strict styles can be hard to understand, because they require a specialised and sometimes obscure bardic vocabulary to provide the words required to rhyme and alliterate in all the right places. The group of poets Edward Evan joined studied and applied these rules in their compositions and competitions. In *Y Fêl Gafod*, Lewis Hopkin's own composition in the twenty-four traditional measures can be seen; his is on the theme of sin, while Edward's was on the nature of God.

The fascinating fact is that it was the 'Grammarians', men of the people, who grappled with the tradition of Welsh poetry and injected new life into it. G. J. Williams considered Edward Evan and Lewis Hopkin the most important of the group in their poetic learning and their mastery of the rules of traditional composition. [19]

R. T. Jenkins contrasted the poetic traditions of Wales and England. While each nation had a comparable, vibrant 'folk' culture, it was the Welsh language, and the people's pride in it, which made the difference.

> Country people in Ceredigion, Penllyn or the *Blaenau* of Glamorgan were so conscious of their language and made such efforts to express themselves in it. They were not content to use it only for day-to-day communication but wanted to play with it and – at a higher level – took 'itchy' delight in the language in a literary way. There was no such 'itch' among the country people of England. Almost all the poets of England were of upper or comfortable class, school educated, or at least benefitted from the quiet and leisure of the vicarage. The history of poetry in Wales, at least in the last three centuries, was very different. [20]

But it wasn't just about the twenty-four complex metres. The poet who wins the midsummer competition in the *Meistersinger* opera first impresses Hans Sachs because he breaks free of the rigid rules and composes 'a spontaneous, free-form, appealing song'. And the Glamorgan poets also wrote in free verse, while keeping elements of the rhyme and alliteration central to traditional Welsh poetry. One of the best-known of these – *Y 'Deryn Pur* – is attributed to Dafydd Nicolas, one of Edward Evan's companions. [21]

Y 'deryn pur â'r adain las	*The pure bird with a wing of blue*
Bydd imi'n was dibryder;	*Will be my trusty herald;*
O brysur brysia at y ferch	*O quickly take a message true*
Lle rhois i'm serch yn gynnar.	*To her who's my beloved.*

Remember that Edward Evan's poetry was said to be as popular in the *Blaenau* as that of Vicar Prichard, and 'yr hen Ficer' wrote in free verse, including the *tri thrawiad* form which Edward used to such effect. G. J. Williams also explains the popularity of Edward's free-verse compositions by comparing them with those of Huw Morys ('Eos Ceiriog'), who lived from 1622 to 1709 and who 'brought into vogue a new metre based on the well-established free accented metres but also containing perfect cynghanedd'.[22]

Among Iolo Morganwg's manuscripts is a letter supposedly written by Dafydd Nicolas to Edward Evan in 1754, which discusses the relative merits of strict-metre poetry and free verse, and refers to the work of Vicar Prichard. It warns that if the old poetry with its rules is lost, it will not be long before the Welsh language itself disappears. G. J. Williams believes this letter is one of Iolo's forgeries, but it is significant that he selected Edward Evan to be its alleged recipient. Edward certainly feared for the survival of Welsh, as he made clear in his message to the readers of the translation of Ecclesiastes into the strict *cywydd* metre.

> Take this piece from the last days of Welsh poetry, before it is
> buried by the total forgetfulness of the Welsh people.[23]

Edward and Lewis Hopkin clearly worked together over the years. They each wrote a poem on the construction of the bridge at Pontypridd in 1756, indeed it may have been a set theme for one of the Grammarians' bardic meetings. One couplet from Lewis's poem is short and sweet:

Pont y Tŷ Pridd, clod iddi,	*Pont y Tŷ Pridd, praise where it's due,*
Ar bynt Europ, top wyti.[24]	*Of all the bridges in Europe, the top one's you.*

Y Fêl Gafod includes poems by the two bards reflecting on the Vanity of the World. When Edward composed a complaint in one of the strict measures about Ann Henry's rejection of him, Lewis responded in kind, with gentle mockery. There are examples where they collaborated, writing alternate verses of a poem, or alternate chapters in the case of *Llyfr y Pregethwr* (Ecclesiastes). They both contributed to the first edition of *Trysorfa Gwybodaeth neu Eurgrawn Cymraeg*, a journal printed in Bristol in 1770. Edward composed a moving elegy in memory of Lewis after his death the following year.[25]

Lewis had an extensive library and may have had a collection of old manuscripts. At some point, Edward studied a manuscript of the poems of Dafydd Benwyn, a Glamorgan poet who flourished around 1600. Both he and John James of Aberdare wrote their names in the book, which was in a collection belonging to Morgan Llewelyn, a prominent dissenter and schoolmaster in Neath.[26] The Llewelyn family were 'the backbone' of the nonconformist congregation at Blaengwrach, where Edward was ordained in 1772 and which was close to Rhigos, the home of his second wife Mary Llewelyn, said to be a descendant of Dafydd Benwyn.

One can imagine Edward Evan's life at Hendre Ifan Goch, learning the skills of carpentry and glazing from Lewis Hopkin. No doubt he helped on the farm and it seems he travelled the *Blaenau* as a freelance mower and reaper in the summer months. He absorbed Lewis's radical religious views and, in the evenings, studied the complex rules of strict-metre traditional Welsh poetry. This was an education which made him the remarkable man he was – multi-skilled and, eventually, a leader of his community in Aberdare.

Iolo Morganwg claimed that Edward Evan and his fellow 'Grammarians' were the inheritors of an unbroken bardic tradition, but this is not true in the way Iolo meant it. He maintained that first Edward, and later he, had been taught the rules of strict metre poetry in the traditional oral manner passed down generation by generation from teacher to pupil. In their case, he claimed, this was from Lewis Hopkin and John Bradford who, he said, had learned from Dafydd o'r Nant and Edward Dafydd, with unbroken links back to the fourteenth century when the art still flourished. So, according to Iolo, Edward and he in Glamorgan, unlike the bards of other regions, had the authentic learning, not something studied from grammars and books written by those who knew nothing of the ancient bardic secrets. In saying this, Iolo conveniently forgot how he had previously described the way he had begun to master the poetic rules as a young man by studying a borrowed copy of Siôn Dafydd Rhys's Grammar. But in that account he also went on to tell a story of his bardic connections in the *Blaenau*.

> There were at that [time] in Glamorgan many others who were
> masters of [these] things, and none besides in any other part

of Wales: Mr. Lewis Hopkin of Llandevodoc ... hearing of my acquirements wrote a very friendly letter to me warmly inviting me to spent [sic] the Christmas holydays with [him]. I with joy accepted this invitation and by him I was initiated into [the] Essoteric literature of [the] ancient Bards ... Mr. L. H. soon after gave some account of me to Mr. John Bradford of Bettws the most learned man that had for more than 200 years appeared in the Principality. I soon after received a letter inviting [me] to spend a week at least at his house where I should meet a few more Bardic friends.

He names Rhys Morgan, Dafydd Nicolas, Lewis Hopkin and Edward Evan 'all of them Bards of Chair or sedarity of Tir Iarll' and claims they admitted him as a bardic 'Pupil of Priviledge'. Later, he says, John Bradford 'invested me with the insignia of the Primitive Order of Bards of the Island of Britain in [the] Chair [of] Glamorgan and Tir Iarll'.

Iolo's biographer, G. J. Williams, sees here 'the romantic bard and druid dreaming', but he acknowledges that behind the fabricated bardic structure there is an element of truth. There *was* a continuus history of poetic meetings or *eisteddfodau* in Glamorgan. Iolo's contact with the Grammarians *was* the beginning of his poetic career and his connection to the literary awakening of the following century. It was in the *Blaenau* that he met people who had been inspired by those who had striven to recover the mastery of the poetic art, people who had collected and studied the work of the old poets.[27]

Iolo honoured only two of the Grammarians with an elegy: Edward Evan and Lewis Hopkin, both of whom he acknowledged as his teachers.[28] In neither case is there even a hint of Bardic mysteries or Druidry; in Edward's only a handsome tribute to his skill, and his roots in the poetic tradition.

Un o fil ag awen faith,	*One in a thousand with great inspiration,*
A gwir ddysg eitha'r gerddiaith;	*Truly learned in the best of poetry;*
E wnai araith yn iraidd,	*His speech full of life,*
Doethineb llym grym a gwraidd;	*A sharp wisdom with powerful roots;*
Awen gain yn ei ganiad,	*A beautiful muse in his singing,*
A grym iaith ym mhob gair mâd.[29]	*And the power of language in every good word.*

In his account of the poet and his background, published in the mid twentieth century, R. T. Jenkins concludes:

> I don't see anyone after him, in his own area, who reached higher ground than he; Edward Ifan, then, is the 'greatest bard' of the Cynon Valley until today. He composed not only in a masterly way, but sometimes very beautifully … There is no doubt some truth in the praise given him for 'maintaining the tradition'; it is likely that his loyalty, geniality and friendliness were quite significant elements in the continuation of the bardic co-operation which kept the old tradition alive.[30]

---

[1] John Miles in *Y Fêl Gafod* (1813); In praise of the poetry of his father-in-law, Lewis Hopkin, and his fellow Glamorgan poets whose work is included in the book.

[2] *Diary of William Thomas*, South Wales Records Society (1995). p.339.

[3] Edward Evan, 'To the Reader', *Llyfr Ecclesiastes neu Y Pregethwr*, Bristol (1767).

[4] Thomas, R., & Chambers, Ll. G., (1959), 'Price, Richard (1723-1791)', *Dictionary of Welsh Biography*.

[5] See Chapter 16.

[6] See G. J. Williams, *Traddodiad Llenyddol Morgannwg* (1948), Chapter 6 for a full account of the Glamorgan Grammarians.

[7] R. T. Jenkins, *Bardd a'i Gefndir*, Trans. Hon. Soc. Cymmrodorion (1948), p.106.

[8] Lemuel James, *Hopkinaid Morganwg* (1909), p.107.

[9] *Traddodiad Llenyddol Morgannwg*, p.228.

[10] *Ditto*, pp.232-5.

[11] Lewis Hopkin Jnr. Quoted in *Hopkinaid Morganwg*, p. 115.

[12] *Traddodiad Llenyddol Morgannwg*, p.230.

[13] G. J. Williams, *Iolo Morganwg* (1956), p.127.

[14] Wiliam Dafydd of Glynogwr wrote a poem urging Rhys Evans to publish his father's poetry, which he did in 1804. See Chapter 20 and *Afalau'r Awen* (1874) p. iv.

[15] Letter from Siencyn Morgan to Iolo (30 Nov 1771), *Correspondence of Iolo Morganwg*, p.62.

[16] Richard Wagner, *Die Meistersinger*, Act 3. Sachs is talking about the culture of the German language, but these lines were taken up by German nationalists and the opera became a favourite of the Nazis.

[17] *Die Meistersinger*, Act 1.

[18] *Geiriadur Prifysgol Cymru*.

[19] *Traddodiad Llenyddol Morgannwg*, pp.288-9.

[20] *Bardd a'i Gefndir* p. 104.

[21] See Daniel Huws's note on 'Y 'Deryn Pur' in the Facsimile edition of *Ancient National Airs of Gwent and Morganwg* by Maria Jane Williams, Notes p.5.

[22] 'Morys, Huw ('Eos Ceiriog')', *Dictionary of Welsh Biography*.

[23] Edward Evan, 'To the Reader', *Llyfr Ecclesiastes neu Y Pregethwr* (1767): 'Derbyn hyn o Brydyddiaeth Gymraeg, ar ei hoes ddiweddaf; a chyn ei chladdu mewn Cwbl angof o blith y Cymru'. Lewis Hopkin echoes Edward's concern a postscript to the main work,'Verses to the Welsh', in which he urges them to respect the *cywydd* form of this translation 'before the rich and joyful *awen* falls silent and dies'.

[24] Lewis Hopkin 'Pont y Tŷ Pridd', *Y Fêl Gafod* (1813), p.69.

[25] Edward Evan, 'In Memory of Lewis Hopkin', *Afalau'r Awen* (1874), p.83.

[26] *Traddodiad Llenyddol Morganwg*, p.228.

[27] *Iolo Morganwg*, pp.117-21.

[28] *Hopkinaid Morganwg*, pp.347-65.

[29] NLW MS 21423E.

[30] *Bardd a'i Gefndir*, p. 143.

CHAPTER 12

1744 – The Farmer's Wife

Gwraig ddawnus hwylus haulwen   *A capable, healthy, cheerful wife*
         - synwyrddoeth,   *- sensible and wise*
Sy'n harddwch i'w pherchen.[1]   *Is the best you could possess.*

Almost nothing is known about the women in Edward Evan's life, not even the name of his mother. Only a little more can be said about his two wives. All that the brief biography in *Afalau'r Awen* reveals about Margaret Thomas, whom he married in 1744, is that she was the daughter of Thomas Howell Thomas of Glynperfedd in the parish of Penderyn, that they were married for thirty years and that they were not blessed with children. Then 'after burying her', Edward lived alone for 'a few years'. As for Mary Llewelyn, his second wife, it's much the same; she was a widow from Rhigos, she had two children, Edward and Rhys, and she was known as 'Pali Toncoch'.

As recently as 1986, Welsh women were described as 'culturally invisible', due to the tendency of male historians to focus on the past deeds of men alone.[2] But later research has begun to fill in some of the gaps in knowledge about women's lives in rural Wales in the eighteenth and nineteenth centuries.[3]

Marriage was usually between a woman and man from the same or neighbouring parishes, which was the case with both Edward Evan's wives. Farmers were particular about whom their daughters married in the interests of the future of the family, and dowries were negotiated on the basis of the bride's father's wealth in land and cattle. When a couple began married life on their own farm (rented in this case), it fell to the husband to supply the agricultural implements while the wife was expected to provide linen, bedding and furniture. No doubt many Welsh readers of *The Cambrian* in 1805 would have agreed with a Scottish farmer when the newspaper quoted his opinion that 'the best animal that could be brought upon a farm was a good wife'.

Legally wives were treated as 'minors' under the 'guardianship' of their husbands, though in practice farming marriages were often a much more equal partnership. Farmer's daughters were brought up to do a range of work, including helping with haymaking, harvest, cows, bird-scaring and work in the dairy. Married women continued to contribute in these ways.

> Of vital importance to the well being of the family economy ...
> was the active co-operation of all members of the household.
> In such an arrangement a wife's work constituted an important
> component of the family's income and hence was essential to
> the family's economic survival. Both husband and wife worked
> together in partnership, for both were needed to fulfil the tasks
> necessary for survival, and to contribute to the 'family purse',
> the proceeds of which went to provide for the family, any surplus
> accrued being ploughed back into the holding for future years.
> Assigned different but complementary tasks, husbands and wives
> usually worked in different parts of the holding. Whilst the men
> were occupied in the fields, women normally stayed within an
> area bordering the farmhouse or cottage, and encompassing
> barn and farmyard.[4]

In addition to child care and other household work, farmers' wives prepared produce for sale at market and made clothing for the family. Their knitting was an important source of extra income, especially in hard times.

Edward was in his late twenties when he decided to give up the bachelor life and look for a wife. In the poem below, he concluded it was better to marry a 'wise and affectionate' companion than continue to run the risk of going astray.

Ffarwel o fynwes Iorwerth Fardd,	*Edward the Bard now says farewell*
I gael darluniad cariad cerdd,	*To the art of writing love songs*
I lawer ceingen hoywen hardd,	*For many a lovely, comely maid;*
'Rwy'n awr yn gw'ardd fy'm gwaith;	*I now renounce my work.*
Ffarwel heb wall i Giwpid ddall,	*Blind Cupid, it's farewell to you,*
At arall bydd ei daith.[5]	*Find targets somewhere else.*

As he contemplated settling down, he received advice from his mentor Lewis Hopkin. The lines at the head of this chapter are from a poem he wrote for his friend on the choice of a bride. It paints a highly conservative picture of the ideal wife, while pulling no misogynistic punches in warning Edward to avoid a woman who might be a 'strumpet', a 'slut', a 'scoundrel', or a 'fool' who doesn't know the value of money and could cost him dear. While Hopkin may have applied the same moral view to a man as to a woman, double standards were common when it came to sexual behaviour, with men often judged far more leniently than women.

Edward himself composed a poem based on three different views of marriage, which he put in the mouths of his fellow poets William Thomas, Rhys Morgan and Lewis Hopkin.[6] Rhys reckons he would have no trouble finding a partner himself if he had Edward's talent with the harp. William's advice is to avoid the marriage trap and stick with the freedom of bachelorhood. Lewis recommends a gentle girl of slender means rather than a wealthy young woman with a high opinion of herself.

Though Margaret Thomas seems to have brought Edward wealth enough to take the lease of the farm at Cefnpennar Isaf, there's no reason to believe their thirty years of marriage were anything but harmonious. His lament at her death sounds like genuine testimony to a lasting love. They were married a few days after his friend and mentor James Jones's wedding, the last occasion, according to Iolo, when Edward played his harp in public. This was a turning point in more ways than one.

It is certainly to be hoped that Margaret escaped the 'chastisement', or worse domestic violence, which was often inflicted on wives by husbands who knew they were unlikely to be held to account and who were often drunk when violent. Edward wrote several poems condemning drunkenness. If, like some local bards, he was ever called upon to write satirical verses to shame a wife-beater in the community, the work has not survived.

Was it all plain sailing? Probably not. One of his most interesting poems in this connection is the dialogue between an angry or 'peevish' wife and a mild or meek husband, who says he would never resort to 'barbaric' violence but warns that if he can't persuade her to change, he would rather leave. His complaint is that her tongue, driven by strong emotions, is wearing him down. He moans about women's foolish 'buzzing' and cites the Apostle Paul's recommendation of Abraham's Sara as the model of what a wife should be. But he gets more than he bargained for when she replies, speaking of her own 'self-respect'.

'Dwy'n prisio am Apostol,	*I don't care for apostles*
na Sara wraig siriol	*or happy wife Sara,*
Nac Abra'm grefyddol,	*Nor religious old Abra'm,*
na diafol na dim;	*nor the devil himself;*
Ni thawaf trwy g'wilydd,	*You won't shame me to silence*
pepwniech fy mhenydd,	*if you try my patience*
A'm dodi dros ddeuddydd	*And treat me each day*
yn ddiddim. [7]	*as worth nothing.*

Despite some predictable assumptions, the poem shows a woman who can stand up for herself and much of the dialogue reflects a mature and balanced understanding of the dynamics of a relationship. In his poem *Few Happy Matches*, which Edward rendered in Welsh, the hymnwriter Isaac Watts listed many causes of unhappy partnerships, including the coupling of a mild and an unkind partner.

Nor let the cruel fetters bind
A gentle to a savage mind,
For Love abhors the sight;
Loose the fierce tiger from the deer,
For native rage and native fear
Rise and forbid delight.

The poem ends with a tribute to love in marriage, though in his version, Edward cuts out Cupid, along with the celestial doves.

Two kindred souls alone must meet;
'Tis friendship makes the bondage sweet,
And feeds their mutual loves:
Bright Venus on her rolling throne
Is drawn by gentlest birds alone,
And Cupids yoke the doves. [8]

The final verse of his tribute to Margaret after her death describes her in almost idealistic terms and suggests that, though they had no children, they enjoyed the company of their wider families in their home.

Yr oedd fy mhriod oreu ei rhyw,	*My wife was the best of her sex,*
Yn caru byw'n ddifyrgar,	*She loved to live a life of joy*
A bod yn llawen yn ei thŷ,	*And to be happy in her home*
Ym mysg ei theulu hawddgar.[9]	*Amongst her kindly family.*

It must have been a lonely life for Edward at Ton Coch after Margaret's death in 1774. Though the biography suggests he lived alone for several years, it was 1776 when he married again. It was common for a widower to remarry, especially if he had children who needed caring for. In this case there were none, but there was a farm to be worked and Edward had been minister at the Old Meeting House for four years. However fond his memories of Margaret, the poem anticipating his second wedding combines a genuine excitement with a mature sense of what the widowed couple could offer each other. And Mary ('Pali') gave her husband what Margaret could not. Their first son was born within a year.

---

[1] Lewis Hopkin, 'Advice to Edward Evan on choosing a life companion', *Y Fêl Gafod* (1813), p.107.

[2] Deirdre Beddoe, quoted by Wilma R. Thomas, *Women in the rural society of south-west Wales, c.1780-1870*, Swansea University thesis (2003). http://cronfa.swan.ac.uk/Record/cronfa42585

[3] Much of the information in this chapter is drawn from Wilma R. Thomas's thesis, cited above. Although she focuses on the three west Wales counties of Carmarthenshire, Pembrokeshire and Cardiganshire, she makes the point that the life of women there was not significantly different from that in other rural parts of Wales before the impact of the industrial revolution, such as upland Glamorgan in the lifetime of Edward Evan's wives.

[4] Wilma R. Thomas, p.63.

[5] Edward Evan, 'Farewell to the Single Life', *Afalau'r Awen* (1874), p.16.

[6] Ditto, p. 41, 'Advice on marriage from three friends'.

[7] Ditto, p.55.

[8] Isaac Watts, 'Few Happy Matches' (1701).

[9] 'Farewell to my Life Companion', *Afalau'r Awen* (1874), p.33.

CHAPTER 13

1744-1798 – Cwm Pennar

'Rwy'n cyfrif hwsmonaeth, yn
sylfaen cynhaliaeth,
I'r holl greadigaeth trwy degwch. [1]

Farming for me is the basis of living
For all of creation in justice.

Edward worked for several years as a carpenter and glazier, presumably continuing in that trade after his apprenticeship with Lewis Hopkin ended. According to the biography published in *Afalau'r Awen* in 1874, his craft took him to seventeen parishes across south Wales. He may have continued to work with Lewis at Hendre Ifan Goch for some time before returning to the family home where he is said to have lived until 1744.

Llwydcoed was where he spent his childhood; Ystradfodwg was where he grew both as a craftsman and a poet under the influence of Lewis Hopkin; Cwm Pennar, above what is now Mountain Ash, was where he spent the rest of his life, from the age of twenty-eight until his death more than fifty years later.

Edward and his first wife Margaret took the tenancy of Cefnpennar Isaf on the hillside below the ridge separating Aberdare parish from Merthyr Tydfil. It was close to Ton Coch and above the estate of Dyffryn House, with which Edward would later be closely connected. Not far away was Pantygerdinen, reputed to have been the home of Edward's fabled ancestor, Hwyel Gwyn y Gôf.

There are no records of their five years at Cefnpennar, only the comment in the brief biography that their landlord was 'the kindest in those days'. Margaret may have faced loneliness and isolation on a hillfarm, with no children, a husband who might have been often away with his trade or, towards the end of her life, on his duties as minister at the Old Meeting

House. It appears that relatives of hers or Edward's may have lived with them, or visited regularly. Otherwise, farmers' wives looked forward to socialising at church, chapel or meeting house, or at markets if they took produce there to sell.

Cefnpennar Isaf was not part of the Dyffryn estate but seems to have been divided between two others, with the holding they rented covering fifty of its acres. The tithe map of 1847 describes most of the fields as pasture or meadow, but several are marked as arable land, so they undoubtedly grew crops there as they did later at Ton Coch where, again, some fields were pasture and others for arable cultivation.

Like any farmer Edward had a keen eye for the weather. One of his poems was prompted by the sight of sheep, all white, in a field of snow. Another by the hard winter of 1775-76, when much of Europe endured what Gilbert White called 'the Great Frost'.[2] In the summer months, Edward looked for promising signs of weather for the harvest.

Wrth wel'd y pryfcopyn,	*When I see the old spider at work*
a'i waith ar yr eithin,	*on the gorse bush,*
Iawn arfod 'rwy'n erfyn	*I pray we've a chance for a spell*
am ronyn o wres,	*of hot days,*
I'r llafur gael sychu,	*For the crops to dry out so the men then*
a'r dynion i'w dannu,	*can turn them,*
A'r heulwen i'w gannu	*While they're bleached by the sun's*
fe'n gynnes. [3]	*warming rays.*

This is just one of many poems which display his roots in the rural society of the *Blaenau* and the pleasure he took in celebrating the skills and artefacts of that life. Just as he praised the old reaper, Rhys Wiliam from Brecknock, who could still 'cut clean', he paid tribute to his sons who followed him in his trade. They may be farm labourers, but they are as deserving of praise as the heroes of ancient epic poetry.

Mae'i feibion dewrion a de	*His brave sons, with their powerful stroke,*
– eu hergyd,	*A true sign of their quality,*
Mewn argoel o'r gore,	*Have come with skill and great success,*
Y deuant, llwyddiant llawdde,	*And cut clean in his place.*
I ladd yn lân yn ei le. [4]	

The fine blade of a scythe was as worthy of celebration as the sword of a warrior. To do their job, the mowers needed the best, like those Edward ordered from the blacksmiths of Llannon.[5]

Serchog ha'rn duriog i dorri,	*Fine blades, hard as steel, to cut*
– rhôsdir,	*the moorland,*
Heb rwystyr na bloesgni,	*They won't stutter as they swing;*
Rhai awchus, hoenus heini,	*Sharp, swift and sweet*
Caledion, croewon eu cri.[6]	*Is the cry of their cutting edge.*

He admired the new bridge at Pontypridd, one of the wonders of Europe. But a well-made wheel for a watermill was equally a thing to be celebrated, along with the work of his fellow-carpenters, who needed long study of their craft, and determination to complete the job.

Rhodd graff, ac argraff,	*What a sight*
gywirgron, – a'r coed,	*– a powerful gift, a perfect circle,*
Fel cedyrn olwynion,	*The strong wooden wheel,*
Rhôd drefnus hwylus yw hon,	*Methodical machine,*
Waith rywiog, yn ei throion.	*A noble work as it turns.*
Grymus a hwylus fydd hi,	*Strong, efficient*
– a gerwin,	*– and fierce*
Yn gyrru'r hen feini,	*To drive the old stones;*
Dyry glod, parod tybi,	*The fame of the fine craftsmen*
Yn y sir, i'r glan seiri.[7]	*Will go far, I warrant.*

Watermills to grind grain were common in the *Blaenau*. The wheel here sounds more like the 'great spur wheel' which drove the millstones than the huge waterwheel on the outside wall of a mill. There were wind-driven mills in the Vale and a surviving mill tower can be seen at Wick, converted to a house, with modern wind turbines in the background. The first time Edward saw a windmill it made an impression on him reminiscent of *Don Quixote*. If not in the Vale, he might have seen one on the hill above the church in Llantrisant, marked 'Hen Felin Wynt' (old windmill) on the Ordnance Survey maps.

Gwelais hen gawres yn gyrru,– dewr bryd,	*I saw an old giant in action*
Bedair braich o bobtu;	*– a fine sight,*
A'r gogledd wynt, croyw hynt cry,	*Four arms spinning on all sides,*
Awch aethus yn ei chwythu.	*The north wind blowing strong,*
	With an edge to take your breath away.

Cno'dd gîl, ddieiddil, addig, – arw lef	*It chewed hard, strong, with an angry noise,*
Ar lafur yn ffyrnig,	*Working like a fury,*
Curodd ei dannedd cerrig,	*Grinding its granite teeth*
A'i chern ddewr yn chwyrnu'n ddig.[8]	*With a terrible roar of its jaw.*

In a poem preserved in two versions in Iolo Morganwg's notebooks, Edward praises Harry, a thatcher. He clearly believed that the working man should be honoured. In an elegy for Shon Jones of Aberdare, he criticised those neighbours who had mocked a poor man who had a hard life.

Gwnewch ddirfawr wahaniaeth rhwng dynion didoraeth,	*You should make a big difference between men who are fickle*
A gweithwyr hwsmoniaeth iawn helaeth eu hynt,	*And workers on farms who give all to their work;*
Fe haedda'r llafurus ei gynnal yn barchus,	*The labourer deserves to be truly respected,*
Drwy bob rhyw anhwylus wan helynt.[9]	*Each day of his life is a struggle.*

These poems, written by a farmer, reveal not a 'druidic bard' wrapped up in ancient mysteries, but Edward Evan, the *bardd gwlad*, the people's poet, immersed in the everyday life of the world in which he lived. In a *triban* discovered and published a century after his death, Edward told the story of a great iron hinge on the door of the baking oven on the Dyffryn estate, which originally came from the main entrance of the house.

Y cleddyf harn ysgymun	*The rejected iron sword*
Sy 'nawr ar ddrws yr odyn	*Which now hangs on the oven,*
Fu gynt gan Ddafydd Ifan Ddu,	*Belonged to Dafydd Ifan Ddu,*
Dechreuad teulu'r Dyffryn.[10]	*The ancestor of Dyffryn.*

Dafydd Ifan Ddu, said to be a gentleman and a poet,[11] had bought the Dyffryn estate for £100 in the sixteenth century. While Edward and Margaret were living at Cefnpennar Isaf it belonged to his descendant John Jones, 'a ruinous sort of man' who was in financial difficulty and mortgaged to the hilt.[12] In 1750 he sold to William Bruce, ancestor of the first Lord Aberdare, who bought up other properties in the area and became a substantial local landlord. It was at this time that the poet became the tenant at Ton Coch, on the hillside above Dyffryn House.

The old road to Aberdare ran up the Pennar valley past Ton Coch. An estate map from the nineteenth century shows the land, including the substantial Dyffryn woods, extending from the Pennar brook as far down the hill as the River Cynon, with one strip cut off by the Glamorgan canal. In 1844, when Edward's son farmed it, four fields were described as arable, the rest were meadow or pasture.

Some said the name Ton Coch ('the red meadow')[13] came from the burning effect of the hot sun on the grass.[14] It seems more likely that the field next to the house, which gave the farm its name, grew the common Red Fescue, *Peisgwellt Coch*, 'one of the most frequent grasses of unimproved meadows', which certainly gives a field a striking russet colour when in seed.[15]

The move to Ton Coch was the start of a long and close family relationship with the estate and the landowners of Dyffryn House. Edward Evan was employed to take care of the trees and other work on the estate.

> The estate had long employed a woodward to ensure that this
> valuable asset was well maintained, and usually this employee
> was one of the tenants of the estate's farms. Whenever money
> was required, this resource could be readily realised for the bene-
> fit of the owner. The timber on the estate was at least as import-
> ant as the farms in terms of the money it could generate.[16]

Thomas Bruce, then vicar of St Nicholas in the Vale, inherited from his father in 1768. Thomas too was interested in arboriculture, sourcing trees and seeds whenever he could and experimenting with new varieties on his upland estate … this timber was to become very important to the estate when developments underway in the 1750s reached fruition in the latter part of the century.[17]

Rev. Bruce would have agreed with an article in Edward Evan's copy of *The Spectator*.

> When a man considers that the putting of a few twigs into the
> ground is doing good to one who will make his appearance in

the world about fifty years hence, or that he is perhaps making one of his own descendants easy or rich, by so inconsiderable an expence; if he finds himself averse to it, he must conclude that he has a poor and base heart, void of all generous principles and love to mankind.[18]

A letter survives from July 1790 which Edward wrote on behalf of himself and Thomas David, another tenant.[19] It was addressed to Rev. Bruce, then in Bath for the summer season, and headed 'Oak, ash and cordwood'. Apart from what it says about the timber, it is one of the few examples of his writing in English and shows clearly that he was not so fluent as in his mother tongue.

> Dear Master, I have put the workmen about the wall according to your direction. The young trees are carefully looked about and kept within good fence. If it will be to your liking you may sell a vast number of ash trees because that they are at full growth, and will not be better; and also many pieces of oak fit for selling. There are also a considerable quantity of cordwood fit for cutting the next winter in Graig Issa if it will be desirable to you. The firs in the Graig are growing so tall that we may see them from Duffryn. Though the cattle only once broke to the young trees I do assure you that no person in the world could value the damage above one shilling.
>
> The garden are kept clean and the young plants thriving well. The house are kept clean and everything therein [according] to your order. Every thing here are kept clean that [we know] of, but the Linen in the cupboard which is in the Great Hall we [know] nothing of, because the key is in your own custody.
>
> [We] are our your most humble servants and tenants, Thomas David [and] Edward Evan.

In 1812, twenty-two years later, a large quantity of 'superior quality' oak was advertised for sale by the Dyffryn estate. More than four hundred trees with a weight of 260 tons were said to be growing on Ton Coch and neighbouring farms, close to the canal 'to which every tree in the lot may be hauled at a very trifling expense'. This was during the Napoleonic Wars and the advertisement described the timber as 'admirably calculated from its particular soundness for navy planks'. It is possible that the trees

Edward Evan had looked after were made into Men of War.[20]

As a Christian, he saw war as a plague, turning the children of one Father against each other. But the poems he wrote in his last years, during the Revolution in France and the war with Britain that followed, cast an intriguing light on his political views and the radicalism for which he was remembered. That political radicalism was inseparable from the dissenting religious tradition which he represented, and which led his Old Meeting House, in the years after his death, to become a centre of radical – and 'heretical' – Unitarianism.

---

[1] Edward Evan, *Afalau'r Awen* (1874), p.62.

[2] Rev. Gilbert White, *The Natural History of Selborne* (1842), pp.310-14.

[3] *Afalau'r Awen*, p.125.

[4] *ditto*, p.64.

[5] Why he should send to Llan-non in Carmarthenshire, or even Llanon in Cardiganshire is imposible to say. There were certainly forges nearer to home.

[6] *Afalau'r Awen*, p.19.

[7] *ditto*, p.118.

[8] *ditto*, p.117.

[9] *ditto*, p.107.

[10] *Yr Ymofynydd* (1892), p.207.

[11] Dafydd ab Ieuan Ddu, owner of Dyffryn House in 1553, was a bard who could compose a *cywydd*, according to *Gardd Aberdâr* (1854), p.80.

[12] It was the diarist William Thomas who described John Jones as 'a ruinous sort of man, who parted with his wife those years past, and mortgaged his estate in vicious living'. *William Thomas's Diary* (25 August 1767), S. Wales Record Society (1995), p.209.

[13] Field number 670 on 1844 tithe map.

[14] 'Catiau Cwta Catwg', *Y Darian* (9 November 1916).

15 *https://www.allthingsrural.co.uk/product/red-fescue/*

[16] Jeremy J. Morgan: 'Henry Austin Bruce, the Duffryn Estate and the development of an industrial society: Mountain Ash 1845-1895', p.36. (M. Phil Thesis, Cardiff University 2016, available online).

[17] Jeremy Morgan, ditto.

[18] *The Spectator*, No. 583 (Vol. 8), p.121.

[19] Thomas David (Tomos Dafydd) was not only a fellow tenant and employee. He was one of the local poets and wrote the first verses of the poem in *Afalau'r Awen* on the

cold winter of 1776, referred to above.

[20] Advertisement in *The Cambrian* (4 April 1812). According to Jeremy Morgan (p.41), the timber sold for £10,700, which paid for the purchase of more surrounding farms. It may also have gone to the ironworks in Merthyr, which were producing material for the war.

CHAPTER 14

Edward Evan's people

Beirdd y byd barnant wyr o galon.[1] *The bards of the world judge men of courage.*

The small, remote parish of Aberdare was Edward Evan's home throughout his long life. But that did not mean that he was cut off from the wider world. And within the *Blaenau*, he knew and honoured people from all walks of life, in a true continuation of an ancient bardic tradition.

Of the poets he met in his youth, Edward left records of only two. The first was his account of the life and early death of Dafydd Thomas in the introduction to the verse translation of Ecclesiastes (*Llyfr y Pregethwr*) he wrote with Lewis Hopkin.[2] The second was his elegy for Hopkin, who died in 1771.

Mae fe 'nawr yn fawr ei fyd,	*He's now in a greater world,*
– gobeithiaf,	*– I trust,*
Mewn bythol ddedwyddfyd;	*In happiness eternal;*
Pam yr wylaf, cwynaf c'yd,	*Why then should I weep and mourn,*
O'm anfodd am ei wynfyd?[3]	*In grief at his felicity?*

During his time as an apprentice at Hendre Ifan Goch he became close to Hopkin's wider family, who lived at nearby Cae'rlan farm, where Lewis had spent much time as a child with his maternal grandfather. A record of his connection can still be seen in the form of a sundial over the porch inscribed 'Tempus irreparabile fugi', 'Lewis Hopkin fecit' ('Time flies and cannot be recovered, made by Lewis Hopkin'), with the date 1749.[4]

Thomas William, Lewis's uncle, inherited the house and Edward Evan commemorated him in a poem after his death in 1757, which is one of the longest he wrote. In the style of a mediaeval bard praising his generous noble patron at his court, he describes Thomas of Cae'rlan as a gentle man and a good neighbour, well known for his generosity, charity and hospitality.

Torodd ei fwyd, wr tirion,   *This kind man would share his food*
I'r rhai tlawd fel brawd o'u bron.[5]   *With the poor, as a brother would.*

It is an impressive tribute in the ancient tradition – in this case to a respected farmer, not a noble. It must have been a treasured gift for the family of the dead man, including Edward's friend and teacher, Lewis Hopkin.

Thomas William left Cae'rlan to Lewis Hopkin's older brother, William Lewis.[6] He was also commemorated in a poem by Edward Evan, after his death in 1784. William, like his uncle, is remembered as a generous man, but Edward, now aged almost seventy, mourns him also as one of his oldest friends – 'tempus fugit'.

'E fudwyd fy nghyfoedion,   *My contemporaries are departing,*
- o'r traian,   *My excellent good friends,*
A'm trwyadl gyfeillion,   *Those talented people, dear to me,*
O ddoniol anwyl ddynion,   *I bid them now farewell.*
Yn iach iddynt o'r hynt hon.[7]

A poem from the 1760s suggests that Edward's political beliefs – like his religion – were not always as radical as they were by the end of his life. But it also shows how he was engaged with the politics of Glamorgan and beyond, long before the French Revolution. In 1761, Sir Edmund Thomas of Wenvoe Castle near Cardiff stood for election as the Member of Parliament for Glamorgan. He was a landowner and a Royalist, friendly with Frederick, Prince of Wales (father of George III), and 'groom of the bedchamber' until the prince's death in 1751. He was a supporter of the Prime Minister John Stuart, third Earl of Bute and father of the future coal owner and first Marquess. He stood again in 1763 and in 1767, though he died during that election.[8] Edward's poem in support of him is remarkable in several ways.

He addresses the residents of Glamorgan as though they all had a voice in choosing a representative in Parliament, which was very far from the case. The poet himself would not have had a vote, but he writes that the law 'favours them' with the opportunity to send a 'skilled debater' to London.[9] The poem praises Sir Edmund not only as a parliamentarian (he had previously represented an English seat) but as a Welshman (*'o hil Brutainiaid'*), perhaps in contrast with the previous MP, Lord Talbot, who was born in England though his mother was from Glamorgan. So far as being a great debater goes, the record shows that Sir Edmund did not speak in the House of Commons after 1761 and did not even vote in a division after 1763, when he was appointed Surveyor General of Woods and Forests.[10] It is clear from other evidence that those without a vote took a close interest in elections and tried to influence their outcome. In this case, for reasons unknown, Edward decided to throw his weight behind the Royalist lord of Wenvoe Castle.

The estate at Penllergaer near Swansea was, for nearly three centuries, the seat of the Price family, descendants of Maenarch, Lord of Brecknock. In 1787, Griffith Price, last of the line, died in London. William Thomas of Michaelstone-super-Ely recorded his death in his diary for 18 August.

> Came over the road this day in a Hearse to be buried at Llangyvelach from London, where he dy'd this nine days past, Griffith Pryce of Penllegaer Esqr., a Councellor at Law and a Solicitor to his Majesty King George the Third. Of about 70 years of age and the father of our County in the Law, being very learned and bold therein.[11]

In an elegy he composed on the death of Griffith Price, Edward Evan echoed Thomas's words about his performance in court in the style of ancient praise poetry.

Gwr cadarn o flaen barnwyr,	*A man strong before judges,*
Gwr da gyda gwycha gwyr,	*A man as good as the best of men,*
Gwr medrus, gwir ei 'madrodd,	*A man of skill, true in his discourse,*
Gwr serchog iawn rywiog rodd.[12]	*A loving man, generous in gifts.*

Price was a judge himself, sitting as Recorder in his ancestral county of Brecknockshire. Both his daughters died, Jane in 1769 and Mary in 1782. After the death of his second child and heiress, Edward sent Griffith a poem which speaks in the voice of the mourning father, again in a style reminiscent of a traditional lament.

Heno 'rwy'n byw fy hunan,	*Tonight I live in silence*
- trwy osteg,	*– alone,*
Mewn tristwch anniddan	*Wretched in grief*
Am fy merch loyw serch lân,	*For my bright, beloved girl,*
Greddfol ac oer wy'n gruddfan. [13]	*Deep and cold my groans.*

Edward's connection with Price is not known. The extensive inventory of his Penllergaer estate, drawn up after his death, shows his interest in literature and includes a number of books in Welsh.[14] The only clue to his political opinions is the fact that his name appears, next to that of Richard Price of Ty'n Ton, on the list of members of the Society for the Abolition of the Slave Trade, formed in the year of his death.[15]

Price, dying without an heir, left the house and estate in Swansea to his relative, John Llewelyn (1756-1817). The name of the property was usually spelt Penllergare, rather than Penllergaer. In *Afalau'r Awen*, it is called Penllwynygaer, which is clearly a mistake; there is no record of such a place name and all the details of Griffith's life confirm that he was certainly the person referred to in Edward's poems.

Considering how little is known of the women in Edward Evan's life, it is noteworthy that several of his poems name women of his acquaintance. In an elegy in memory of Ann Williams of Penwern he describes her as 'my friend'.

Mor wych yw coffadwriaeth y cyfion wiwlon waith,	*How fine 'tis to remember the righteous and their works,*
Mor rhydd o'u holl drallodion 'nol dod i ben eu taith.[16]	*How free they are from all their woes at their long journey's end.*

There are two poems to women giving advice on how to live a good and happy life. One is addressed to Margaret Williams of Sychbant, which was the name of a farm in the parish of Llangynwyd. The other is for Pegi Williams of Blaenau Gwent, who may have been one of the old-established family of Cwm Nant y Groes, a farm above Abertillery.[17] Similar advice is given in the poem addressed to the sons of Dafydd Edward who were going to England, with all the risks that entailed. At far greater peril, in Edward's opinion, was William John Howell, his farmhand, who had decided to join the crew of a privateer, one of the ships licensed to attack and sack enemy vessels during the wars with France.[18]

He wrote a poem for Richard Watkins of Pantyfid, a farm neighbouring

Hendre Ifan Goch, who had sold Cae'rlan to William Thomas, Lewis Hopkin's uncle.[19] Watkins had lent Edward a copy of *The Wars of the Jews* by the first century Jewish historian Josephus, which includes an account of the Roman destruction of the temple in Jerusalem. It had been translated in 1760 by William Whiston, a Newtonian in science and an Arian in religion. In his poem Edward, like many Christians of the time, interprets the history as divine vengeance on the Jews for the crucifixion of Jesus.[20]

He sent a newly-sharpened razor to Rev. Philip Charles, of the Old Meeting House at Cefncoed y Cymmer, along with a poem praising its edge:

Ddim gwell arf ar dy farf di.[21]   *No better blade for your beard.*

A gravestone originally standing outside the east window of St John's Church in Aberdare recorded the death of a murderer, William Owen, a 'pauper' aged twenty-nine, who was hanged on the gibbet on Stalling Down in 1787 after murdering his sweetheart in Merthyr Tydfil. The original Welsh inscription wore away long ago, but Edward translated it in an English verse included in *Afalau'r Awen.*

> My lovely passions, turn'd to furious rage,
> Have brought me here in the bloom of age,
> Yet not despised of pardon from my sin,
> By true repentance, from the heart within.[22]

If Owen did repent, that might explain how his body came to be buried in hallowed ground after being left to hang as a warning to others on the hilltop above Cowbridge. The burial is recorded in the Parish Register on 21 April 1787.

Edward Evan's original gravestone was replaced by a family memorial which stood in the churchyard until 1972, when it was moved to the edge of the burial ground, where it can no longer be found.[23] Still to be seen on the outside wall of St John's Church is a memorial to Rev. Owen Rees, minister of the Old Meeting House in Aberdare from 1756 to 1768.[24] It is now badly weathered but the inscription was in the form of an acrostic poem by Edward Evan, in which the first letters of each line form the name of the dead man. It is a meditation on the transience of earthly life.

O ddyn ar derfyn bron darfod, - ystyr,
Wir destyn myfyrdod,
Elw i'r byw ni welir bod
Na Sylfaen hir breswylfod.

O *man, at life's end, remember*
What is vital to be learned;
Enduring riches are not in this world,
Nor is there here an abiding city.

Rhybyddiais ddyfais wir ddwyfol, - orchwyl,
Erchais ar fy mhobol,
Er neb i drysori 'nol,
Sail addas a sylweddol.[25]

Recall the godly message which
Ever I preached to my people;
Everyone may store up treasure
Solely on a sure foundation.

Between 1768 and 1770, Owen Rees was briefly succeeded at the Old Meeting House by two ministers. But according to Iolo Morganwg, it was his wish that Edward Evan should succeed him as he did, following his ordination in 1772.[26]

---

[1] Aneirin, *Y Gododdin*, 6th century.

[2] See chapter 15.

[3] Edward Evan, *Afalau'r Awen* (1874), pp.83-84.

[4] See Illustration in RCAHM Wales, Glamorgan, Vol. IV, Part 2, p.XXX. 'Tempus fugi' is an error (by Lewis Hopkin) for 'Tempus fugit'.

[5] *Afalau'r Awen*, pp.95-98. The poem is more than 120 lines.

[6] Lemuel James, *Hopkiniaid Morgannwg*, pp.103ff.

[7] *Afalau'r Awen*, pp.49-50.

[8] *Diary of William Thomas* (12 October 1767), S. Wales Record Society (1995), p.194.

[9] Jeremy Morgan (in a note to the author) suggests it is possible that Edward Evan had a vote, since the forty-shilling freeholder qualification contained many elements of property. 'Certainly, many of his friends like Lewis Hopkin would have. It might be considered that, as a tenant farmer and skilled craftsman, Edward Evan and those in his circle were at least the elite of the working class. That he was woodward to an upper-class Anglican vicar alone suggests he was not excluded from employment by his religion. He held, in effect, the role of agent to the Dyffryn estate, which was not a petty employment. Anglicans in such positions would have been the parochial officers and have had a place in the running of the locality. While by no means wealthy, Edward Evan and his circle need to be considered in this light. There were many poorer than them.'

[10] L. Namier & J. Brooke (eds.), *History of Parliament: The House of Commons 1754-1790* (1964).

[11] *Diary of William Thomas* (11 August 1787), South Wales Records Society (1995).

[12] *Afalau'r Awen*, pp.109-10.

[13] *Ditto*, p.82-3, 'Verses sent by the author to Mr Price, of Penllwynygaer, after the

death of his only daughter and heir'.

[14] Jeff Childs, 'Inside Penllergaer House Two Hundred Years Ago', Gower Society, No. 41, (1990).

[15] *List of the Society for the Abolition of the Slave Trade,* London (1788), p.40. The report of the committee points out that they are campaigning for abolition of the trade, not of slavery itself.

[16] *Afalau'r Awen* pp.37-8. I have been unable to trace Penwern.

[17] Daniel Lewis, *The History of Aberystruth Parish in Monmouthshire* (1838), translated by Colin Morgan, Blaenau Gwent Heritage Forum (2009), p.18.

[18] *Afalau'r Awen*, pp.62-3.

[19] 'Meisgyn and Glynrhondda', Llantrisant and District Local History Society, New Series Vol. X, No.2 (March 2018), p.28.

[20] *Afalau'r Awen*, pp.50-51.

[21] *Ditto*, p.90

[22] *Ditto*, p.121.

[23] In addition to Edward Evan, the gravestone recorded the names of his wife Mary ['Pali'] (d.1821), Rees [Rhys] Evans (d.1867), his wife Mary (d.1871), Edward [son of the bard] (d.1862), Howell Evans [son of Rhys], (d.1867), Elizabeth Evans [wife of Howell] (d.1889), Jane Evans [daughter of Howell and Elizabeth] (d. 1891). Also buried in the grave was Elizabeth Anne, daughter of Thomas and Ann John (d.1865, aged 14 months); her mother was probably Ann(e), a daughter of Rhys Evans. The details of the gravestone are No.784 in the record of the graves at St John's Church.

[24] Owen Rees's son Josiah must also have been well-known to Edward. He was the editor of *Trysorfa Gwybodaeth neu Eurgrawn Cymru*, a journal published in Bristol in 1770, which included poems by Edward Evan and Lewis Hopkin.

[25] *Afalau'r Awen*, pp.105-6.

[26] R. T. Jenkins, *Bardd a'i Gefndir*, Trans. Hon. Soc. Cymmrodorion (1948), p.126.

CHAPTER 15

1772 – The Old Meeting House

Er cymmaint o enwau sy' nawr	*There are so many sects*
yn ein dyddiau.	*with their different names,*
'Does neb rhyw gynheddfau	*But the truth is their virtue*
ond ffrwythau tra ffraeth,	*is seen by their fruits;*
Drwy ffydd wironeddol	*It is genuine faith and*
a bwriad 'tifeiriol,	*a heartfelt repentance*
A wna'n gadwedigol deg odiaeth.[1]	*That will bring the salvation of souls.*

Edward was fifty-six years old in 1772 when he was installed as minister at what became known as the Old Meeting House (*yr Hen Dŷ Cwrdd*) in Aberdare. Almost two hundred years later a young Eric Jones arrived in the town to take up the post. He would be the last minister to the Welsh speakers of the *Hen Dŷ Cwrdd*, and to another Unitarian congregation at Highland Place, where he held services until he retired in 2003.

When I met him, sixty years after he came to Aberdare, he recalled how he was received by other religious leaders in the town, where there was still a large number of chapels.

> They had a meeting to decide whether I should be invited to be part of the Ministers' Fellowship and they decided they couldn't invite me to join. There was one minister who would refuse to shake hands with me.[2]

Their objection was that, as a Unitarian, Eric Jones was a 'heretic', not a true Christian. This hostility arose from the theological journey which the ministers and members of the Old Meeting House had travelled in the previous two hundred years. And Edward Evan's own religious development was a key part of that journey.

Why should this matter, especially to a non-religious reader? There are three reasons. First, Edward's beliefs were at the centre of his life as a man with a mission. Secondly, those beliefs are reflected in much of his poetry and explain its popularity among devout readers in the nineteenth century. Thirdly, the 'leftward' journey of radical nonconformity was a very important factor in the political radicalism of that century, as later chapters will show.

To make sense of all this, it is necessary to venture briefly into the deep waters of protestant theology. There is a risk of oversimplification here and the reader who requires more detail is referred to authoritative sources which are available.[3]

In the register of those he baptised at the Old Meeting House, Edward often signed himself 'Edward Evan, Dissenting Minister of the Gospel'.[4] Those few words very simply sum up his religious beliefs, in what can be a complex and confusing theological discussion. In his poetry and his religious publications it is clear that Jesus's teaching, a message of love and salvation set out in the gospels, was the basis of Edward's faith. And the congregations with whom he developed his understanding of Christianity were Dissenters, nonconformists.

Again, the words say it all; these were people who 'dissented', who refused to conform, who rejected the religious order of the Establishment in the form of the Church of England. In the case of the Old Meeting House it was that dissent which led, in the years after Edward's death, to a clear 'Unitarian' position which many mainstream Christians condemned as heresy.

The story begins three hundred years before Eric Jones's arrival in Aberdare, with the persecution of Dissenters under the 1662 Act of Parliament which ruled that 'there could be no social and political harmony without strict religious uniformity'.[5]

Religion and politics had been inseparably linked in the English Reformation and the Civil Wars of the seventeenth century. Parliamentarianism and Puritanism went hand in hand, in opposition to the supposed 'Divine Right' of the king and the hierarchy of the Established Church. Puritan missionary activity in Wales during the years of war and the Commonwealth saw the establishment of small but significant communities of

Dissenters, including one which put down deep roots on the mountain between Merthyr Tydfil and Aberdare.

Writing in the 1760s, the rector of Merthyr complained to his bishop that hardly anyone attended his services, for which he blamed those who had overthrown church and king a hundred years earlier.

> We have very few communicants, not above ten or twelve, more is the pity. The occasion whereof is our having so great a number of dissenters, who before the Grand Rebellion, were not so many, but in those unhappy times of usurpation multiplied apace, took firm footing and overspread this part of the country in every way.[6]

In the face of persecution after the restoration of Charles II, the farmhouse at Blaencannaid, close to the rocky road (*yr heol gerrig*) between Merthyr and Aberdare, became a haven for the local Dissenters. This was one of 'the clandestine congregations ... which perpetuated the Dissenting message in post-restoration Wales'.[7] Following the 'Glorious Revolution' of 1688, which saw the Catholic James II replaced by the Protestants William and Mary, a new meeting house at Cwm-y-glo, close to Blaencannaid, was licensed under the Act of Toleration of 1689. This congregation was the origin of several later non-conformist meetings in the *Blaenau*, including the Old Meeting House in Aberdare. Eric Jones felt a strong link to that period.

> When I visited Cwm-y-glo on the mountain between Aberdare and Merthyr Tydfil, to find a location down in a dingle and realise how careful people had to be when they met for their worship, and I was told about people standing out in the fields keeping watch for the law, I realised the sacrifice people had made in those days so that we could get to where we were in the 1960s. It had quite an influence on me. I feel a direct connection to those people, those very radical people in the early days, who put their lives on the line.[8]

According to Thomas Rowlands ('Idris Ddu'), Edward Evan was the last person to preach at the historic meeting house at Cwm y Glo, whose roots went so deep into the history of nonconformity.[9] Edward himself made a connection to 1689 and the new regime which William and Mary's reign had introduced in religion and politics. In a poem which highlights the continuing dissatisfaction of those who did not conform to the rules and rites of the established church, he reveals how alive these issues remained for more than a century.[10]

First he welcomes the expulsion of James and the 'papist' Stuarts, but he regrets that this 'reformation' did not go far enough. Too much 'popish rubbish and folly' remain in the Church of England; the clergy are more interested in wealth and privilege than in Christ's teaching; they neglect their flocks and leave them in the hands of poorly-paid curates; bishops are described as complacent, money-grubbing and aggressive.

In a satirical section he puts words into the mouths of these bishops, who complain that Jesus's teaching is too restrictive for those who desire riches, greatness and honours. Dissenters, whom they dismiss as puritan 'Roundheads', are warned to keep their mouths shut and be grateful for such limited freedoms as they have.

Edward echoes the widespread and long complaint of nonconformists against the tithe – a tenth of their income – which they were still forced to pay to the Anglican Church. This became a particularly burning issue following the French Revolution of 1798,[11] was taken up by the Chartists in the 1840s, and was not finally resolved until the Disestablishment of the Church of England in Wales in 1920.

Despite his later nonconformity, Edward was undoubtedly baptised in the Anglican church of St John's in Aberdare; he was married, though a nonconformist, in the Anglican church in Penderyn, with the apparent support of Theophilus Evans, an Anglican clergyman 'very antagonistic towards Dissent'.[12] His body was buried, with his ancestors, in the church-yard of St John's, although by that time the Old Meeting House had its own burial ground. Nothing is known about his early religious beliefs or practices, but he is believed to have joined the congregation at Cwm-y-glo in around 1748. It seems likely his 'conversion' was the result of Lewis Hopkin's influence during the years that he lived with him at Hendre Ifan Goch, when he may well have attended the meeting at Cymmer where Hopkin was a deacon.

The congregation at Cwm-y-glo divided in the late 1740s, with new causes established in and around Merthyr Tydfil. Members from Aberdare may have continued to cross the mountain to gather there even after the lease of the meeting house expired in 1749. Eventually, and probably for reasons of convenience rather than doctrine, they founded their own *Tŷ Cwrdd*, 'a meeting house ... for Protestant Dissenters', at Trecynon, Aberdare in 1751, with Edward Evan among its first members.[13]

A century later, in 1858, just before it was demolished and replaced with an impressive new building, the original Old Meeting House was described by an anonymous visitor.

> At a little distance you would take the chapel for a labourer's cottage; on coming closer ... you might suppose it to be an inn of the humbler sort. The tiled roof is extended over a porch, within which a flight of stone steps on one side leads up into the gallery ... Inside, the chapel looks like a building of two storeys with a square aperture cut in the upper storey for the pulpit to stand in ... The chapel will hold perhaps 250 people.[14]

The service was entirely in Welsh. The unaccompanied singing was 'superior to what might have been expected; the voices were melodious and the performances pleasing.' Bread and wine were shared among the congregation '*er cof am ein Harglwydd Jesu Grist*' ('in memory of our Lord Jesus Christ').

By 1858 when their visitor described the service in the Old Meeting House, it had been Unitarian for half a century. In their communion 'our Lord Jesus Christ' was revered as a teacher but not as God, and the bread and wine were shared in his memory but by no means as his divine 'body and blood'. In a history of Unitarianism in Merthyr Tydfil and Aberdare, the position is summed up in this way:

> That Jesus had no existence before his perfectly natural birth and was not divine. Rather, he was a man 'blessed of God'. To this school of thought, the [Trinitarian] idea of a Divinity composed of Three Persons which remained indivisibly one God was irrational, untenable and unnecessary to a life of piety and reason in partnership ... In summary, it became a premise of the emerging Unitarian movement that Jesus was an enlightened teacher blessed of God, but fully human nonetheless.[15]

This was a very long way from the theology which had been at the heart of early Protestant dissent, and from the beliefs held when Edward Evan first joined the 'Presbyterian' congregation at the Old Meeting House. Here it becomes necessary to engage briefly with the description of three or four 'isms', theological approaches to Christianity which have, between them, generated libraries of books. These are Calvinism, Arminianism, Arianism and Unitarianism.

Calvin, like all orthodox Christians, believed in the Trinity of the Father, Son and Holy Spirit, three 'persons' of one Godhead. He taught that every human was tainted by the 'original sin' of Adam and Eve, and that only those 'elected' by God would be saved from eternal damnation by the redeeming blood of Christ, the second person of the Trinity. Nothing a Christian could do or say would achieve their salvation; their eternal fate was predestined.

Historians have described how 'the tough-minded chapels' of the *Blaenau* 'went over to liberal Presbyterianism on their route to Unitarianism',[16] 'elevating the doctrine of justification above the harsher demands of predestination and election'.[17] Justification refers to salvation through faith, repentance and good works, and so was an important divergence from Calvinist teaching, and a matter of eternal life or death. This became the great divide between Calvinism and Arminianism. While Calvin's teaching remained a powerful force in Wales, especially among Methodists, Arminius had taught that humans had free will and that God's grace was available to all who repented of sin.

In his 1763 report to the bishop, the rector of Merthyr wrote:

> Above three-quarters of the ... inhabitants are Presbyterians, professing themselves for the most part Arminians. There are a few Calvinists and fewer Baptists and among all these, I am afraid, are too many Deists ...[18]

The 'Deists', as he calls them, were probably Arians, followers of a doctrine based on the ideas of Arius who was condemned as a heretic in the fourth century. This was the next 'dangerous' step on the road from Arminianism to Unitarianism. For Arians, Jesus was secondary to the Father and not truly God 'of himself'. This amounted to a denial of the Trinity and was 'a radical departure from orthodox belief.'[19]

Between 1748 and the end of his ministry in 1796, Edward Evan had travelled that long distance and stood, as an Arian, on the threshold of outright Unitarianism, the creed which became the bedrock of religious and political radicalism in Aberdare and Merthyr in the following century.

It is impossible to date most of Edward's poems, but references within them can be seen as steps in the radicalisation of his religious beliefs. When it comes to Calvinism, there is nothing to suggest that he was ever a hardline follower. The original sin of Adam and Eve is an essential element of Calvinist doctrine, but in his poem on 'The Fall of Adam',[20] Edward makes no mention of 'election' or predestination. He clearly sees Jesus as saviour, messiah, the second Adam who 'bought' human salvation at the cost of his death. But equally clearly, 'a gate of hope has been opened for all who are repentant', through the grace of Christ and the immeasurable, loving mercy of God. This is only one of several poems on religious themes which speak of the mercy available to all who repent.[21]

He certainly sounds like an Arminian and R. T. Jenkins believes he was influenced at this stage by the the theologian Richard Baxter, who held that Christ had died for all and that faith and repentance are the conditions for salvation.[22] Further evidence can be seen in his first religious work, published in Carmarthen in 1757, fifteen years before his ordination as a minister. This is a Welsh version of *Lectures to Children and Young People* by Samuel Bourn, who was also influenced by Baxter.[23] Bourn states clearly that 'the Terms of Salvation' as declared in the Gospel are repentance (a return to God), Faith (owning or accepting Jesus Christ), Holiness, Righteousness, and Obedience to Christ and his Gospel.[24]

Bourn would later publish *A Vindication of the Principles and Practice of Protestant Dissenters*, designed to help parents explain to their children 'the true grounds of non-conformity'. Bourn's lectures and Edward Evan's translation are in the form of 'catechisms', questions and answers about Christian belief which young people were encouraged to learn. The introduction, included in Welsh, puts a great emphasis on the importance of moral education by parents, and Edward's decision to translate the work reflects a similar commitment, which can also be seen in several of his poems advising young people on how to live a good life. The fact that it was published, years before his ordination, is a remarkable tribute to this farmer's reputation, his commitment to learning, and to his mission.

Arminian influence can be seen in the verse translation of Ecclesiastes (*Llyfr y Pregethwr*) which he and Lewis Hopkin published in 1767. It includes a tribute to their friend Dafydd Thomas and represents the first publication of any poetry written by Edward Evan. It was Edward who wrote the introduction, in which he explains that their interpretation of this book of the Old Testament is based on the work of Simon Patrick, the Bishop of Ely, who was criticised for his Arminian beliefs.[25] Edward clearly respected his theology, despite the fact that the bishop had supported the penal laws against nonconformists.

The first record of Edward Evan preaching at the Old Meeting House in Aberdare comes from some years earlier, in June 1763, when he took as his text Job chapter seven, verse sixteen, which speaks of the 'vanity' of life, a theme he explored more than once in his poetry.[26] This was still nine years before his ordination and the question now arises whether he studied formally before becoming a minister. If he did, it was at the Academy in

Carmarthen, where his successor Eric Jones was a student in the 1960s alongside more orthodox Baptists and Congregationalists. By Edward Evan's day its leadership had moved from Arminianism to Arianism under Jenkin Jenkins. [27]

In view of his age, experience and learning – self-taught or otherwise – it may not have been considered essential for Edward Evan to gain formal theological qualifications before his ordination. But there certainly was an Edward Evans at Carmarthen between 1768 and 1771 and no other student of that name has been traced. The main reason for doubting that he attended is the fact that the Presbyterian Fund Board in London, which supported students, had an age limit of twenty-three and Edward was fifty-two by this time. On the other hand, his colleague Thomas Morgan, ordained alongside him in 1772, was definitely a student at the academy in those years and was supported by the fund, even though he was thirty-two. R. T. Jenkins, who investigated the question in great detail, remained of the opinion that Edward probably did not study at Carmarthen, though he left the question open. In light of all the evidence he uncovered, however, it is certainly possible that Edward left the farm in Margaret's care and joined the students at the academy during term time.[28] She probably had help on the farm; in one poem Edward tries to dissuade a man from leaving the land to go to sea 'after he had worked for me for a time'.[29]

Jenkin Jenkins, an Arian and tutor at the academy, was one of the six 'ministers of the gospel' who took part in the ordination of Edward Evan and Thomas Morgan at Blaengwrach in July 1772. Of the others, David Williams 'veered towards Arminianism and Arianism'; Samuel Davies 'defected' to Arminianism (or Arianism); Josiah Rees, 'an Arian from his early days' became a Unitarian; Joseph Simmons was said to be a Calvinist but was later criticised by Edmund Jones, for having taken part in the ordination of the 'heretical' Edward Evan.[30] Josiah was the son of Owen Rees, Edward's predecessor as minister of the Old Meeting House from 1756 to 1768. Edmund Jones, known as 'the Old Prophet', blamed him for the falling away from Calvinist orthodoxy. 'See now in Edward Evans the consequences of Owen Rees's apostasy from evangelical truths'.[31]

Edward was minister at the Old Meeting House from 1772 until 1796, when he reached the age of eighty. According to one report, he was paid a salary of eight pounds a year (only a thousand pounds today).[32] The formal membership was never large, although the old building could hold more than two hundred. But the curate of Aberdare, reporting on nonconformity in the parish in 1781, wrote: 'They do increase of late because they love to be dissenters.'[33]

The year after he took over the ministry at the Old Meeting House, Edward translated into Welsh an important document in the history of Calvinism and Arminianism in Wales. This was Charles Winter's account of the dispute among the Baptist congregation at Hengoed in 1730, which led to his excommunication. Winter went on to establish an Arminian Baptist church, in line with his belief that God's grace and salvation were available to all. After his death, the Calvinist Baptists refused to ordain his successor. It was the liberal Presbyterians, including Edward Evan and several of those who had taken part in his ordination, who stepped in to conduct the cermony.[34]

Edward's reputation as a preacher spread far. In 1775 he was invited to preach at a meeting of ministers at Y Drewen near Newcastle Emlyn, seventy miles from Aberdare and two days' ride on horseback. His sermon, two hymns he composed and his translation of psalm 148 were published that same year at Carmarthen, with a quotation from a poem by Vicar Prichard printed below the preacher's name.[35] Edward's message to 'those who would be servants of Christ' is entirely consistent with his Arminian belief in a loving God. Crucially, in the context of the movement, in the 'Age of Reason', towards a 'rational' religion, Edward Evan emphasises that the service of God depends upon understanding and sound judgement. He has no time for the 'enthusiastic' and emotional appeal of the Methodism which was beginning to take hold in Wales.

> First and foremost, Christ taught a religion of understanding ...
> The service of Christ is an intelligent service, not a service of
> excitable and unruly emotion. [36]

It was common for ministers to preach to each other's congregations and no doubt Edward was widely invited. Edmund Jones would not have singled him out for criticism if his influence had been confined to one remote meeting house. Jones enlarged on Edward's alleged 'heresy', reporting that his congregation wanted him to invite Morgan Jones of Cymmer to preach at the Old Meeting House. 'He wrote to come, but ordered him not to preach or speak of Election, Original Sin, the Trinity, the Deity of Christ, the atonement or satisfaction'. R. T. Jenkins is cautious, in view of Edmund Jones's strong Calvinist views, but taking this along with other evidence, he accepts that Edward Evan finally came very close to the Unitarianism which took firm root in Aberdare only a few years after his death.[37]

Iolo Morganwg, who later founded the South Wales Unitarian Association, described his old friend and mentor as 'a professed Unitarian'.[38]

This does not mean that he was narrow-minded or exclusive in his views. In a poem describing the different Protestant sects which he encountered as a young man, he finds good and bad in them all. His conclusion, quoted at the head of this chapter, is that a vine is to be judged by its fruits, and his sincere belief is that all can be saved through Christ's mercy. In the end, it is this tolerance, and the foundation of his mission in the teaching of Jesus, which shines through in the writings of Edward Evan, 'Dissenting Minister of the Gospel'. However his theology is defined, he lamented Christian sectarianism.

> Every faction's opinion is in a sort of fetters. And because even the wisest of us in this world can see only through a glass darkly, love should teach us to sympathise with each other's frailty, until such time when we hope to know as we are known.[39]

Not everyone was so enlightened, and strong feelings resurfaced about the political implications of religious non-conformity. After the French Revolution in 1789, dissenters came under the same suspicion as had led to their persecution in the 1660s. Samuel Horsley, Bishop of St Davids, pointed the finger, declaring that 'the principles of a Nonconformist in religion and a republican in politics are inseparably united'.[40]

The integral link between religious and political dissent is at the heart of the analysis of Gwyn A. Williams, who describes how Dr. Richard Price of Ty'n Ton, 'son of an old Glamorgan family of Cromwellian Puritans' became 'perhaps the most celebrated political Dissenter', a Unitarian, and defender of the American and French revolutions. He had links with an extremely radical group associated with the Earl of Shelburne and 'a propagandizing unitarian circle' in Essex Street, London, which Iolo Morganwg and John Bradford, both close associates of Edward Evan, also attended. As Williams shows, the world from which Price emerged was that which had produced Iolo Morganwg and, earlier, John Bradford, Lewis Hopkin, and Edward Evan who, he believes, 'became the first Unitarian minister in the hill country'.[41]

---

[1] Edward Evan, 'A poem written by the author in his youth concerning various Creeds', *Afalau'r Awen* (1874), pp.98-101.

[2] Rev. Eric Jones, interview with the author (2023).

[3] E.g. David L. Davies, *They Love to be Dissenters: The Historical Background of Unitarianism in Merthyr Tydfil and Aberdare, with specific reference to Hen Dŷ Cwrdd, Trecynon* (2011).

[4] Glamorgan Archives, DBR/X/1.

[5] D. Densil Morgan, *Theologia Cambrensis*, Vol. 1, p.203.

[6] Rev. Thomas Price (1763), in *They Love to be Dissenters*, p.30.

[7] *Theologia Cambrensis*, Vol. 1, p.205

[8] Eric Jones interview.

[9] Thomas Rowlands (1855); NLW MS 22673D. His source was Lewis ap Richard Shincin (born 1764).

[10] *Afalau'r Awen*, p.39, 'A Survey of the form of Government in England when William and Mary came to rule'.

[11] Cathryn A. Charnell-White, *French Poetry of the French Revolution*, p.399.

[12] *Theologia Cambrensis*, Vol. 1, p.378.

[13] For the background and detailed history of the Old Meeting House (Hen Dŷ Cwrdd Trecynon, Aberdare) see *They Love to be Dissenters*.

[14] *Swansea & Glamorgan Herald* (15 December 1858), in *They Love to be Dissenters*, p.59.

[15] *They Love to be Dissenters*, pp.76-77.

[16] Gwyn A. Williams, *The Search for Beulah Land* (1980), pp.14-15. 'A Dissenting network dating from Cromwell's time ... linked comfortable congregations in the Vale [of Glamorgan], wide open to the trade winds and to the liberal and scientific currents which coursed through eighteenth century Dissent from its often heretical academies, to the tough-minded chapels of the hill country [the Blaenau] which, with their congregations of smallholders, auctioneers, artisans, opening up to the master colliers, engineers, skilled puddlers and ironstone miners of the new iron complex, went over to liberal Presbyterianism on their route into Unitarianism.'

[17] Geraint H Jenkins, *Literature, Religion and Society in Wales 1660-1730*, p.184.

[18] *They Love to be Dissenters*, p.29.

[19] *They Love to be Dissenters*, p.76.

[20] *Afalau'r Awen*, p.104-5.

[21] See for example *Afalau'r Awen*, pp. 86-8, 'A Debate between the Body and the Soul'.

[22] https://en.wikipedia.org/wiki/Richard_Baxter

[23] Samuel Bourn the Younger, *Lectures to Children and Young People*, 2nd ed. Birmingham (1739).

[24] *Lectures to Children and Young People*, p. 97.

[25] Simon Patrick, *A Paraphrase upon the Books of Ecclesiastes and the Song of Solomon*, London (1685).

[26] *Yr Ymofynydd* (1892), p.206.

[27] 'Jenkins, Jenkin (d.1780)', *Dictionary of Welsh Biography*.

[28] R. T. Jenkins, *Bardd a'i Gefndir*, Trans. Hon. Soc. Cymmrodorion (1948), p.149 concludes his lengthy discussion of the issue by leaving it up to the reader to make up his or her own mind.

[29] *Afalau'r Awen*, p.62.

[30] For these see *Dictionary of Welsh Biography*.

[31] *Bardd a'i Gefndir*, p. 125.

[32] *Y Darian* (5 December 1918).

[33] *They Love to be Dissenters*, p.34.

[34] *Yr Ymofynydd*, Vol 1. No. 7 (1848), pp. 149-53. See also entry for 'Charles Winter (1700-1773)', *Dictionary of Welsh Biography*.

[35] Edward Evan, *Golwg ar Gynheddfau Gwasanaeth ac Anrhydedd Gwasanaethwyr Crist*, a sermon delivered to a meeting of ministers at Y Drewen, Newcastle Emlyn (1775), published in Carmarthen the same year.

[36] Ditto.

[37] *Bardd a'i Gefndir*, pp. 130-31.

[38] Iolo Morgannwg, letter to Theophilus Lindsey (10 Feb 1797); *Correspondence of Iolo Morganwg*, letter 444.

[39] *Golwg ar Gynheddfau Gwasanaeth*, p.18.

[40] *They Love to be Dissenters*, p.23.

[41] Gwyn A. Williams, *When Was Wales?* (1988), p.168.

CHAPTER 16

1793 – 'Death lays his icy hand on kings'[1]

O dofa di'r gormeswyr,	*Mad tyrants tame,*
a thorr di fwriad hy	*break down the high,*
Bob talcen balch ac uchel	*Whose haughty foreheads*
sy'n curo'r awyr fry.[2]	*beat the sky.*

In the last ten years of Edward Evan's life poetry, religion and politics came together amid the turbulence of the French Revolution and the wars between Britain and France which followed. It is no coincidence that it was in the year of the Revolution, 1789, that the Bishop of St Davids condemned Dissenters as republicans disloyal to King and Country, and Edmund Jones recorded his condemnation of Edward as a heretic.

> When the French Revolution broke out, the most advanced lovers of freedom among Nonconformists at once responded to the demand, that at first went out from France to all lands, for justice and liberty to all.[3]

Aberdare may have been a remote parish in the *Blaenau* of Glamorgan, but the reverberations of events in France, London and even Yorkshire reached Edward at Ton Coch in the years when Iolo Morganwg and his Gorsedd of Bards made 'Liberty' and the 'Rights of Man' their slogans. The strongest evidence of Edward's engagement with the radical politics of the revolutionary years can be found in a poem he wrote 'in the time of War and Tumult, in the year 1794', which connects him with the activities of campaigners accused of treason and sedition.

During the wars with France, patriotic Britons were encouraged to take part in 'fast days', and to pray for the nation and the king. One such was 28 February 1794, when an organisation called the Friends of Peace and

Reform held a large public meeting in Sheffield in opposition to the fast day. As part of the proceedings a hymn, composed for the occasion by the radical James Montgomery, was sung 'in full chorus by the assembly consisting of several thousand persons'. Afterwards eleven resolutions 'of a strong character' were passed and the whole proceedings were reported in a pamphlet, with a copy sent to the London Corresponding Society, which campaigned for democratic reform of Parliament.[4]

The Yorkshire pamphlet was among the documents seized when the society's secretary, Thomas Hardy, was arrested in London along with twelve others. They were accused of treason and Hardy was imprisoned in the Tower. The correspondence with Sheffield became part of the evidence against him and two others when they were tried at the Old Bailey in October 1794. The hymn 'composed by one Montgomery' was cited in court as one of the documents seized at Hardy's home. The Attorney General led for the prosecution, but the jury acquitted all three, in a humiliation for William Pitt's government. While Hardy was in custody, his home had been attacked by a 'Church and King' mob and his terrorised wife subsequently died in childbirth.[5]

Iolo Morganwg attended the trials of Hardy and John Horne Tooke, in which the playwright Richard Brinsley Sheridan gave evidence for the defence. He reported it in a letter to his wife, Peggy.

> I was at the Old Baily, an eye and ear witness to Pitt's prejury on the trial of Horne Tooke and of the evidence that was given by Mr Sheridan at the same time, and by the Duke of Richmond on Hardy's trial, in direct contradiction of what Pitt said. This is probably an information that you have not yet found in the rascally ministerial papers that are taken in Glamorganshire.[6]

Iolo's poem 'Trial by Jury', printed as a broadsheet, was recited during celebrations of Hardy's acquittal at the Crown and Anchor tavern in London on 4 February 1795.

> Boast, Britain, thy Juries! thy glory! thy plan!
> They treat the *stern Tyrant* with scorn!
> O! bid them descend, the best Guardians of Man,
> To millions of ages unborn.[7]

Edward Evan was clearly aware of the trial and the background events in Yorkshire, either through Iolo or his connections with radicals in Merthyr Tydfil. Like Hardy, James Montgomery suffered for his political views. He was twice imprisoned on charges of sedition. In 1795 he was jailed for printing 'A Patriotic Song' which included a view of the war with France which was seen as far from patriotic by the magistrates.

> Europe's fate on the contest's decision depends;
> Most important its issue will be,
> For should France be subdued, Europe's liberty ends,
> If she triumphs the world will be free.[8]

Edward translated Montgomery's Sheffield 'Hymn', which is included in its original English in *Afalau'r Awen* alongside the Welsh poem. Two verses of the original sum up its powerful opposition to tyranny and slavery.

> O Thou, whose awful word can bind
> The roaring waves, the raging wind,
> Mad tyrants tame, break down the high,
> Whose haughty foreheads beat the sky.
>
> Burst every dungeon, every chain,
> Give injured slaves their rights again;
> Let truth prevail, let discord cease,
> Speak – and the world shall smile in peace.[9]

When Edward's poem was published in the first collection of his poetry, it was described as 'a hymn composed by a respectable person in the time of War and Tumult, in the year 1794'. The war with France was not over when Rhys Evans, almost certainly with the help of Iolo Morganwg, first published his father's work in 1804; Nelson died in the Battle of Trafalgar the following year. Was the term 'respectable person' an attempt to disguise the radical and subversive connections of the poem? Or was it an acknowledgement that Montgomery and his colleagues deserved political respect?. Bearing in mind the whole story surrounding the piece, this is perhaps the strongest evidence of Edward's political sympathies and his reputation as a radical, which clearly resonated with the Chartists forty years later. Thomas Evans ('Tomos Glyn Cothi'), who succeeded him as minister of the Old Meeting House in 1811, also wrote a translation of James Montgomery's 'seditious' hymn. He was imprisoned for his political views in 1803.

§

Hear the voice of the Bard!
Who Present, Past, & Future sees
Whose ears have heard
The Holy Word,
That walk'd among the ancient trees.[10]

The fascinating and controversial figure of Iolo Morganwg (1747-1826) stands at the centre of the story in Glamorgan in the turbulent years of the Revolution and its aftermath. It was in 1789 that he cast Edward Evan in the mythical role of 'the Last Bard' in order to authenticate his claim to ancient authority. Iolo's radical religious and political views were combined in what Gwyn A. Williams called his 'Gorsedd of druidical, Jacobin and masonic Bards'.[11] His bardic and political activities became inseparable and, during the years of war with France, attracted the hostile attention of the authorities. Repressive laws against 'treasonable and seditious practices and attempts', passed in 1795 and 1799 explain the close eye kept on Iolo's *gorsedd* meetings.

> The air was full of suspicions at the time. The events that had taken, and were taking, place on the continent, leading to great political upheavals, involving the fate of kings, made the English King and Government keenly sensitive to the possibility of a similar upheaval taking place in these Islands.[12]

Strange though it may seem, Iolo's road to radical political and religious dissent had begun with his interest in the ancient traditions of Welsh poetry. As a young man, he had been greatly influenced by the Glamorgan 'Grammarians' and had learned the rules of strict metre bardic poetry from Lewis Hopkin and Edward Evan. Like many of the older poets with whom he associated, Iolo was a craftsman and a religious dissenter; he would go on to found the South Wales Unitarian Association in 1803.

He was, in his own phrase, 'a rattleskull genius',[13] an itinerant stonemason, an expert on agriculture, a poet, an antiquarian with an interest in all aspects of Welsh culture, a collector of ancient manuscripts, a prolific letter writer, a radical nonconformist, and a supporter of the Rights of Man. He was a Glamorgan 'nationalist' and took the bardic name Iolo Morganwg from the county.[14] He was determined to prove that the true heritage of Wales was represented by the culture of south, not north, Wales. To support that case he engaged in extensive and convincing forgeries, which extended to the whole structure he built to 'prove' the connections between ancient Druidism, the mediaeval Bardic traditions, Liberty, religious Nonconformity and the modern 'Gorsedd of Bards of the Island of Britain'.[15]

> Iolo became obsessed with the notion that the strict-metre Welsh bards were the descendants of the ancient Druids, the sages and, according to some authorities, the priests of the early Celtic and Brythonic world.[16]

An interest in 'Celticism' and 'a theory of Celtic origins' was widespread in the 18th century and 'druidism' was an aspect of this. In his introduction to 'Songs of Experience', William Blake expressed his deep engagement with these ideas, as the lines quoted at the head of this section show. Ancient stone circles were interpreted by many as sites of druidic worship; thus, in 1740, the antiquary William Stukeley entitled his study, 'Stonehenge, a temple restor'd to the Druids'.[17]

Iolo built his druidic-bardic structure on these foundations, again seeking to prove that archaeological sites in Glamorgan were far more important than those in north Wales highlighted in Henry Rowlands's influential volume about the history of Anglesey.[18] In 'The Mountain Shepherd', this is how he depicts the Garth, scene of his Gorsedd meetings in 1797 and 1798, 'deemed sacred by Druids of old', with its 'barrows and cromlecks'.[19] The poem encapsulates the essentials of Iolo's 'bardism', including its contemporary resonance with 'Liberty' and the Rights of Man. The poem ends with a thinly-disguised attack on George III, cautiously attributed to the shepherd of the title.

> He laughs at all monkeys who riches adore
> And says a good conscience can never be poor;
> Let him laugh at all bloc[k]heads for 'tis a good thing,
> But sure he's a fool, for he laughs at the king.
>
> He calls him a nin[n]y – sure that cannot be –
> Yet this shepherd by Jove is far wiser than me,
> 'Tis treason I fear, I was taught so at school,
> To laugh at poor George or to call him a fool.[20]

One of the many contradictions in the complex character of Iolo Morganwg was that while he vigorously promoted republicanism, he was also also obliged to seek the approval of royalty and nobility. His English collection *Poems, Lyrical and Pastoral* was 'by permission, and with the respect of gratitude, dedicated to His Royal Highness George Prince of Wales, by his most humble servant, Edward Williams'.[21]

The intricate elements of Iolo's bardism and the Gorsedd ceremonies which expressed it were summed up in the preface to an edition of ancient Welsh poems, which highlighted the political radicalism and republicanism which Iolo increasingly emphasised.[22] It included details of the ceremonies, distinct 'orders' of bards, and the religious beliefs underpinning bardism, which was described as 'a system embracing all the leading principles which tend to spread liberty, peace and happiness amongst mankind'.

> In terms of content and shape, in its intricate interweaving of fact and fiction, past and present, and in the sheer diversity of its basic elements, bardism was an expression of the complicated and controversial nature of its mastermind, Iolo Morganwg. Wales's genuine poetic tradition and its structures, informed by received learning on druidism, antiquarianism and primitivism, provided its basic framework. But other intellectual interests also shaped bardism: Jacobinism, Freemasonry, orientalism, Unitarian theology, and the history and literature of his native Glamorgan.[23]

The 'Gorsedd of Bards' would become an integral element of the revived (and respectable) National Eisteddfod in the nineteenth century, thanks to Iolo's success in combining the arts of Welsh music and poetry with his druidic bardism. In 1946, Princess Elizabeth (the future Queen) was invested into the Gorsedd at the 'Royal' National Eisteddfod in Mountain Ash.[24] In the 1790s, Iolo's Gorsedd meetings (sometimes referred to as an *eisteddfod*) were those gatherings on hilltops in Glamorgan, which included recitation of poems on specific themes and an increasing emphasis on 'Liberty', the Rights of Man and opposition to monarchy. Among the bards who attended was Edward Evan's successor, the radical Unitarian, Tomos Glyn Cothi.

When Iolo announced his plans to hold a gathering on the Spring Equinox of 1796, the first name on the list of those invited to attend was *Iorwerth Gwynfardd Morganwg* ('Edward the Druid of Glamorgan'), a bardic name for Edward Evan. It is not known for sure whether that Gorsedd, on Stalling Down, actually took place.[25] A poem inviting Edward to attend a forthcoming 'eisteddfod' was published in 1797 and is believed to have referred to the Gorsedd held on the Garth Mountain on 21 June that year. Both Edward Evan (on this occasion 'Iorwerth Ifan') and his son Rhys

Evans ('Rhys ab Ifan')[26] were listed on the scroll prepared by Iolo earlier in 1797, naming those expected on the Garth on Midsummer Day the following year.[27]

Later in 1797, at the autumn equinox, the 'Bard of Liberty' and his followers attracted unwelcome attention from the authorities. They had reason to be suspicious of the loyalty of those attending the meeting, as the Gorsedd members were devising a suitable bardic coat of arms for Napoleon, who only a month later was given command of the army to fight England! According to Iolo, twelve magistrates and one hundred soldiers from the Cowbridge Volunteers kept a close eye (and ear) on the proceedings, watching for any sign of opposition to the king. Iolo complained to his friend William Owen Pughe in London about this 'harrassment'.

> We (the bards of Glamorgan) have been as severly [sic] persecuted by Church and Kingists as our glorious predecessors were by Edward the Bardicide [Edward I]. Many of our young disciples have been intimidated and have withdrawn themselves from our Gorsez. I am in hopes however that a few will meet on Garth Mountain next Alban Hefin [21 June 1798]. I intend then to recite some ancient trïoedd [triads], [to] deliver a short araith [speech], to recite something in verse, &c. The transactions of our Gorsedd I will send to [the] Cambrian Register as an appeal to the public, exhibit[ing] ourselves as men of peace and social order, and not th[e] seditious persons that some suppose us to be.[28]

Undeterred, at the Gorsedd on 21 March 1798, he recited his poem '*Breiniau Dyn*' ('The Rights of Man'), echoing the famous work of the republican Tom Paine, whom he had met in London and who had been burned in effigy in Cardiff in 1792. It was sung to the tune of 'God Save the King', like Robert Thomson's 'New Song', on which it was partly based.

> Let us with France agree,
> And bid the World be free –
> Leading the way.
> Let Tyrants all conspire,
> Fearless of sword and fire,
> Freedom shall ne'er retire,
> Freedom shall sway! [29]

It was in the pages of the *Cambrian Register*, referred to in Iolo's letter, that his mission to combine a revival of the Welsh poetic tradition with druidic support for 'Liberty', the Rights of Man and 'democratic principles' came in for the most vituperative criticism. The anonymous writer in 1799 mocks the idea that 'the bardic succession has been preserved to the present time, among the hills of Glamorgan and Gwent'. If his abilities were not so 'extravagant', Iolo 'the harlequin of the farce', might usefully be employed in the service of Welsh literature, rather than in attempting 'to revive the religious, but ridiculous mummeries of ancient druidism:'

> An attempt that every true lover of British poetry will despise, and cannot avoid condemning – that most admirable science needs no support, receives no additional splendor, or courts applause from meretricious ornaments, from senseless pantomime, or from "Alban Hevin". Exhibitions to make the vulgar stare, and the worshipful magistrates tremble for the fate of the nation. The British muse is as respectable, and certainly a more comfortable companion, by the fire-side, as on the top of a hill[+].
>
> [+]*This alludes to a silly attempt lately made in Glamorganshire, to hold something like a poetic session upon a hill, preceded by a ridiculous advertisement or hand bill, which the magistrates, knowing the harlequin of the farce to be of democratic principles, apprehended might endanger the peace of the kingdom; they therefore very properly prevented his rising in the world, lest when he got to the summit he might beckon to Buonoparte, and bring him over the British channel to the top of the Garth.*[30]

Fears of a French landing on the Welsh coast were not without foundation; it had happened in 1797, in the last invasion of British soil. Two thousand French troops were brought by ship to the coast of Pembrokeshire as part of an abortive scheme to divert attention from a planned invasion of Ireland which, the French believed, would be supported by the Catholic Irish population. While the invasion of Ireland never happened and the landing near Fishguard was quickly neutralised, fears of further incursions were widespread and religious Dissenters, in Pembrokeshire and elsewhere, were suspected and persecuted for their alleged – and unsubstantiated – collaboration with the French invaders.

Although the stories of Edward Evan's bardic inheritance and Druidic succession were repeated many times in the century after his death and created a potent myth, there is no evidence that he himself ever made any claim to ancient Druidic or Bardic ancestry. There is nothing in his poetry which smacks of Druidism. When a brief biography was included in the fourth edition of his poetic works, it described him as 'a famous bard of the Chair of Glamorgan', which had by that time acquired respectability within the revived National Eisteddfod. Iolo occasionally referred to him as '*Gwynfardd*' – 'Druid' – the highest order of the Gorsedd of Bards, but his obituary poem which praises Edward's integrity and poetic skill, makes no mention of druids or bards. Nevertheless, thanks to Iolo's pervading influence, it was often in this guise that he was remembered and honoured in the century after his death. As late as 1908 Edward was still credited with the preservation of the 'bardic cult'.

It is not known for certain whether Edward actually attended any of the hilltop Gorsedd meetings, in spite of the evidence of his invitations. After all, by the late 1790s he was in his eighties and might have had difficulty travelling and reaching the summits. Clearly, though, Iolo wanted to enlist him in his Gorsedd with its radical political agenda, both as an active participant and as the supposed authentic link to its supposed druidic roots.

§

Evidence of Edward Evan's reaction to political developments in France, the execution of the French king, and the wars which followed, can be found in his poetry, including his reflections on the 'Glorious Revolution' of 1688.

> It was widely considered that, by diminishing the influence of the pope and the Roman Catholic Church in matters of state, the French people had done no more than imitate Britain's Glorious Revolution of 1688 ... thus firming the nation's Protestant foundations in the settlement of 1689 that established a constitutional monarchy whereby the monarch's power was restricted by the Houses of Commons and the Lords. [31]

The London society founded to celebrate the Glorious Revolution of 1688 invited Richard Price to give a lecture in 1789, shortly after the fall of the Bastille in France. He celebrated 'the dominion of kings changed for the dominion of laws, and the dominion of priests giving way to the dominion of reason and conscience'. Like Edward Evan in his 'Survey of the form of Government in England when William and Mary came to rule',[32] Price considered that the 'Glorious Revolution' was 'by no means perfect' although it had delivered the people of Britain from 'popery and arbitrary power'. Nevertheless, he saw it as the first in a historic series.

After sharing in the benefits of one Revolution, I have been
spared to be a witness to two other Revolutions, both glorious
… Be encouraged, all ye friends of freedom, and writers in its
defence! The times are auspicious. Your labours have not been in
vain. Behold kingdoms, admonished by you, starting from sleep,
breaking their fetters, and claiming justice from their oppressors!
Behold, the light you have struck out, after setting America
free, reflected to France, and there kindled into a blaze that lays
despotism in ashes, and warms and illuminates Europe!

Tremble all ye oppressors of the world! Take warning all ye
supporters of slavish governments, and slavish hierarchies! …
You cannot now hold the world in darkness. Struggle no longer
against increasing light and liberality. Restore to mankind their
rights; and consent to the correction of abuses, before they and
you are destroyed together.[33]

It is in this context that Edward Evan's poem on the form of government
under William and Mary features as the first in an extensive collection of
poetry in Welsh in response to the French Revolution.[34] His 'frustration
with the limited success of the 1689 settlement to effect religious freedom'
can be seen as reflecting on how France could show the way for the
restoration of ancient liberties in Britain through the 'reformation' of the
form of government established by the 'Glorious' Revolution.[35]

Enthusiasm for the Revolution in France was dampened by the days
of Terror under 'Madame la Guillotine' and the execution of the king
in January 1793. This, more than anything, cast suspicion on radicals
who continued to express sympathy for the revolutionaries. Soon after the
death of Louis XVI, the execution of Charles I, 'King and Martyr' was
commemorated in Britain with sermons preached throughout the land
in Anglican churches. It is significant therefore that Edward Evan chose
to translate a poem entitled 'Thoughts upon Death, after hearing of the
murder of King Charles I'.

There is no way of knowing when Edward's translation was written,
but the suggestion is that it was after the the execution of the French king.
Its original author, James Shirley, was a Royalist and certainly intended
his work as a lament for the death of Charles. But the poem is also a
meditation on Death 'the Leveller' and the transience of 'the glories of
our birth and state'.

Sceptre and crown
Must tumble down,
And in the dust be equal laid,
With the poor crooked scythe and spade.

It is striking that in his translation, Edward Evan expands on these lines with a specific and negative reference to the corpse of the king:

Ei goron a'i deyrnwialen	*His crown and his sceptre*
a syrth yn llwch y llawr,	*shall fall into dust*
Ac yn y ddaear briddlyd,	*And when his vile body's rotted,*
'nol symmyd ei gorph sâl,	*they shall lie in earth,*
Ni bydd ef ronyn harddach,	*No better than a scythe or spade.*
na phladur pur neu bâl. [36]	

In those years, 'imagining' the death of the king became a treasonable offence in Britain and celebrating the death of any king would be a dangerous step to take. Shirley has the 'victor victim' bleeding on death's purple altar, but again Edward expands the line with the conqueror 'bleeding in his guilt'. It does not seem far-fetched to see how the poem could be read as a reference not to Charles but to Louis XVI, 'in order to fulfil the egalitarian sentiment implicit in the trope of "death the leveller".'[37]

One other poem of Edward's deserves mention, bearing in mind his strong Christian faith and belief in the 'brotherhood of man'. This strict-metre *cywydd* 'composed in the time of war between us and France' is an impassioned plea for peace and a condemnation of the anger, greed and dishonesty which has brought destruction, like a plague.

Plant i'r un tad, rhoddiad rydd,	*Children of the one father, our generous*
Gwelwn yn lladd ei gilydd! [38]	*benefactor,*
	See them now, killing each other!

The poem ends with lines which echo Isaiah and his prophecy that 'nation shall not lift up sword against nation, neither shall they learn war any more'. But it was many years after his death in 1798 that the war with France ended and Edward Evan's peaceful vision became reality, of a kind, in Britain and Europe.

Amser sy'n syber nesáu: - i'r cloddiau　　*A noble time is coming to the land;*
Daw'r cleddyf yn sychau,　　　　　　　*The sword will become a ploughshare,*
A'r gwaywffyn o'r bryn brau　　　　　　*And spears from the harsh hill*
A dorrir yn bladuriau.　　　　　　　　*Shall be beaten into scythes.*

---

[1] Edward Evan, *Afalau'r Awen* (1874), p.78.

[2] 'In the time of War and Tumult', *Afalau'r Awen*, p.60.

[3] Rev. David Davies, *The Influence of the French Revolution on Welsh Life & Literature* (1926), p. 22.

4 John Holland & James Everett, *Memoirs of the Life and Writings of James Montgomery* (1854), p.164.

5 See 'Thomas Hardy (1752-1832)' and 'London Corresponding Society' entries in *Dictionary of National Biography.*

[6] *Correspondence of Iolo Morganwg* (2007), letter 309, p.660. The letter is wrongly dated 19 February 1794 (Hardy was arrested in May 1794; his trial began on 28 October).

7 Edward Williams, *Trial By Jury – The Grand Palladium of British Liberty* (4 Feb. 1795); National Library of Scotland: https://digital.nls.uk/english-ballads/archive/74898133
See also Iolo's account to his wife in *Correspondence*, Letter 357, p.725.

8 *Memoirs of the Life and Writings of James Montgomery*, p.192.

9 *Memoirs of the Life and Writings of James Montgomery*, p.165. The text in *Afalau'r Awen*, p.60, is slightly different.

[10] William Blake, Introduction to *Songs of Experience* (1794). See Jon Mee, '"Images of Truth New Born": Iolo, William Blake and the literary Radicalism of the 1790s', in Geraint H. Jenkins (ed.), *A Rattleskull Genius, the many Faces of Iolo Morganwg* (2009).

[11] Gwyn A Williams, *The Merthyr Rising* (1988), p.73.

[12] *The Influence of the French Revolution on Welsh Life & Literature*, p. 233.

[13] Iolo Morganwg's own words (NLW MS21387E, no.25), *A Rattleskull Genius*, p.1.

[14] Something like 'Glamorgan Eddie'.

[15] A woman was admitted to the bardic fellowship at the first meeting in London in 1792, but there is no evidence of women joining the Glamorgan bards at their mountain meetings later in the decade.

[16] Ceri W. Lewis, 'Iolo Morganwg and Strict-metre Welsh Poetry', in *A Rattleskull Genius*, p.88.

[17] Branwen Jarvis, 'Iolo Morganwg and the Welsh Cultural Background', ibid. p.30.

[18] Henry Rowlands, *Mona Antiqua Restaurata*, 2nd ed. (1766).

[19] See Chapter 3.

[20] Iolo Morganwg, 'The Mountain Shepherd' (NLW 21285E), in Ffion Mair Jones, *The Bard is a Very Singular Character* (2010), pp. 196-7 & 284-5.

[21] Edward Williams ('Iolo Morganwg'), *Poems, Lyric and Pastoral*, London (1794). The

story of the agonising drafting of that sentence is told in Mary-Ann Constantine, '"This Wildernessed Business of Publication": The Making of Poems Lyric and Pastoral (1794)', in *Rattleskull Genius*, p.132.

[22] William Owen, *The Heroic Elegies of Llywarç Hen* (1792), p. xxiv.

[23] Cathryn A. Charnell-White, *Bardic Circles* (2007), p.9.

[24] See Chapter 23.

[25] Geraint & Zonia Bowen, *Hanes Gorsedd y Beirdd* (1991), p.40.

[26] After his father's death, Rhys was formally invited by Iolo to join the Gorsedd as a bard in his own right but, for reasons unknown, declined the honour. See the biography in *Afalau'r Awen* (1874), p.170.

[27] *Hanes Gorsedd y Beirdd*, p.41.

[28] Iolo to Wm. O. Pughe (12 May 1798), *Correspondence of Iolo Morganwg*, Letter no. 472.

[29] Robert Thomson, 'A New song, to an old tune, viz. "God save the king"', in John Mee, *Print, Publicity, and Popular Radicalism*, p.80. Iolo's Welsh poem reprises this song by the Radical Thomson; see M-A. Constantine & E. Edwards, '"Bard of Liberty": Iolo Morganwg, Wales and Radical Song', in J. Kirk et al. (eds.), *United Islands? The Language of Resistance* (2012), p.64.

[30] *Cambrian Register* for 1796 (published 1799), p. 465. According to Mary-Ann Constantine (note to the author), the anonymous writer was Theophilus Jones, from whom Iolo Morganwg, 'the harlequin of the farce', later sought legal advice. Jones also came into possession of the manuscript of *Y Gododdin*, with which Edward Evan was said to be associated. (See Chapter 17).

[31] Cathryn A. Charnell-White, *Welsh Poetry of the French Revolution 1789-1805* (2012), p.9.

32 *Afalau'r Awen*, p.39.

[33] Richard Price, *A Discourse on the Love of Our Country* (delivered on 4 November 1789).

[34] *Welsh Poetry of the French Revolution*, p.65.

[35] Ditto, pp. 9-10 & 12-13.

[36] *Afalau'r Awen*, pp. 78-9. It is interesting to note that the poem is said in *Afalau'r Awen* to be by Samuel Butler and the version Edward translated is indeed the one wrongly attributed to Butler, another Royalist, in a volume published in 1715. This explains why the text differs in places from James Shirley's original and is another indication of how Edward was in touch with works by some of the big names of English literature.

[37] *Welsh Poetry of the French Revolution*, p. 23.

[38] 'A cywydd composed in the time of war between us and France', *Afalau'r Awen*, pp. 71-73.

CHAPTER 17

The Lost Book of Aneirin

Gwŷr a aeth Gatraeth,
oedd ffraeth eu llu,
Glasfedd eu hancwyn a gwenwyn fu,
Trychant trwy beiriant yn catáu,
A gwedi elwch tawelwch fu. [1]

Cavalry rode to Catterick,
their host was swift,
Fresh mead was their feast and it was bitter,
Three hundred fighting under command,
And after the cry of jubilation
there was silence.

Twelve hundred years before the wars of Edward Evan's old age, a band of Welsh warriors rode out of their fortress in Edinburgh to attack a superior English force at Catterick in Yorkshire. This is the story behind the *Gododdin*, 'the earliest Welsh poem of any considerable length',[2] composed not long after the battle of Catraeth, sometime around 600 C.E. It is attributed to the bard Aneirin and survived in one mediaeval manuscript, now preserved in the National Library of Wales. According to the legend circulating in the nineteenth century, Edward Evan, the bard of Aberdare was at one time its keeper.

Llyfr Aneirin, the Book of Aneirin, deserves appreciation far beyond the borders of modern Wales. It is evidence of a history unknown to most of the inhabitants of the British Isles, a history which could – and should – transform the understanding of the communities of modern Britain. What was a band of 'Welsh' warriors doing in Edinburgh around the year 600? Why should the tale of their doomed adventure have survived in a manuscript in Wales? Who were these English soldiers whom they attacked in a newly founded kingdom with the Welsh name of Deira? How many in Scotland, England or Wales know that as late as the early eleventh century, Welsh may have been the language of Strathclyde? [3]

The poet Aneirin is remembered in mediaeval Welsh sources as

Aneirin Gwawdrydd Mechteyrn Beirdd – 'Aneirin of Glowing Verse, High King of Bards'. His poem the *Gododdin* incorporates all the evidence which has survived from which we can deduce the basis for this exalted reputation. Much of it has been preserved in a very early form of the Welsh language, and it has been handed down through the ages as an integral part of the literature of Wales; indeed it may justly be said that the verse of Aneirin combined with that of his contemporary Taliesin form the twin corner-stones of the Welsh poetic tradition.[4]

The Welsh of the *Gododdin* is far closer to the modern language than 'English' poetry of the same period such as *Beowulf*, the Old English of which is more or less impenetrable to a modern English speaker. It is interesting, though, to note the similarities in the poetry of these opposing peoples. The Irish poet Seamus Heaney, himself deeply versed in the traditions of Celtic literature, commented on the themes, poetic form, and the role of the traditional singer in *Beowulf*. He might have been describing Aneirin, warrior poet in his lord's household.

> The singer as we are told is a carrier of tales, a keeper of the traditional corpus, and all this is taking place in an oral culture, where the poet's word hoard is full of what the scholars call formulaic phrases, word tesserae, pieces of verbal jigsaw, which he uses to fit his new theme to a strict metre, entwining his words.[5]

> Meanwhile, a thane
> of the king's household, a carrier of tales,
> a traditional singer deeply schooled
> in the lore of the of the past, linked a new theme
> to a strict metre. The man started
> to recite with skill, rehearsing Beowulf's
> triumphs and feats in well-fashioned lines,
> entwining his words.[6]

Just so does the poet of the *Gododdin* praise the brave warriors who rode from Edinburgh to their doom. Apart from its historic significance, the poem is important evidence of the deep roots of formal Welsh poetry, containing many of the elements of internal rhyme and alliteration which Edward Evan and his fellow 'Grammarians' studied and practised twelve centuries later, and which survive to this day in the form of strict metre *cynghanedd*. Although the only surviving mediaeval manuscript was written by a scribe in Wales in the thirteenth century, the language is a much older survivor of centuries of oral transmission from bard to pupil.

> During these centuries it appears that the *Gododdin* enjoyed high esteem as an essential piece for recitation in bardic competitions (the indirect ancestors of the modern Eisteddfodau).[7]

Was Edward Evan really one of those who handed down through the ages this integral part of the literature of Wales? That was certainly a story told of him in the century after his death, another powerful legend worthy of recognition and investigation.

Copies of the original thirteenth century manuscript were made and circulated in the sixteenth, seventeenth and eighteenth centuries. When one of these came into the hands of Evan Evans ('Ieuan Fardd') around 1758, his mentor Lewis Morris wrote:

> Who do you think I have at my elbow, as happy as ever Alexander thought himself after a conquest? No less a man than Ieuan Fardd, who hath discovered some old MSS [manuscripts] lately that no body of this age or the last ever as much as dreamed of. And this discovery is to him and me as great as that of America by Columbus. We have found an epic poem in the British [Welsh] called Gododin, equal at least to the Iliad, Aeneid or Paradise Lost.

It was not until 1801, three years after Edward Evan's death, that a version of the text was published in the *Myvyrian Archaiology of Wales* by Iolo Morganwg's collaborator Owen Jones ('Owain Myfyr'). It was based on earlier copies, because the original manuscript had been lost in the late eighteenth century. This is where Edward's involvement in the story of its transmission belongs.

On one of the blank pages at the beginning of the recovered ancient manuscript, Theophilus Jones of Brecon, writing sometime after 1807, wrote that it was 'given me by Mr Thomas Bacon who bought it from a person at Aberdâr'.

Just as a legend of 'druidic' bardic descent became attached to the memory of Edward Evan, so did the story that he was the person who had preserved the precious manuscript of the 'High King of Bards'. Surprisingly it is in the United States that the earliest printed source for this legend is to be found. David Cadwgan ('Cadwgan Fardd') was born in Wales in 1815 and died in Pennsylvania in 1895. He had been 'ordained' as a bard by the 'archdruid' Myfyr Morganwg (Evan Davies)[8], a friend of Edward Evan's son Rhys, at the famous Rocking Stone above Pontypridd and recalled how his father had told him about the eisteddfod held there by Iolo Morganwg in 1817.[9] This was his account of the *Gododdin* manuscript (often spelled 'Gododin' at the time).

> The poem was the property of the Gorsedd of the Glamorgan Bards. It was in the custody of the bard Edward Evan, Ton Coch, Aberdare, who died in 1798. He had given the 'Gododin' to a Mr Bacon, Aberaman, and he lent it to Mr Jones, the historian, of Breconshire.[10]

A different version of this story was later told by the historian Charles Wilkins who reported that Anthony Bacon, owner of the Cyfarthfa Ironworks in Merthyr, moved to Aberdare 'where he took a lively interest in bardic doings, and was a personal friend of many of the Aberdare poets.'[11]

> Amongst his friends was an old bard, named Evans, who was held in great repute far and near, but was, like the majority of bards, as poor as a church mouse. Bacon helped him in his need, and the poet gave him, as he felt the hand of death upon him, the greatest treasure he possessed, a copy of the 'Gododin', the famous 'Iliad' of the Welsh Homer – Aneurin. … Bacon, in the close of his Welsh career, was visited by the indefatigable historian of Brecon, Theophilus Jones, who borrowed the book, and forgot to return it … In justice to the memory of Theophilus Jones, he stated that it was given him by Mr. Bacon.[12]

We are in the realm here of the 'tales that are told', fascinating tales about a man who had become a legendary figure. Perhaps not surprisingly, the story recorded more than a hundred years after Edward's death raises as many questions as it answers. The detective work in unravelling it is as interesting as the legend.

The first point to make is that Theophilus Jones wrote in the manuscript that he had it from *Thomas* Bacon. The man in Wilkins's story was Anthony Bacon, Thomas's father, the owner of Cyfarthfa ironworks, who died in 1786 twelve years before Edward Evan. If the gift had been to the father, it could not have been made at the poet's deathbed. What is more, Edward did not retire from his ministry at the Old Meeting House until 1796; if he had given the manuscript to Anthony Bacon before 1786, it is unlikely that he felt the hand of death upon him at that time.

There is another flaw in the story. Cadwgan Fardd reportedly said that Edward passed the manuscript to 'a Mr Bacon of Aberaman' and Wilkins also has Anthony Bacon living at Aberaman House when he moved to Aberdare Parish. But Edward could not have given the manuscript to any Mr Bacon at Aberaman. The house remained in the hands of the Matthews family until 1806, when it was sold to Bacon's son, Anthony Bacon *II*, brother of Thomas. Thomas and his daughters were frequent visitors to the house, which was sold after Anthony II's death in 1827.

W. W. Price, who investigated Wilkins's account, claimed there was no evidence that Anthony Bacon ever lived in Aberdare Parish. [13] However, Bacon bought the lease of the Hirwaun Ironworks in 1780 and either built, or enlarged for himself, a mansion at Hirwaun village, known as Tŷ Mawr.[14] The house was just beyond the Aberdare Parish boundary, but there is every likelihood that he spent time in the area and may well have known Edward Evan – particularly if, as claimed, he took an interest in the activities of the local bards.[15] On that basis, it is possible that Edward could have passed on the manuscript to him, but only if he had it before 1786.

The date presents a further problem. Gruffudd Antur, research fellow at the Centre for Advanced Welsh & Celtic Studies, has worked closely with the world expert on Welsh manuscripts, Daniel Huws of the National Library of Wales, whom he consulted on this question.[16] Dr. Antur pointed out that the manuscript disappeared from the great library at Hengwrt near Dolgellau sometime before 1785. Assessing the evidence for its transmission, he believes it very unlikely that it could have reached Edward Evan in Aberdare and been passed on before Anthony Bacon's death in 1786.

In any case, it is *Thomas* Bacon who is mentioned by Theophilus Jones. Could he have had the manuscript from Edward in the years between his father's and Edward's death? Thomas was born in 1778 and raised in England. It is not known whether he visited his father in Wales, though that must be possible, bearing in mind that his brother Anthony chose to settle at Aberaman House after selling his share of the iron empire which the brothers inherited on their father's death. Anthony sold the Cyfarthfa ironworks to Richard Crawshay in 1794. Thomas came into possession of the Hirwaun Ironworks (and presumably Tŷ Mawr mansion) on his majority in 1799. If he knew he was going to own it, could he not have spent time in the Aberdare area before Edward Evan's death in 1798? Was he interested in Welsh and Welsh poetry? It appears his father was, and in any case a wonderful ancient manuscript would have been something to possess.

All these possibilities depend on the arrival of the Book of Aneirin in Aberdare before 1798. If it came to Edward Evan, how did it reach him from north Wales? In the light of all the unanswered questions, the accounts of Edward's role in the preservation of the Book of Aneirin begin to look more like another legend attached to his name after his death, than a factual account. If a person at Aberdare had the book, who else would it have been but the 'druidic' bard of Ton Coch? 'Perhaps the mystery can never be cleared up', concluded W. W. Price.[17]

§

Torr bob rhyw garchar tywyll,
a phob rhyw gadwyn gas,
Rho'r caeth yn rhydd o'i rwymau,
tryw rydd-did gwir dy ras. [18]

Burst every dungeon, every chain,
Give injured slaves their rights again.

The thirteenth century manuscript of the *Gododdin* is kept in the National Library of Wales.[19] Whatever his interest in it, Thomas Bacon must be acknowledged as one of those who preserved it. What is not well known is that the Book of Aneirin passed through the hands of a family of ironmasters whose wealth derived from slavery, which was a burning issue in the later years of Edward Evan's life.

Opposition to the slave trade led to the formation in 1787 of a society campaigning for its abolition. Among the subscribers were Richard Price of Ty'n Ton and another acquaintance of Edward Evan, the prominent London lawyer Griffith Price of Penllergaer. In the society's prospectus, its chairman wrote, 'The voice of humanity calls loudly for the extinction of a traffic, which no plea of policy or interest can justify in the eye of reason or conscience', though he was at pains to emphasise that the society's aims (at that stage at least) did not include the abolition of slavery as an institution.[20]

In 1792 a pamphlet was published (in Welsh) by a number of Carmarthen printers, including John Ross who had printed Edward Evan's sermon at Newcastle Emlyn. Its anonymous author, 'a Welshman opposed to all oppression', urged his compatriots to avoid sugar, treacle and rum on the grounds that they were the products of slavery in the West Indies, where more than 200,000 slaves worked on Jamaica's sugar plantations alone. This boycott was one of the tactics used by the abolitionists. The pamphlet also advertises a poem available from a printer in Bristol, which consists of verses written in the voice of slaves complaining of their sufferings in the 'Sugar Islands'. The only surviving copy of that broadsheet is in the papers left by Iolo Morganwg.[21]

Iolo's early biographer, Elijah Waring, claimed that Iolo had advertised the sugar he sold in his shop in Cowbridge as 'East India Sweets, uncontaminated with human gore'.

> A somewhat credulous and uncritical biographer, Waring took his cue from his subject in producing what has become a familiar and enduring portrayal of Iolo and his views on the question of slavery. He depicted the Glamorgan bard as an unremitting idealist and an unbending abolitionist … This is an image that would appear to befit the self-styled Bard of Liberty, the irreverent social critic and the author of anti-slavery verse who proudly and ostentatiously listed 'Humanity's Wilberforce' among the subscribers to his Poems, Lyrical and Pastoral.[22]

At the first meeting of his Gorsedd on Primrose Hill in 1792, Iolo read from his bardic ode condemning slavery, which was quoted in a contemporary report of the event.

> Join here thy Bards with mournful note,
> They weep for Afric's injur'd race,
> Long has thy Muse, in worlds remote,
> Sung loud of Britain's foul disgrace.[23]

The historian Andrew Davies points out that, as with his attitude to royalty, Iolo's condemnation of the 'most horrid traffick in human blood' concealed contradictions.[24] His three brothers had emigrated to the West Indies and become wealthy through the exploitation of enslaved workers. Iolo always insisted that he had refused all offers of financial help from them because of his abhorrence of slavery, but his biographer, G. J. Williams, believed his account of their relationship was 'wholly misleading'. On several occasions during the 1790s and 1800s, he received small sums from his brothers, and Davies reveals that John Williams left Iolo and his three children £100 each in his will, which itemised his estate, including 'Negroes' valued at almost £7,000.

Iolo, who was in financial difficulty, consulted a lawyer about the possibility of emigrating to Jamaica to take control of his brother's estate. He may have intended to free the enslaved workers, but he had clearly compromised with his previous insistence that he would have nothing to do with the wealth produced by the 'diabolical traffic' in human beings. By this time, 'whenever the subject of his brothers' money was raised, the vocabulary of morality disappeared entirely from his letters and was replaced by legal jargon.' In the end, some at least of the legacy was paid. 'Who knows' asks Andrew Davies 'what private anguish Iolo, the fervent abolitionist, had endured by this point and what was to follow if indeed he later accepted "the contaminated gains of that detested slave trade".'[25]

When it comes to Thomas Bacon, one-time owner of the Book of Aneirin, neither Wilkins nor Price reports on the source of the family's wealth. But Anthony Bacon's sons cannot have been ignorant of it. In his will he left to his half-brother a share of 30,000 acres in Virginia which he owned with 'sundry gentlemen', along with the enslaved people on them. Born in Whitehaven in Cumberland in 1717, he has been described as 'one of the greatest merchants and industrialists of the eighteenth century, who rose from ordinary beginnings ... to become a Member of Parliament and one of the richest commoners in England'.[26]

As a young man he travelled to America and worked in the tobacco industry before returning to England, where by 1740 he was master of a ship carrying criminals to Maryland where they would be put to work alongside African slaves. The vessel returned with a cargo of tobacco. By 1757 he was in business with George Washington, the future president and slave-owner, acting as his agent in the sale of tobacco. Bacon and Washington became partners in a huge project to reclaim swampland to grow hemp and tobacco. These were the 30,000 acres referred to in his will. Each member of the Dismal Swamp Company was to provide five slaves; Bacon supplied ten.

Back at his base in London, Bacon won a government contract to supply forts in Senegal, west Africa. From there he entered the infamous triangular trade, selling 'seasoned, able and working negroes' to the islands of the West Indies and carrying sugar or tobacco on the return voyage to Britain. Between 1760 and 1763 four of his ships delivered enslaved Africans to the American colonies.[27] Between 1764 and 1766 another of his vessels, 'The King of Bonny', transported more than 700 hundred slaves to Barbados and St Kitts in the West Indies. He contracted with the government in London to supply slaves for work on the islands of Grenada, the Grenadines, Tobago, St Vincent and Dominica. Between 1768 and 1776 he and his partners were won government contracts worth nearly £67,000 (around £9 million in today's equivalent).[28] 'The commerce in slaves had taken him into the ranks of the super-rich'.[29]

Anthony Bacon's older brother, Thomas, became an Anglican minister and emigrated to Maryland where he encouraged slaves to attend his church. Preaching to an enslaved congregation in the 1740s he told them their passage across the Atlantic was evidence of God's mercy, bringing them 'out of a Land of Darkness and Ignorance, where your Forefathers knew nothing of Him to a Country where you may come to Knowledge of the only true God'. He instructed them that they must obey their masters, whether they were gentle and mild, or peevish and hard.[30]

Anthony Bacon invested his capital in the iron industry of south Wales, developing the Cyfarthfa works in Merthyr, which would become the largest in the world by 1800. He specialised in the manufacture of cannons and became the main supplier to the government's Board of Ordnance, delivering hundreds of guns during the War of American Independence.

> The shifting of his interests from African and West Indian commerce to south Wales iron making is an extremely clear (if not necessarily common) example of the migration of capital from slave-based commerce to domestic industry.[31]

There is a fascinating twist to the story explored in this chapter, linking Edward Evan of Aberdare, a sixth century Welsh poem, and the exploitation of enslaved Africans. The lawyer Iolo Morganwg first consulted about his brother's slave estate in Jamaica was none other than Theophilus Jones, fervent critic of 'the harlequin of the farce', his Unitarianism, radical tendencies and druidic inventions. This was the man who came into possession of the Book of Aneirin and wrote: 'This copy Mr Davies … supposed to be that mentioned by Llwyd, and said to have been lost out of the Hengwrt Library; it was given me by Mr Thomas Bacon who bought it from a person at Aberdâr'.[32] That, according to Wilkins, was 'the old bard named Evans' on his deathbed.

---

[1] Aneirin, '*Y Gododdin*' *Britain's Oldest Poem*, A. O. H. Jarman (1990), p.7.

[2] *Y Gododdin*, Jarman, p.ix.

[3] Kenneth Jackson, *Language & History in Early Britain* (1953), p.219.

[4] Rachel Bromwich, 'The Oldest Scottish Poem: The Gododdin' (Review) in *Medium*

Aevum, vol.39, no. 2 (1970), p.160.

[5] From 'Seamus Heaney – The Translator', Part 4 of 'Four Sides of Seamus Heaney', BBC Radio (10 September 2023).

[6] Seamus Heaney, *Beowulf: A new translation* (1999), p.28.

[7] Rachel Bromwich, p.161.

[8] 'Davies, Evan ('Myfyr Morganwg' 1801 - 1888)', *Dictionary of Welsh Biography*.

[9] *Aberystwith Observer* (14 December 1889).

[10] *Western Mail* (2 June 1884).

[11] Charles Wilkins, *The South Wales Coal Trade and its allied Industries* (1888), p.379.

[12] Charles Wilkins, *History of the Iron, Steel, Tinplate and Other Trades of Wales* (1903), p.59.

[13] See W. W. Price, 'The Legend of Anthony Bacon' in *Bulletin of the Board of Celtic Studies*, xi, pp.109-12.

[14] Nansi Selwood, *A History of the Villages of Hirwaun and Rhigos* (1997), pp.50-1. See also https://webapps.rctcbc.gov.uk/heritagetrail/english/cynon/hirwaun.html

[15] Jeremy Morgan (note to the author): 'It is certainly true the gentry and industrialists were closely linked and connections with the Bruce family might have led to this acquaintance. As a minister of religion – even a dissenter – Edward Evan would have been a notable local figure recognisable to most inhabitants. Did the Bacon's speak Welsh – my guess is they must have had at least a little knowledge given their workforce was overwhelmingly Welsh speaking.'

[16] Daniel Huws produced *A Repertory of Welsh Manuscripts*, published by the National Library of Wales in three volumes (2022). It covers a thousand years of history, describes more than 3,000 manuscripts, includes biographies of 1,500 scribes and features over 1,000 specimens of script.

[17] 'The Legend of Anthony Bacon', p.112.

[18] Edward Evan, 'A Hymn composed by a respectable person in the time of War and Tumult, in the year 1794', *Afalau'r Awen* (1874) p.60. The English is from James Montgomery's Hymn, quoted here with Edward's translation. See Chapter 16.

[19] The National Library of Wales published a fine facsimile in 1989 and the manuscript can be viewed online in high quality via the library's website: http://hdl.handle.net/10107/4651067

[20] *List of the Society, instituted in 1787, for the Purpose of effecting the Abolition of the Slave Trade*, London (1788).

[21] See Andrew Green, *Wales in 100 Objects* (2018), p.106.

[22] Andrew Davies, '"Uncontaminated with Human Gore"? Iolo Morganwg, Slavery and the Jamaican Inheritance' in Geraint H. Jenkins (ed.), *A Rattleskull Genius* (2009), p. 293. Another subscriber to Iolo's book was Rev. Edward Evans [sic] of Aberdare.

[23] *Gentleman's Magazine* (1792), p.957, 'The following (an Apostrophe to Liberty) is extracted from Edward Williams's Ode'. For more on Iolo's abolitionist poetry, see Rhys Kaminski-Jones, *Reframing Welsh Revivalism: True Britons and Celtic Empires, 1707-1819*.

[24] Mary-Ann Constantine (in a note to the author) points out that Iolo was by no means alone among contemporary abolitionists in holding contradictory positions

– much like many of those in the twenty-first century concerned about the environmental crisis.

25 *A Rattleskull Genius*, pp. 311-313.

[26] http://www.whitehavenandwesternlakeland.co.uk/people/anthonybacon.htm

[27] https://www.slavevoyages.org/voyage/database#searchId=3pVJ8iz2

[28] https://www.bankofengland.co.uk/monetary-policy/inflation/inflation-calculator

[29] Chris Evans, *Slave Wales* (2010), pp.55-60.

[30] *Slave Wales*, p.75. For the life of Rev. Thomas Bacon see: https://msa.maryland.gov/megafile/msa/speccol/sc2900/sc2908/000001/000075/html/am75np--1.html

[31] 'Bacon, Anthony (bap. 1717, d. 1786), merchant and ironmaster.' *Oxford Dictionary of National Biography*.

[32] Theophilus Jones was the grandson of Theophilus Evans, who signed Edward Evan's marriage licence and who was author of *Drych y Prif Oesoedd*, the reprint of which was advertised in the first edition of Edward's poetry, published in 1804.

CHAPTER 18

1798 – The Call of the Cuckoo

Mae llais y gog yn canu,   *I hear the cuckoo calling*
Trwy'r goedwig fawr o ddeutu,   *In the wide woods on the hillside,*
Yn rhoddi i ni bromis braf   *A promise clear to one and all*
Fod 'nawr yr haf yn nesu.   *That summer is upon us.*

Bydd llawer llencyn 'smala,   *Many healthy, merry lads*
Sydd 'nawr yn iach mewn tyrfa,   *Out in the crowds this season,*
Yn ei feddrod wrtho'i hun,   *Will lie in cold and lonely graves*
Cyn cano'r flwyddyn nesaf. [1]   *When cuckoo calls next springtime.*

Edward Evan died on Midsummer Day, when the grass in the meadows around Ton Coch may have had the reddish colour that gave the place its name. He wrote these lines about the cuckoo just a few weeks before his death. There was a superstition that hearing the cuckoo's call could be a good or a bad omen, depending from which side it was heard.[2] The two verses of Edward's poem seem to reflect these two interpretations of the cuckoo's song – promising on the one hand, threatening on the other.

Did he ask his son Edward to play the harp for him in his final days so he could hear it in his bed? Was it the same instrument the old man himself had played for many years, at home with his family and friends long after he gave up playing in public? Perhaps he played *Gwêl yr Adeilad*. It's slow, with a gentle rhythm; rather sad in its way, but peaceful, which seems fitting.[3] And one of the poems which the dying man had set to this tune was 'Advice from a Father to his Son'.[4]

Edward had given up his ministry at the Old Meeting House only two years before his death. Another poem, which he wrote in the days before he died, shows his faith was still strong:

Fy ngwendid heb lid sy'n ymledu,	*From day to day, I feel more weak*
– o ddydd	*But feel no sense of anger;*
I ddydd yn helaethu,	*O gentle Lord, grant me your grace –*
Duw, o'th ras cyweithias cu,	*Hold up my soul in safety.*[1]
Fy enaid dal i fynu.	

There is no picture of him.[5] Photography had yet to be invented and he would not have had his portrait painted, even though he was a well-known poet and preacher. We are left with the legacy he left in poetry and legend.

§

Un o fil ag awen faith	*Inspired as one in a thousand*
A gwir ddysg eitha'r gerddiaith	*With true learning on his tongue;*
E wnai araith yn iraidd	*Full of life in his speaking,*
Doethineb llym grym a gwraidd,	*His wisdom sharp and rooted deep;*
Awen gain yn ei gariad,	*Love shone in his bright muse*
A grym iaith ym mhob gair mâd.[6]	*And the power of language in each good word.*

---

[1] Edward Evan, *Afalau'r Awen* (1874), p.167.

[2] See Lilija Kudirkiene, "The Image of the Cuckoo in Folklore', in *Tautosakos Darbai* (2004), pp.55-69. See also 'Superstition Relating to the Cuckoo', 1930s Schools' Collection (Gort Uí Chluana, Beanntraí) www.duchas.ie

[3] 'Gwêl yr Adeilad': https://abcnotation.com/tunePage?a=trillian.mit.edu/~jc/music/abc/mirror/jodecjames.home.att.net/gwel_yr_adeilad/0000

[4] 'Advice from a father to his son to the tune "Gwêl yr Adeilad"', *Afalau'r Awen* (1874), p.74.

[5] The illustration on the cover of this book is an imagined portrait of Edward Evan's successor at the Old Meeting House, Rev. Thomas Evans ('Tomos Glyn Cothi').

[6] Iolo Morganwg, 'Elegy for Edward Evan', National Library of Wales MS 21423E.

CHAPTER 19

1837 – Old Songs in a New Land

Llais Bardd, llais prif-fardd profwch, – llais caniad,	*The voice of a bard, of a master-poet – listen,*
Llais cynydd diddanwch,	*A voice of song which brings delight,*
Llais Athro trwyddo treiddiwch	*The voice of a teacher from the past,*
Llais Iorwerth lanwerth o'i lwch. [1]	*The voice of Edward in his wisdom.*

Forty years after Edward Evan's death, his poetry made a remarkable impact in Merthyr Tydfil and Aberdare, the area described by Gwyn A. Williams as 'the heartland of Chartism and the home of the Welsh Chartist press in both languages' – *Udgorn Cymru* in Welsh and the *Advocate & Merthyr Free Press* in English. [2] These papers, edited by Morgan Williams and David John, supported the six points of the Charter, 'repudiated violence, advocated temperance and attacked tithes and church rates'. [3]

It was in September 1840 that Williams printed Edward's poem condemning the worship of the 'false gods' of anger, avarice, pride and gluttony. [4] On the face of it, the poem might be considered unobjectionable, but the newspapers and their publishers were not. At the end of the following month the Home Office received a copy of a letter written by the manager of the iron works at Abersychan in Monmouthshire, which shared intelligence alleging that the Chartists were threatening rebellion all across the iron country of south Wales around the anniversary of the bloody 1839 march on Newport.

> Through the agency of spies it has been discovered that there are regular meetings held by the leading men amongst them, throughout the whole of the Welsh district, and that it has been determined that there shall be throughout the winter nights

detached parties deputed to commit outrages of all kinds on property and persons.[5]

Morgan Williams and David John were certainly 'leading men' amongst the Chartists; both were delegates representing the movement in south Wales at national conventions held in Manchester and London. Williams by 1840 was 'the chief working-class leader in Wales' and a member of the national executive of the National Chartist Association. He went into hiding in 1842 after the others had been arrested.[6]

In November 1840, the magistrates of Merthyr, led by John Bruce Pryce of Dyffryn, sent the Home Secretary a copy of the *Advocate*, which included an outspoken attack on 'the political corruption of our Rulers, the dishonesty and fraud of Mammon-seeking men'.[7] They also sent the latest issue of the *Udgorn* with translations of the articles that worried them. They highlighted one which criticised 'the waste of the people's money' in payments to idle officials who do nothing of value in return. Another was David John's letter, which likewise complained that the labour of working people paid to keep a wasteful and profligate government on its feet. 'O workers', he asked, 'how long will this continue?'[8]

It was the magistrates at Caerphilly who sent the Home Secretary a copy of the *Udgorn* which included Edward Evan's attack on 'false gods' as well as 'instructions for the organisation of the Chartist Association throughout the Kingdom'. The Marquis of Normanby probably paid little attention to poetry in Welsh, even if it could be read as an attack on the powerful and wealthy. But its publication in a Chartist newspaper at this time is clearly significant.

Edward Evan's poems were first published in 1804, six years after he died, but it is the third edition which provides solid evidence of his impact on a world very different from his own. Morgan Williams and David John would have found the poem they reprinted in 1840 in their own copies of the poet's work, published three years earlier. What is striking is that they and many of the leading radicals of Merthyr and Aberdare had subscribed to make the publication possible.

> The Welsh poems of the late Edward Evan of Toncoch, Aberdare (Iorwerth ab Ieuan). The above Work being out of Print, and a large number of persons being anxious to obtain it, it is proposed to publish a third edition, if sufficient names can be obtained to remunerate the Publisher.

This advertisement on the front page of the *Glamorgan, Brecon and*

Monmouthshire Gazette in April 1837 attracted sufficient interest to support republication of *Afalau'r Awen,* later that year. The list of subscribers included in the book reads like a 'Who's Who' of politics and industry in Aberdare and Merthyr at this critical time. As a result, the poems of Edward Evan, 'the old bard' of Ton Coch, found a new Welsh-speaking audience in industrial south-east Wales, which pulled in between two thirds and three quarters of the existing Welsh population during the nineteenth century.

Both Merthyr and Aberdare were centres of the iron industry, but it was in 1837 that coal in Aberdare began to rival the iron of Merthyr. In June that year, Matthew Wayne, one of the book's subscribers, sank a pit at Abernant-y-groes, within sight of Ton Coch, launching an industry which would make the Cynon Valley the dominant force in the booming market for steam coal. The mine was on land owned by William David, another subscriber. Wayne had cut his teeth as furnace manager for Richard Crawshay at Cyfarthfa in Merthyr, going on to establish his own iron works at Aberdare in 1827. Significantly, he was a religious Dissenter, a member of the Unitarian Meeting House at Cefn Coed, closely linked to the *Hen Dŷ Cwrdd* at Trecynon where Edward Evan had been minister until 1796.

Unitarians were at the heart of intellectual and political life in Merthyr and Aberdare. The historian Gwyn A. Williams wrote that 'the roll-call of Merthyr Unitarians is a register of the men who shaped the town' and that by 1831, 'whoever pronounced himself Unitarian pronounced himself radical'.[9] Many of the radicals whom Williams names, like Matthew Wayne, can be found in the list of subscribers to Edward Evan's poetry, including all those mentioned below.

One was William Williams, father of the *Udgorn*'s editor and son of Edward Evan's old friend, the weaver Morgan Williams of Penyrheolgerrig. William was a Unitarian, chief engineer at the Cyfarthfa ironworks, and a leading member of the Cyfarthfa Philosophical Society, whose members subscribed to buy scientific instruments and 'used to read Tom Paine, Voltaire, Volney, d'Holbach in secret on Aberdare Mountain'.[10] In his later life, Morgan Williams recalled 'a little knot of men, sturdy old Republicans', who would meet at his father's home at Penyrheolgerrig, including two whose names appear in the list of subscribers to *Afalau'r Awen*, Thomas Evans of Cyfarthfa, 'philosopher, astronomer and mathematician', and John Lewis of Gethin.[11]

Christopher James, another subscriber, was a succesful businessman, a member of Merthyr's 'radical dynasty par exellence'. His brother Job was a bookseller and admirer of William Cobbett. The family was linked by marriage to the Williamses of Penyrheolgerrig and to William Howell of the Patriot Inn, also on the list. The Patriot was the first venue for a new, urban eisteddfod tradition which took off in the 1820s. Iolo Morganwg, whose son Taliesin lived in Merthyr, had succeeded in combining these poetic meetings with the invented ceremonies of his Gorsedd of Bards, in whose genealogy he had cast Edward Evan as an essential link to the ancient 'druidic' past.

Another radical subscriber from the world of the eisteddfod was John Thomas ('Ieuan Ddu'). He had been co-editor with Morgan Williams of an earlier newspaper, *Y Gweithiwr (The Workman)*, which, like the *Udgorn* and the *Advocate*, so alarmed the magistrates that they had sent a copy to the Home Office in 1834, demanding prosecution for sedition. Thomas had worked with Zephaniah Williams, one of three leaders transported to Australia after the Chartist march on Newport in 1839. Gwyn A. Williams described John Thomas, like Morgan Williams, as 'a Unitarian and directly descended from the Republicans of the time of the French Revolution'.[12]

Thomas established an eisteddfod society in Merthyr in 1831, which took its name, the Free Enquirers, from the Zetetics, subscribers to the radical journal *The Republican*. They met at the Swan Inn (owned by Christopher James's brother, William), where they held several eisteddfodau between 1831 and 1834.[13] Edward Evan's son and editor, the Unitarian and poet Rhys Evans, adjudicated at an eisteddfod there in 1833. The landlord of the Swan, Edward Williams, subscribed for thirty copies of *Afalau'r Awen*, no doubt for distribution to the network of poets and followers who attended eisteddfodau at his establishment.

On the other side of the mountain in Aberdare, a similar society of 'Freethinkers' was established by William Williams, another Unitarian, who took his bardic name, 'Y Carw Coch', from the Stag, the tavern he owned from 1837. His wife, Margaret, was a descendant of Edward Evan's brother, Rhys ab Ifan.[14] Williams had worked at Llwydcoed as an iron ore miner and continued to be described as such as late as 1841. He must be the 'Mr William Williams, Miner', listed in *Afalau'r Awen*. Like John Jones, 'druggist' at the sign of the White Horse, also on the list, Williams had absorbed Unitarian and Chartist beliefs from two of Edward Evan's successors as ministers at the Old Meeting House in Trecynon, Rev.

Thomas Evans ('Tomos Glyn Cothi') and Rev. John Jones.[15]

Tomos Glyn Cothi, who died in 1833, owned one of the few surviving copies of the first edition of Edward Evan's poetry. He was a close associate of Iolo Morganwg and was jailed for singing a revolutionary song in 1797. Rev. John Jones was another of the leading players in the radical politics of Aberdare and Merthyr, and Edward Evan's sons were leading members of his congregation. He is listed as a subscriber along with his Unitarian colleagues, Rev. Owen Evans of Cefncoed and Rev. David John at Twynyrodyn. David John was a blacksmith, a mathematician and father of the younger David John, publisher of *The Advocate* and *Udgorn Cymru* with Morgan Williams.

Both John Jones and Owen Evans lectured to the Cyfarthfa Philosphical Society, Jones on astronomy and Evans on 'the use of the globe'.[16] John Jones, 'a social democrat before the term was invented',[17] had spoken powerfully at a meeting on Aberdare Mountain organised by Morgan Williams during the General Election of 1835[18]. There the ironworkers, who had no vote, made clear their opposition to the Tory candidate for Merthyr and Aberdare and forced him to withdraw. This was the moment, wrote Gwyn A. Williams, when 'nonconformist radicalism in its most intransigent form gripped Merthyr Tydfil'.[19]

Clearly the poetry of Edward Evan resonated with the radicals of Merthyr and Aberdare. But not only with Unitarians and Chartists. Perhaps surprisingly, the list of subscribers to *Afalau'r Awen* in 1837 includes prominent establishment figures and enemies of Chartism, who also supported publication of the book. Unlike 'Mr' Morgan Williams and 'Rev.' John Jones, they are identified as 'Esqr.'.

One was Henry Scale, ironmaster at the Aberdare works in Llwydcoed, who wrote regularly to the Lord Lieutenant, the Marquis of Bute, in late 1839. He warned that 'a Chartist Rebellion in Wales will be more formidable than in any other part of the Kingdom'[20] and criticised the response of his fellow ironmasters and the magistrates.[21] He particularly refused to accept that the Aberdare and Merthyr Chartists were committed to using 'moral force', not violence, to achieve their aims although he reported, after the the armed march on Newport, that they had voted not to join their Monmouthshire comrades.[22]

Scale regularly targeted Morgan Williams in his letters to Bute and was particularly outraged at his plans to establish the *Udgorn* and the *Advocate*.

The fellow is now returned from London, where he took himself a few days before the outbreak at Newport, to do what think you my Lord? To establish a Chartist Newspaper!!! – that to add fuel to the fire not smouldering but burning.[23]

A rival of the Scale family was Rowland Fothergill, owner of the Abernant ironworks, who eventually took over the Aberdare works. During the Merthyr Rising of 1831 his house had been ransacked by angry workers. He was active as a magistrate in the aftermath of the Newport Riots and later became High Sheriff of Glamorgan. In 1842 it was reported that he had dismissed some of the leading men in his works 'in consequence of their political views.' He subscribed for two copies of Edward Evan's poems.

Fothergill was one of five magistrates, listed as subscribers, who were involved in the aftermath of Newport, including Williams of Garth Hall and Rev. Charles Maybery, Rector of Penderyn and a descendant of ironmasters at Hirwaun and Tredegar. John Bruce Pryce of the Dyffryn estate in Aberdare and William Thomas 'squire' of the Court at Merthyr, had been in the thick of the Rising of 1831. On the eve of that outbreak, three thousand people forced Bruce to release a prisoner whom he had committed to jail. Later, he and Thomas had been confronted by a mob of two thousand, and Bruce had read the Riot Act while the crowd brandished a red flag.[24] Bruce was involved in the hunt for men wanted after the Newport march in 1839, and in one letter to the Lord Lieutenant he pointed the finger at a 'Socinian Preacher', one of the three Unitarian ministers, 'whom I have long suspected'.[25]

William Thomas reported to Bute on Chartist activity in Merthyr before the Newport march and identified Morgan Williams as their leader. 'The weaver in question is occasionally having Meetings held near his house at Aberdare Hill, but there is nothing connected with them to excite any fear', he assured his Lordship.[26] Despite his Tory beliefs and his role as a magistrate, Thomas seems to have had a soft spot for the editor of the *Udgorn* and to have respected his commitment to 'moral force' Chartism. Years after his flight from Merthyr to avoid arrest, Morgan Williams revealed that it was 'Squire' Thomas who had given him the tip-off in time for him to escape.[27]

Perhaps there is a clue here that something united these inhabitants of Merthyr and Aberdare, despite their political differences. Did they share some values which might explain the appeal of Edward Evan's book across the divide? In the case of Bruce Pryce, there was a close relationship.

Although Rhys Evans, son of Edward and editor of his poems, was a member of the 'Socinian' (Unitarian) congregation at the Old Meeting House, he was also a tenant of Bruce's Dyffryn Estate, as his father had been. And, like Edward Evan, he worked as estate foreman, enjoying a relationship of apparent mutual respect with Bruce and his family, including the future Lord Aberdare.[28]

There are several reasons which might explain Edward Evan's appeal to this diverse audience in the iron towns of Aberdare and Merthyr, forty years after his death.

Chartists would have known that he was remembered and respected by Morgan Williams as a political radical from the days of the French Revolution. The congregations at the Old Meeting Houses in Aberdare and Merthyr would have seen him as a vital figure in the transition from Arianism to the radical Unitarian creed which took root in the years after his death. And, in a world where old moral certainties were challenged in the uprooted 'frontier' society of the new industrial Wales, Edward Evan's 'Godly and Moral Songs' would have had a nostalgic appeal, representing the values of a simpler and kinder age, and echoing the popular verse of the 'Old Vicar' Prichard, to whom he was compared.

Most obviously, his poetry appealed because it was written in Welsh, the language spoken by most of the migrant workers who gravitated towards the booming iron towns. It was clearly the language of all the subscribers, divided though they were by politics and class. The revival of the eisteddfod was an important anchor for Welsh culture in troubled waters and Edward Evan was intimately connected with the roots of this revival. He had been one of the Glamorgan poets who showed a new interest in the old poetic forms and from whom Iolo Morganwg had learned the art. And, according to Iolo at least, he had been a key figure in the creation of the Gorsedd of Bards, whose ceremonial role became central to the new eisteddfod tradition. The verses at the head of this chapter are a tribute from Gwilym Morganwg, one of the leading figures in the revived eisteddfod movement in Glamorgan, 'ordained' by Iolo and called by Taliesin ab Iolo 'my only brother druid'. To Gwilym, Edward was a '*prif-fardd*', a chief bard, deserving a title given to the great and famous poets of the past and to those who win the crown or chair at the modern National Eisteddfod.

[1] Gwilym Morganwg, tribute to Edward Evan, *Afalau'r Awen* (1874), p.v.

[2] Gwyn A Williams, 'Dic Penderyn', *Llafur* Vol 2. No.3 (1978), p. 110.

[3] Joe England, *The Crucible of Modern Wales – Merthyr Tydfil 1760-1912* (2017), p.133.

4 *Udgorn Cymru*, Rhif 7. Cyf. 1, (Sept. 1840), p.6.

[5] 'Extract from a letter (30 October 1840) from Mr. William Wood, manager of the British Iron Company's Works at Abersychan near Pontypool, addressed to the Managing Directors of that Company', National Archives: HO1840/57, p.1002.

[6] Joe England, 'Morgan Williams: Merthyr's Forgotten Leader,' *Journal of Merthyr Tydfil Historical Society* (2014), pp.144-146.

[7] *The Advocate* no. 5 (Nov 1 1840), p.1. National Archives: HO1840/57, p.1030.

8 *Udgorn Cymru*, Rhif 9, Cyf. 1, (November 1840), David John, p.2 & p.10.

[9] Gwyn A Williams, *The Merthyr Rising* (1988), p.75 & 64.

[10] *The Merthyr Rising* p.73.

[11] Morgan Williams, *Red Dragon* (September 1882), p.98.

[12] Gwyn A. Williams, 'Eyewitness 1 May 1834', *Rebecca* (May 1982), p.30.

[13] *The Merthyr Rising*, p.86.

[14] R. T. Jenkins, *Bardd a'i Gefndir*, Trans. Hon. Soc. Cymmrodorion (1948), p. 99.

[15] D. L. Davies, 'Llwybrau'r Carw', in *Cwm Cynon*, ed. Hywel T. Edwards (1997), pp.98ff.

[16] Andrew Green, 'The Cyfarthfa Philosophical Society': https://gwallter.com/history/the-cyfarthfa-philosophical-society.html

[17] *The Merthyr Rising* p.74.

[18] See *The Crucible of Modern Wales*, pp.122-123.

[19] *The Merthyr Rising*, p.227.

[20] Scale to Bute (19 December 1839), CCL Bute XX.140 (Cardiff Central Library).

[21] Scale to Bute (14 November 1839), CCL Bute XX.69.

[22] Scale to Bute (15 November 1839), CCL Bute XX.72.

[23] Scale to Bute (19 November 1839), CCL Bute XX.75.

[24] *The Merthyr Rising*, p.120.

[25] Bruce Pryce to Bute (21 November 1839), CCL Bute XX.78.

[26] William Thomas to Bute (18 August 1839), CCL Bute XX.20.

[27] Joe England, *Journal of Merthyr Tydfil Historical Society*, 2014, p.137.

[28] See Chapter 21.

CHAPTER 20

1804-1874 – 'Give this little Book to the World'

Gwna frys yma Rhys ac ymrho	*Make haste Rhys and complete*
– i'th dasc,	*the job,*
Mae dysgwyl am dano,	*That everyone's expecting,*
Dalir trwy barch lle delo,	*It will meet with respect in all of Wales,*
A'i dderbyn mewn bryn a bro.[1]	*And be welcomed in the hills and vales.*

Few of Edward Evan's poems were published in his lifetime and they reached only a limited audience. The century following his death saw four editions of his poems published in a Glamorgan transformed by industrial, social and political changes which created a new and engaged readership. The dates of each edition are points of punctuation in this process of transformation. It was his son Rhys who oversaw publication of the first three – in 1804, 1816 and 1837.

While Edward Evan can be seen, in many ways, as a representative of the pre-industrial age, he saw the first iron works in Wales established at Hirwaun in 1757 and those opened in Merthyr two years later. But he could hardly have imagined the scale of the changes which were to come during the lifetime of his son and his grandchildren who saw to the printing of his work.

In 1804, the year Rhys Evans first published his father's poems, Glamorgan witnessed an event which symbolised the new era. Richard Trevithick's steam engine pulled ten tons of iron nine miles from the Penydarren works in Merthyr to the head of the canal at Abercynon. This was the first locomotive-hauled railway journey in the world and would have a profound effect on the Aberdare valley which became, in the middle of the century, the main source of coal for steam engines on land and sea. It was a new world into which Edward Evan's poems were published.

The previous year Iolo Morganwg had 'work to do' at Merthyr Tydfil, which would keep him there for about three weeks. In a letter to William Owen Pughe in London, he explained that he was hoping to bring out a collection of south-Walian songs, which would be printed in the town. In the same letter, he included proposals for printing the poetry of Edward Evan and suggested that Pughe could collect the names of subscribers to the volume.

> Perhaps half a dozen names may be picked up in London. I say perhaps: there are but few south Walians in London, and North Walians have for a very long time entertained a very illiberal and very illfounded prejudice against south Walian poetry.[2]

Pughe replied with enthusiasm to Iolo's proposed collection of songs and put his name down for twenty copies of the works of Edward Evan, for which 'I will be answerable'.[3] Iolo had actually written to him about the publication of Edward's poetry the previous December, saying the book was already 'in the press' at Merthyr. It was to be printed on good paper, sewed, and priced at two shillings.[4]

It is clear that Iolo played a part in its eventual publication, though his own proposed volume of songs never saw the light of day.[5] Rhys Evans gave the collection a religious title: *Caniadau Moesol a Duwiol*, 'Moral and Godly Songs', with the subtitle 'Commendations to Live Well and to Behave with Love towards all Humanity'. It included around fifty poems, along with the verse translation of Ecclesiastes (*Llyfr y Pregethwr*) begun by Dafydd Thomas, completed by Edward Evan and Lewis Hopkin, and first published in 1767.

The title *Caniadau Moesol* ('Moral Songs') echoes that of one of the editions of the work of the famous hymn-writer, William Williams Pantycelyn, published in 1764. It was a title used again in the nineteenth century to describe works by other poets and hymnists, and was clearly intended, along with the sub-title in this case, to appeal to a religious audience with a nostalgia for the work of the Old Vicar. Later editions of Edward's poems retained the original lengthy wording on the title page, but used a more appealing headline: *Afalau'r Awen*, ('The Fruits of the Muse'), which echoed the bardic use of the word 'awen' for poetic inspiration.

As previous chapters have shown, there is more to Edward's poetry than heavy moralising or dry religious themes. All editions followed the first by opening with a sequence of love poems and although his work as a *bardd gwlad* (a people's poet) is represented more fully in the later printings, verses reflecting everyday life in the *Blaenau* were included from the start.

The fact that the first edition was printed on the newly-established press in Merthyr Tydfil, and that Iolo was also planning to print there, is an indication of the changes brought by the industrial revolution. The population of Aberdare was only 1,486 in 1801, but on the other side of the mountain, the iron industry had made Merthyr the biggest town in Wales, with 7,700 inhabitants.

The changing printing scene in Wales in the previous century is reflected in the history of the publication of Edward Evan's works during his lifetime. The earliest was his translation of Samuel Bourn's *Lectures to Children*, printed in Carmarthen in 1757 by Evan Powell,[6] who included his own poetic tribute to the translator at the end of the book. Powell had printed the 1752 edition of *Canwyll y Cymry*, the work of Vicar Prichard, to whose poetry Edward's would later be compared. In his tribute to Edward Evan, Powell described him as *wir ficer*, 'a true vicar', in an apparent reference to the Old Vicar.

On the far side of the Severn Estuary, Bristol was far bigger than any town in Wales in the eighteenth century, with a population growing from 20,000 in 1700 to more than 60,000 by 1800. It was here that Lewis Hopkin and Edward Evan went to publish the original edition of *Llyfr y Pregethwr* in 1767. Farley's was the press which had printed the first collection of Pantycelyn's hymns in 1751. Between 1698 and 1775, the Farley family built up a considerable printing and publishing operation in Bristol, Exeter and the west of England, including a number of newspaper titles.[7] It was Sarah Farley,[8] a pioneer of women in printing, who ran the press when *Llyfr y Pregethwr* was published. Her name survived into the nineteenth century in the title of *Sarah Farley's Bristol Journal*.

Llyfr y Pregethwr is extremely rare and the copy in the National Library at Aberystwyth has evidence of an interesting history. It is bound with several religious works and on the inside cover is a quotation in Greek from Luke's gospel below the name 'The Revd. Mr Evan Evans'.[9] A separate hand has written a translation of the Greek, 'One thing is needful' and, in Welsh, that the handwriting is that of Evan Evans, 'Brydydd Hir'. Evans (1731-1788) had a colourful career and is described as 'undoubtedly the greatest Welsh scholar of his age'.[10] The book later belonged to Peter Bailey Williams (1763-1836), Rector of Llanrug in Caernarvonshire, another Welsh scholar. Interestingly, he was an opponent of the French Revolution and was praised 'for his discernment in seeing that Iolo Morganwg's claims about the "Gorsedd of Bards" were false'.[11]

The first publication of individual poems by Edward Evan had come in 1770, in a volume edited by the son of Owen Rees, his predecessor as minister at the Old Meeting House in Aberdare. Josiah Rees's *Trysorfa Gwybodaeth neu Eurgrawn Cymraeg* ('The Treasury of Knowledge or Welsh Magazine') was printed by John Ross, who had set up in Carmarthen in 1763 and brought out the expanded collection of Pantycelyn's hymns in 1764. The printer advertised himself as a time-served London professional with high quality equipment, 'the only printer in these parts regularly brought up to the craft'.[12] Ross went on to print Edward Evan's sermon delivered at Y Dref Wen in 1775.

It seems unlikely that Edward would have chosen to publish a collection of his poetry himself. In a revealing letter to Iolo Morganwg, written a few years before he died, the old bard commented on the two volumes of Iolo's English poetry, *Poems, Lyric and Pastoral*, printed in London in 1794.

> I received your letter and had a look at your two books with a fair and uncontentious spirit. I look upon them as the fruit of an intelligent mind and of diligent reflection, but I cannot see a great scarcity of new books among the inhabitants of our country, with the exception of schoolbooks, which are like a mantle worn daily. I have read many apologists' books. I received much learning and solace from so many of them as to show that the essence and attributes of God are the basis of every religious truth.
>
> I have read much of the writings of learned men in English poetry but, indeed (compared to the work of Alexander Pope), many of them were not an atom more delectable to the appetite of my intellect than the kiln-dried bread of Cardiganshire to the appetite of my mouth.
>
> True is the old proverb, that there is no purpose in producing many books.[13]

Though he may have damned Iolo's work with faint praise, he ended with a poem, a *triban*, signed 'Iorwerth ab Ioan'.

Dewch attaf mewn dewraf daith,	*Visit me on your bold travels,*
Dda naws, i'm ddiddan noswaith	*For a friendly evening conversation,*
Mewn diogel wîr dawel dôn,	*Safe in a truly peaceful mood,*
Am roeso di ymryson.	*A welcome, and no disputation.*

It is highly probable that Iolo (who was indeed a bold and extensive traveller) visited Ton Coch in Edward's lifetime and later when Rhys Evans was preparing his poetry for publication and seeing it through the press; he certainly visited Rhys in later years. No doubt Iolo encouraged him to publish his father's work with news of support from London. The poem quoted at the head of this chapter and printed at the front of the 1804 edition, was also intended as encouragement, in this case from William Dafydd, a poet who had been mentioned along with Edward, in connection with an eisteddfod or bardic meeting at Llantrisant in 1770.

The first printing press in Merthyr, which Iolo referred to in his letter to Pughe, was established in 1801 by William Williams, who had run a bookshop in the growing town since the previous year. In 1803 he brought out a new edition of *Drych y Prif Oesoedd* by Theophilus Evans, the Anglican cleric who had witnessed Edward's marriage licence sixty years earlier. In his history of printing in Wales, Ifano Jones gives a possible explanation of why *Caneuon Moesol a Duwiol* had apparently been 'in the press' since 1802.

> Not having been brought up to the craft, William Williams found considerable difficulty for some years in carrying out the business of printing in Merthyr owing to the scarcity of Welsh compositors; but he had a good knowledge of Welsh; and by dint of great pains at correcting proofs and instructing his Welsh employees, he overcame his difficulties, and produced a large number of well-printed books.[14]

The surviving copies of the first edition of Edward Evan's poems bear out the quality of Williams's work. The typography and layout are superior to the later editions printed in Merthyr and Aberdare. There are some fine capitals and ornamentation. It is impossible to know how many copies were printed, but this edition is extremely rare and only to be found in the National Library in Aberystwyth, at Bangor University, and in an incomplete copy in the Salisbury Collection at Cardiff University.

One of the two copies in the National Library belonged to Rev. Thomas Evans ('Tomos Glyn Cothi'). On the title page is written 'Thomas Evans from Rees Evans' and below that, in a different hand, 'His brother'. While Tomos Glyn Cothi had a brother, Rees Evans of Tonyrefail, it seems more likely that this was a gift from Rhys Evans, son of the poet, whose name was often also spelled 'Rees'. He was a leading member of the congregation at the Old Meeting House where Tomos Glyn Cothi became minister in 1811 and his father had certainly known the recipient.[15]

This copy of *Caneuon Moesol a Duwiol* is bound with *Y Fêl Gafod*, a collection of poetry published by Lewis Hopkin's son-in-law, John Miles, in 1813 and also printed by William Williams in Merthyr. Along with poems by Hopkin, are others by his fellow 'Grammarians', including some by Edward Evan which were not in the 1804 collection. Whether Rhys omitted them, or did not have them at the time, is not clear, but their inclusion in *Y Fêl Gafod* may have been one of the things which prompted him to bring out an expanded, second edition in 1816. The more attractive title of Miles's collection ('The Shower of Honey' or 'Manna') may also have prompted him to name the new book *Afalau'r Awen*.

In 1816 William Williams printed the second edition of Edward Evan's work in Merthyr during a period of industrial strife in the iron country. The first great strike came that year, after wages were cut at a time of rising prices. Men marched on Merthyr from Tredegar, shutting down all the furnaces on the way. Shots were fired by special constables at the Dowlais works, whose owner John Guest barricaded himself in his house, while Crawshay of Cyfarthfa fled to the hills. A painting by Penry Williams captured the stand-off between the strikers and troops brought in to quell the riot.[16] In the end, the ironmasters agreed not to cut wages any further and peace was restored.

The new edition, with its new title, included an additional twenty-two poems of varying length, ending again with the verse translation of Ecclesiastes. The address to the reader from Rhys Evans was omitted, but William Dafydd's poem, originally addressed to Rhys, was included, now as one of several poems of praise for the work of 'the late famous bard'. The book was priced at two shillings and sixpence.

After many years of searching for a copy of Edward Evan's work, this was the edition which I found, online, from a second-hand bookshop in Yorkshire. It was unbound, having been separated by the seller from a number of other works in Welsh, of a religious nature. I had it restored, at considerable expense, by a traditional bookbinder near St Paul's in London. On the first leaf its owner inscribed her name, Jane Owens of Minffordd, a house near Llangefni on Anglesey, and (in Welsh), 'This book was given to her as a remembrance by her son Owen, who was going to London' in 1837. At the back, Thomas Owen of Minffordd recorded (in English) the arrival of John Owen from India and China on 25 November 1844.

The third edition was launched into a world of even greater turmoil than that of 1816. The advertisement seeking subscriptions in April 1837 announced that it would include 'several Poems, Englynion, &c. not contained in either of the former, the Manuscripts having only recently been discovered'.[17] The book was again printed in Merthyr, this time by Thomas Price who had set up a press there as early as 1822. William Williams, printer of the first two editions had moved to Brecon after selling his Merthyr business to Job James, the follower of William Cobbett, in 1819.[18]

The list of subscribers in 1837 is remarkable not only for its range but also as an indication of how Welsh continued to be spoken and read by all classes in the industrialised *Blaenau*. In addition to the Chartists and 'Esquires' discussed in chapter 19, there were several shopkeepers, inn keepers, a collier, a glazier, shoemakers, a 'serjeant', a gardener, a carpenter, a miller, a mason and the well-known clockmaker William Williams, as well as many individuals who cannot now be traced.[19] The subscribers ordered two hundred and fifteen copies in total, so perhaps five hundred would have been printed.

Just a few years later, a visitor could still describe the 'beautiful, rural looking village of Aberdare', but by 1851 the population was ten times what it had been at the turn of the century. There were outbreaks of typhus, cholera and smallpox.[20] A report submitted to the Board of Health in London in 1853 painted a picture of overcrowding and 'immorality', high rates of disease and infant mortality, lack of clean water and sanitation.

> There are whole rows of houses without any privy at all, the inmates having no place to go excepting the fields ... All sense of decency is lost for want of proper convenience and the moral effect of this practice is very bad.[21]

In 1861 Aberdare was said to be 'less dirty than most of the adjoining iron districts', thanks to the establishment and effort of a Local Board of Health. There was a fine new parish church, but industrial waste scarred the environment.

> The narrow valley is blocked up to a great extent by enormous black banks of cinder, which are composed of refuse from the works, and additions are being made to these tips hourly thus filling up and covering a considerable space of ground in a few years. As the tips in progress are composed of hot cinders, they are on fire from nearly top to bottom and glow like lava. The

scene is strange and impressive in broad daylight, but when viewed at night it is wild beyond conception.[22]

By 1874, when the fourth and last edition of *Afalau'r Awen* was published in Aberdare, the population had grown to almost 40,000 and the valley contained forty seven coal mines producing around two million tons of steam coal a year. The growth from a village of under 1,500 at the turn of the century had brought not only industrial and political strife, but serious social and environmental stress, whose effects were still complained of.

> The Valley of Aberdare has become a trough full of human beings as its bottom, deep underground, is full of superior steam coal ... the bowels of the earth are torn out and thrown on the surface; the sides of the mountains are rent and made to pour out hills of swarthy rubbish; trains that seem of interminable length are ever conveying towards the sea coal and iron extracted from these cavernous depths for the behoof of all lands ... At certain hours, the 'pits', all but bottomless, belch out their myriads of grimy, blackened human forms, each with a Davey lamp in hand, who hasten to their humble homes to wash, feed, and rest.[23]

There had been a printing press in the town since the 1850s. Josiah Jones (1799-1873), who had served as Independent Minister to various congregations around Wales, was also a printer and publisher who established several newspapers in Aberdare. After his death in 1873, his son continued the business of Jones a'i mab (Jones & Son) and printed the fourth edition.[24] This included the brief biography of the poet referred to previously and a much longer biography of his son, Rhys Evans who had died in 1867. Rhys's daughter Mary Kingsbury of Fforchaman and his son, Rhys Evans of Penygraig, Llanfabon, were the instigators of the new publication.[25]

For many years it was impossible to buy a copy of the 1874 edition, but more recently it has been scanned and is readily available online. It is even possible to buy well-bound printed facsimile copies, at a reasonable price, from booksellers in India. Edward Evan's 1775 sermon at Y Dref Wen is available online, as is his translation of Samuel Bourn's *Lectures to Children*. There's no explanation for why and how these works were selected for scanning, unlike, for example, Lewis Hopkin's *Y Fêl Gafod*, but the result is that Edward Evan's writing, composed in the remote hills of eighteenth century Glamorgan, is now accessible worldwide thanks to the internet and the original commitment of the poet's descendants to bring his work out in print.

[1] 'Give this little book to the world': William Dafydd of Aberglynogwr, 'Entreaty to the publisher of the work' [Rhys Evans], included in Edward Evan, *Caniadau Moesol a Duwiol* (1804), p.iv.

[2] Edward Williams (Iolo Morganwg) to William Owen Pughe (7 June 1803); *Correspondence of Iolo Morganwg* (2007).

[3] William Owen Pughe to Edward Williams (Iolo Morganwg) (30 June 1803), *ditto*.

[4] Edward Williams (Iolo Morganwg) to William Owen Pughe (19 December 1802), *ditto.*.

[5] See Mary-Ann Constantine, 'Songs and Stones: Iolo Morganwg (1747-1826), Mason and Bard', *The Eighteenth Century*, Vol. 47, No. 2/3 (2006), pp. 233-251.

[6] Ifano Jones, *A History of Printing and Printers in Wales to 1810* (1925), pp.72-74.

[7] 'Farley family', *Oxford Dictionary of National Biography*.

[8] 'Farley, Sarah', *The Women's Print History Project, 2019*: https://womensprinthistoryproject.com/person/3947

[9] ὀλίγων δέ ἐστιν χρεία ἢ ἑνός Luke 10:42 'But one thing is needful: (and Mary hath chosen that good part, which shall not be taken away from her)'.

[10] 'Evan Evans (Ieuan Fardd or Ieuan Brydydd Hir 1731 - 1788)', *Dictionary of Welsh Biography*.

[11] 'Peter Bailey Williams (1763 - 1836)', *ditto*.

[12] *A History of Printing and Printers in Wales*, pp.113-116.

[13] Edward Evan to Edward Williams (Iolo Morganwg) (1796?), English translation of letter from *Correspondence of Iolo Morganwg*, letter 405. '

[14] *A History of Printing and Printers in Wales*, pp. 167-176.

[15] See Appendix 1 for details of other owners of the various editions of Edward Evan's published works.

[16] https://www.peoplescollection.wales/items/9688

[17] *Glamorgan, Monmouthshire and Brecon Gazette & Merthyr Guardian* (15 April 1837).

[18] *A History of Printing and Printers in Wales*, pp.167-176.

[19] For the full list of subscribers to the 1837 edition, see Appendix 2.

[20] See *Old Aberdare*, Vol. 2 (1997), p.76.

[21] Report by the Inspector of the General Board of Health 1853, see *The Land Our Fathers Possessed* (2011), pp.71-74.

[22] *Bristol Mercury* (24 August 1861), see *ditto*, pp.83-85.

[23] Thomas Nicholas (1874), see *ditto*, pp.86-87.

[24] *Aberdare Times*, 'Death of the Rev. Josiah Thomas Jones' (1 February 1873).

[25] *Aberdare Times*, Advertisement for a new edition of the poetry of Edward Evan (12 Sept 1874.)

CHAPTER 21

1777-1869 – The Sons of the Bard

Ys gwelaf achos galar	*I have good cause for mourning*
I'm o waith colli'n car,	*Since I have lost my friend,*
Rees Evans, hir oes a safodd,	*Rees Evans, who lived so long,*
A byw fu'n fardd wrth ein bodd.	*A bard who brought much pleasure.*
Un call oedd Evans, Toncoch,	*Wise was Evans of Toncoch,*
A gwiwddoeth, fel y gwyddoch;	*And worthy as you know;*
Ei hanes fydd yn enwog	*His story will be famous*
Tra'r bryniau a'r creigiau crog.[1]	*While hills and cliffs endure.*

The life of Edward Evan's son Rhys spans the period of industrial revolution punctuated by the publication of his poetry. He was born at Ton Coch in 1779 and lived there until his death in 1867. His life represented 'almost a history of the parish of Aberdare ... certainly a history of its new age, the beginning of its development of priceless treasures in iron and coal'.[2]

The Abernant ironworks, just up the valley from Ton Coch, opened in 1800 at the same time as the Aberdare works in Llwydcoed, where Edward Evan's birthplace became Tregibbon, the site of the ironworkers' houses. Around 1810 work began on the Aberdare Canal which ran close to Ton Coch's land and led to a development in which Rhys Evans was directly involved.

His father had looked after the woods on his landlord's Dyffryn estate and Rhys Evans continued the tradition, serving as estate foreman for the owner John Bruce Pryce.[3] Around 1808 a man called Dafydd Siôn

Rhys wanted to build a house and an inn on land belonging to the estate, near the old river crossing and half way along the new turnpike road and the canal linking Aberdare with Navigation House at Abercynon. It was potentially a prime location for passing trade and a site meeting was held at which Dafydd Siôn Rhys, Mr Bruce, his wife Sarah, and Rhys Evans discussed the plan. What would the new tavern be called? The landlord, predictably, suggested 'The Bruce Arms' in line with common practice. Mrs Bruce pointed to a tree which would have to be felled to make way for the buildings and asked what it was called. Rhys Evans told her it was a rowan or mountain ash and she persuaded her husband to give the inn that name. As a community grew around the place, it became first the hamlet and later the town of Mountain Ash, centre of a booming iron and coal industry downstream of Aberdare.[4]

John Bruce Pryce, Stipendiary Magistrate and pursuer of the Chartists in 1839, would play an important part in the life of Rhys Evans and his daughter Mary. He was the great nephew of the Rev. Thomas Bruce, whom Edward Evan had served, and continued to expand the estate he inherited. In 1807 he married Sarah Austin of Barbados, whose family was deeply involved with slavery in the West Indies. Although her father Hugh Williams Austin, Rector of St Peter's Barbados, does not appear to have owned enslaved people himself, her grandfather, Col. Thomas Austin, who died in 1806, owned slave estates in Demerara, now Guyana.[5] Sarah's uncles, John and William Austin, inherited from him and were paid £40,000 compensation in 1836 (the equivalent of £3,775,000 today) when more than eight hundred enslaved workers were finally freed.[6] Another uncle, Rev. Richard Austin owned two hundred and fifty enslaved people in Surinam.[7]

John and Sarah Bruce's daughter Margaret was born in 1811 and their son, Henry Austin Bruce (later Lord Aberdare), in 1815. Margaret married in 1835 and renewed her mother's connection with the West Indies. She and her husband, Charles Thomas Alleyne, lived on Barbados, where in 1820 he had inherited from his father slave estates valued at £44,000. He received compensation totalling £15,000 (worth £1,400,000 today) for the liberation of six hundred enslaved workers. The couple moved to Bristol after emancipation.[8]

Whether Rhys Evans was aware of the connection to slavery is not known, though it would certainly have gone against his principles. He composed a series of *tribannau* in honour of the wedding of Margaret and Charles Alleyne at Dyffryn, addressing the father of the bride as 'my dear loving master' and wishing his daughter and her husband health and happiness, 'wherever they should go'. The poem ended with a request that Rev. William Knight, uncle of the bride and a poet himself, should compose verses in reply. Knight ('Gwilym o Fargam'), later Dean of Llandaff Cathedral, obliged with a series of *tribannau* which are a testimony to Rhys's ability and reputation as a poet.

Y prydydd prydferth serchog,   *You fine and loving poet,*
Ti genaist yn galonog;   *You sing with true conviction;*
I ateb it' nid wyf ond gwan,   *I am too weak to answer you,*
O awen analluog.   *And lacking inspiration.*

Yr wyt ti'n bêr ganiedydd,   *You are a fine composer,*
Ac eto'n fab i brydydd;   *And son to a great poet;*
Yr eos wyt mewn hyfryd gân,   *Your song sounds like the nightingale,*
O'r fro hyd flaen y mynydd.[9]   *From vale to mountain summit.*

Rhys Evans adjudicated at eisteddfodau, including the one held at The Swan in Merthyr in 1833. R.T. Jenkins believed Edward Evan would have been pleased by the literary renewal in Merthyr and Aberdare, 'a renewal in which his son Rhys played a considerable part; a renewal which later became an inspiration for men like William Williams ('Carw Coch') and David Williams ('Alaw Goch') to hold eisteddfodau in Aberdare'.[10] Although Rhys Evans's own poetry was never published as a collection, several examples and extracts are included in the biography printed in the fourth edition of his father's work in 1874. Like Edward Evan he started young, composing at the age of eleven a *triban* similar to his father's poem about Tabitha, in this case referring to a man who was working in a small quarry at Ton Coch.

Mi welais fachgen echdo'   *T'other day I saw a boy*
Ar ben y Gwar yn gweithio;   *Up working in the quarry;*
'Roedd ganddo ffroc a phicys trwm,   *He had a smock and heavy pick,*
A'i enw Twm Llandeilo.   *They call him Tom Llandeilo.*

When Rhys was a boy it appears there was still little schooling available in Aberdare and he was taught a range of subjects by his father. In later life he was said to be a great reader, having studied the works of Pope, Dryden and Milton in detail. He could apparently recite from memory the whole of *Paradise Lost* in English and Welsh.[11] This seems a truly remarkable feat, but there is evidence of others who have achieved it.[12] He used to entertain his family around the fire in winter, in a domestic 'eisteddfod', reading, reciting, and singing.[13]

His education was sufficently effective to allow him to set up for a time as a schoolmaster at Gwernifor in what is now Mountain Ash. When he was twenty-five he married one of his former pupils, sixteen-year-old Mary Williams, whose father Howel farmed at Aberffrwd, not far from her new home. She spent the rest of her life at Ton Coch, where she lived with her husband, his mother (who died in 1823) and his brother Edward. She gave birth to ten children, five girls and five boys, one of whom was stillborn. Despite what must have been an exhausting life, Mary Evans lived at Ton Coch until 1871, when she died at the age of 83. The biography of 1874 reports that she played an active part on the farm alongside her husband.

> He and his wife were well-versed in the principles of agriculture as can still be seen today on the farm where they lived. Their knowledge of the principles and theory of agricultural chemistry was a great advantage to them in achieving beneficial outcomes, which kept their family happy and comfortable.[14]

Iolo Morganwg encouraged Rhys in his poetry and visited him at Ton Coch, but he failed to persuade him to accept 'ordination' as a bard 'by right and descent'. It is tempting to think that Rhys was negatively influenced by the way that Iolo had mythologised his father. As late as 1866 he again refused the honour when it was offered by Myfyr Morganwg (Evan Davies), who had come 'deeply under the influence of the Druidic "fever" that affected some persons at that time' and who claimed to have succeeded as archdruid after the death of Iolo's son Taliesin Williams in 1847.

The biography recites an intriguing tale of an attempt by Rhys Evans and Myfyr Morganwg to erect a stone circle on the mountain at Cefnpennar above Ton Coch, with the aim of holding an eisteddfod there. While at work they were set upon by a band of 'wicked and malicious' men. Rhys left Myfyr, promising to return quickly with a piece of poetry to recite over the stones, but instead of going back up the mountain, he stayed at home. How Myfyr managed is not reported, but that was the end of that eisteddfod.

Rhys's older brother Edward was also something of a poet and wrote under the bardic name 'Cynfab' ('Firstborn'). When he was born, his father, then sixty-one, feared he would not live to guide his child to adulthood.

O fy maban olwg wiwlan,   *O my lovely newborn baby*
Nid wyt ond bychan yn y byd,   *You have just come to this world;*
Rhag fy ngalw ar fyr i farw,   *In case death should call me quickly,*
Gadawa i'n groyw wrth dy grud,   *Let me now, beside your cradle*
Ddewis rybudd didwyll dedwydd *Leave you this, my best advice;*
Ar i ti beunydd tra f'ech di byw,   *Every day, whatever happens,*
Blygu'n isel os cei dy hoedel,   *To act justly, to love mercy*
I rodio yn dawel gyd â Duw. [15]   *And walk humbly with your God.*

Edward junior was a harpist, like his father, and it is almost certainly he that Robert Griffiths refers to in his history of the harp in Wales as 'a fairly famous harpist' and composer who flourished around 1830.[16] He had travelled to America as a young man with three others from Aberdare. The story was told in an obituary of one of his companions, Edward Thomas of Cefnpennar, who died in 1859.

> The adventurers meditated a long stay in the States and they had provided themselves before hand with hatchets, billhooks, and pickaxes ... But Welshmen who leave their country from merely sentimental motives soon get homesick; and this proved the case here. After they had been three weeks in the States, they paid a visit to a country churchyard. Here they observed that many of the people had been cut off in the flower of their youth, and the fact begot serious reflections. At length Edward Thomas said, 'Boys, people die very young in this country. Let us go home'. And thereupon they agreed to return, and did so.[17]

Both Edward Thomas and Edward Evans avoided an early death; the former lived to be seventy-four, and the harpist of Ton Coch died in 1868 at the age of eighty-five. He lost his sight in the last years of his life, which is no doubt the origin of a long-lived family legend about a blind harpist.

Rhys and Edward Evans were leading members of the Old Meeting House where their father had been minister. Under his successors, Thomas Evans ('Tomos Glyn Cothi') and John Jones, it became, in the words of historian David L. Davies, 'a kind of college of freethinking, and prominent in matters of church and state'. Rhys was praised by the poet Gwilym Gellideg as 'a freethinker and a lover of the truth', and he was undoubtedly connected to the radicals of Merthyr.[18] In later life he attended the new Unitarian meeting house at Abernantygroes, closer to Ton Coch and the ironworks and coal mines of Cwmbach.

Several collieries were opened on Dyffryn Estate land near Ton Coch in the 1840s and 1850s. The Evans brothers, farming on the hillside, would have been acutely aware of the mining disasters which cost the lives of many men and boys. In 1849, fifty-three were killed at Lletyshenkin, fourteen of them boys. Three years later, fifty men and fifteen boys were killed at the Middle Duffryn pit just below their farm.[19] Between 1845 and 1860 one hundred and thirty-three miners died in the three Duffryn collieries.[20] John Bruce Pryce was paid a royalty for every ton of coal mined from under his land and was keen to expand his holdings, as he did in 1860 when he bought the farm belonging to Rhys Evans's daughter Mary. Her dramatic story involves the legal battle of a widow and single mother against powerful and wealthy landowners who made a killing out of coal.

---

[1] Gwilym Gellideg, 'In Memoriam Rees Evans', *Aberdare Times* (7 September 1867).

[2] Obituary, *Y Gwladgarwr* (14 September 1867).

[3] Variously known as John Bruce Knight, John Bruce Bruce and John Bruce Pryce, father of Henry Austin Bruce, first Lord Aberdare.

[4] Jeremy J. Morgan: 'Henry Austin Bruce, the Duffryn Estate and the development of an industrial society: Mountain Ash 1845-1895', p.41. (M. Phil Thesis, Cardiff University 2016, available online).

[5] 'Col. Thomas Austin', *Legacies of British Slavery database*, http://wwwdepts-live.ucl.ac.uk/lbs/person/view/2146661105

[6] 'William Austin', *ditto*, http://wwwdepts-live.ucl.ac.uk/lbs/person/view/2146630745
'John Austin', *ditto*, http://wwwdepts-live.ucl.ac.uk/lbs/person/view/8650

[7] 'Rev. Richard Austin', *ditto*, http://wwwdepts-live.ucl.ac.uk/lbs/person/view/2146647831

[8] 'Charles Thomas Alleyne', *ditto*, http://wwwdepts-live.ucl.ac.uk/lbs/person/view/6849

[9] Biography of Rhys Evans, *Afalau'r Awen* (1874), pp.175-6.

[10] R. T. Jenkins, *Bardd a'i Gefndir* (1948), p.144.

[11] *Paradise Lost* translated by William Owen-Pughe as *Coll Gwynfa* (1819).

[12] Including the literary critic Harold Bloom: https://www.cbc.ca/radio/sunday/the-sunday-edition-for-october-20-2019-1.5325821/remembering-harold-bloom-the-yale-scholar-who-searched-for-literary-genius-1.5325834

[13] Biography of Rhys Evans, *Afalau'r Awen* (1874), p.170.

[14] *Ditto*, p.170.

[15] Ditto, p.25, 'A poem for Edward my first son in his cradle'.

[16] Robert Griffiths, *Llyfr Cerdd Dannau* (1913), p.196.

[17] *Cardiff and Merthyr Guardian & Brecon Gazette* (2 July 1859).

[18] See Chapter 19.

[19] Jeremy Morgan (note to the author): 'There are ruins of the colliery at the side of the main road through the valley, an unusual survival.'

[20] See Cynon Valley History Society, *Cynon Coal*, (2001), chapter 7.

CHAPTER 22

1845 – Mineral Rights and Wrongs

Our earth, though plundered to exhaustion,
Still has the strength to answer back.[1]

Between 1840 and 1844, four collieries were opened by Thomas Powell on land belonging to the Dyffryn Estate. Powell's 'Duffryn' mines formed the nucleus of what became 'the greatest single undertaking in the South Wales coal trade'.[2]

These collieries were mining the Four Feet seam of top-quality steam coal which had been struck by Thomas Wayne when he sank the first pit in the valley at Abernantygroes in 1837. The Evans family would have been well aware of these developments close to Ton Coch.

In 1845, Rhys Evans's daughter Mary Kingsbury found herself enmeshed in a court case over the ownership of coal below the farm which had been left to her young son when her husband died. The legal battles saw her arrested as a debtor and eventually forced to sell the land to John Bruce Pryce of Dyffryn.

Mary Evans had married Jenkin Kingsbury of Fforchaman on the other side of the valley from Ton Coch in 1827 but he died just eight years later, leaving her with the farm and three young children. It was not until 1856 that Fforchaman colliery was opened, but the legal action started more than ten years earlier. The presence of the Four Feet seam below the farm was either known or predicted and Mary Kingsbury wanted to assert her rights as a coal owner.

For centuries the ownership of land in Glamorgan had focused on the surface: sites for building, fields for crops, meadows, woods and coppice. The growth of the iron and coal industries changed everything; real value now lay below the surface in the 'mines', the minerals, which often belonged to large estates who stood to make a fortune. When land was sold, even before the iron and coal boom, the mineral rights were usually 'reserved' to the original owner and the conveyance or 'release' would make this clear.

Mary Kingsbury's battle with the landed gentry made her something of a local hero. The popular story was that she had taken on 'Lord Aberdare' and lost. The true story is different, though the end result was the same; Fforchaman did become the property of Lord Aberdare and the former landowner Mary Kingsbury was, by 1880, the oldest tenant of the Dyffryn Estate.

In her legal battle she found herself in front of a special jury at the Glamorgan Assizes, up against one of the heirs of the formerly great Aberaman estate, which had been divided between three daughters in 1788 when the last male of the Matthews line died. Fforchaman farm fell to Eleanor Matthews, wife of one Major Hugh Lord.

In 1799, Thomas Jenkin Gibbon, the tenant at Fforchaman, and the man who built Tregibbon, bought the freehold of the farm from Major Lord. His son-in-law, Thomas Kingsbury, and his grandson, Jenkin Kingsbury, both died young leaving Mary and her children in possession of the land. The court case hinged on the evidence of what Thomas Jenkin Gibbon had, or had not, legally purchased.

In the division of the Matthews estate the mineral rights had been kept as one, in the interests of all three inheriting parties. But Mary Kingsbury insisted that Hugh Lord had sold his third share of the 'mines' under Fforchaman to Thomas Jenkin Gibbon, so she was entitled to a third of any royalties on coal to be extracted.

Each side was represented in court by Queen's Counsel and Colonel Arthur Lord, son of Hugh and Eleanor, sought to have Mary Kingsbury 'ejected' from her claim to the minerals. His Q.C. maintained they could not have been sold without the consent of all three Matthews heirs. But he conceded that Hugh Lord 'being an imprudent man, had disposed of his right, by which it came into the hands of the defendant.' Neverthless he insisted that the court should rule against her, since her title was bad.

The judge stated that a document in Mary Kingsbury's possession made it clear that Hugh Lord had 'fully intended' to convey the mineral rights to Thomas Jenkin Gibbon, whether he had the right to do so, or not.

> The deed produced on behalf of Mrs Kingsbury … showed a clear conveyance, not only of the surface, but of Major Lord's third share of the minerals.[3]

This deed must have been the document later seen by a Q.C. acting for John Bruce Pryce, who commented that the 'abstract' of the original conveyance did not reserve the mineral rights.[4]

In the end, the court ruled that Hugh Lord had had no right to sell the minerals under Fforchaman and gave the verdict in favour of his son. But the judge left it to the High Court in London to decide whether the case should fall because no coal had yet been mined.[5]

The name of the case of 'Lord v. Kingsbury' may well have fed the legend that Mary's legal battle was with Lord Aberdare. But there was no such lord until Henry Austin Bruce was made a peer in 1873. It was his father, John Bruce Pryce, who eventually took possession of Fforchaman in 1860, when Mary's accumulated debts forced her to sell.

It seems highly likely that the legal battle had contributed to her financial difficulties. Hiring a Q.C. has always been expensive. In 1848 Colonel Lord had Mary Kingsbury arrested for non-payment of costs associated with the case. This must have been the origin of the story that she spent a night in jail. She was one of a number of 'insolvents' brought before the court. It is not clear whether the costs in question concerned the original hearing or a subsequent appeal to the High Court, of which there is no record. In this case, though, Lord's arguments were rejected and Mary, the insolvent, was discharged.[6]

Over the following years, she and her son leased land to the colliery which was opened at Fforchaman but they never benefitted from royalties. They sold parcels of land for housing as the mining village of Cwmaman grew around the mine. But they also borrowed money by mortgaging the farm and in 1859 the lenders demanded repayment.

It is no surprise that John Bruce Pryce was interested in buying Fforchaman. He had steadily extended his estate and owned adjoining land. The Evans family had strong connections with Dyffryn; not only was Mary's father Rhys employed on the estate, her brother Rhys had been the tenant of the Mountain Ash Inn. It would make sense to keep the Kingsburys as tenants at Fforchaman under the new arrangements.

When Lord Aberdare's son married in 1880, celebrations were held at Dyffryn House and Mary Kingsbury, now aged seventy-five and the oldest tenant on the estate, was given the honour of presenting the newly-weds with a silver salver.[7] As a former landowner in her own right, she must have had mixed feelings.[8]

The descendants of Edward Evan remained tenants at Fforchaman until

1982, when the fourth Lord Aberdare sold the farm back to a Kingsbury, Mary's great-grandson. Fforchaman colliery, which opened in 1856, closed in 1965. The ancient farmhouse, once an isolated whitewashed cottage like Ton Coch, still stands in a row of terraced houses built for the families of miners who worked the coal for just over a hundred years.

---

[1] Harri Webb, 'Dyffryn Woods', *Collected Poems* (1995), pp.83-84.

[2] Morris & Williams, *South Wales Coal Industry 1841-1875* (1958), pp.106-7.

[3] *Cardiff & Merthyr Guardian* (19 July 1845).

[4] Abstract title of Rees Kingsbury (1859), Glamorgan Archives DBR/23.

[5] Reported in *The Cambrian* (19 July 1845) and the *Cardiff & Merthyr Guardian* of the same date.

[6] *Cardiff & Merthyr Guardian* (30 September 1848).

[7] *South Wales Daily News* (6 August 1880).

[8] Mary Kingsbury died in 1889, a few months after the birth of her great grandson, the author's grandfather, Evan Jenkin Kingsbury (1889-1981).

CHAPTER 23

2024 – The Woods of Glyn Cynon

Aberdâr, Llanwynno i gyd,	*In Aberdare, Llanwynno,*
Plwy Merthyr hyd Llanfabon,	*In Merthyr and Llanfabon,*
Mwya adfyd a fu erioed	*The worst affliction ever came*
Pan dorred Coed Glyn Cynon.	*When they cut the trees of Cynon.*
Llawer bedwen las ei chlog	*Many a birch with cloak of green*
Ynghrôg y bytho'r Saeson!)	*(The English – we should hang 'em!)*
Sydd yn danllwyth mawr o dân	*Is now a roaring, flaming fire*
Gan wŷr yr haearn duon. [1]	*Thanks to the men of iron.*

Edward Evan's grandson Rhys, who wrote the poem on the leaving of Ton Coch, moved to a small farm called Penygraig when he married in 1852. It was in the parish of Llanfabon, which is mentioned in the above lament for the lost woods of Glyn Cynon composed by an anonymous poet in the sixteenth century.

The story of Edward Evan and his legacy is a story rooted in the landscape of Glamorgan. A year after my search for the remains of 'the old home of the bards' on Mountain Ash golf course, I went looking for Rhys Evans's home on the mountain above Cilfynydd, a former mining village not far from the junction of the rivers Cynon and Taff. Edward Evan's great granddaughter Elizabeth lived at Penygraig until 1932. An ancient track leads uphill towards the summit where the farmhouse stood. On the right hand as you go up, the fields and hedges are exactly as shown on the earliest Ordnance Survey maps, the boundaries unchanged for hundreds of years. On the left are huge, unrestored colliery tips eroded by the wheels of off-road motorcycles. Penygraig, which was marked on

OS maps as late as 1948, is buried under thousands of tons of black coal waste from the colliery in the valley below. It's a striking illustration of the physical impact of industry on the landscape and the historical record of the *Blaenau* of Glamorgan.

In his essay *The Lie of the Land*, the poet Nigel Jenkins refers to 'the complex reality of an inhabited, worked over, ever-changing landscape' and describes the 'fall from ecological grace' which coincided with the arrival of the first farmers in Wales six or seven thousand years ago. No part of the country has escaped that impact and only isolated fragments of 'primary woodland' survive.

> One of the Stone Age farmer's chief labours would have been felling trees to carve out plots for cultivation, and it is at this juncture that the ecological equilibrium of the earlier nomadic Stone Age begins to be lost. With their slash-and-burn clearances these farmer-pastoralists inaugurated an epoch of unprecedented human landscape-making which we are still living through today. The ecological vandalism of opencast coal mining in Glamorgan or the dumping at sea of raw sewage has its genesis in a psychology of environmental mastery that sprang from the blade of a polished stone axe over four thousand years ago.[2]

Jenkins describes how oak and birch woodland on higher ground was the first to be felled by the early farmers because it was much more accessible than the 'tangled, swampy forest' of the river valleys. And this pattern of land use and settlement can still be seen in the location of hillside farms in the *Blaenau*. Names like Edward Evan's birthplace, Penyrallt ('Hilltop') and Penygraig ('Top of the Rock') prove the point, and it's likely that farms like these and Ton Coch occupied land worked for thousands of years before the time of Edward Evan and his ancestors. It was only with industrialisation that the valleys, rather than the hills, became the defining feature of upland Glamorgan.

In 1903 Jenkin Howell described the process of deforestation and clearing in the Cynon Valley, which had produced (in his opinion) 'one of the most beautiful and level vales in the country'.[3] He lamented the impact of industry in defiling that man-made beauty, but also reported memories of a thriving wooded landscape still populated by wild boar before they were hunted to extinction.

I have heard an old inhabitant say that his grandfather remembered helping in the hunting of the wild boar … They would wait a few weeks after the acorns had fallen in the woods, to give the boar time to fatten before attacking them. Then at daybreak they would climb the edges of the nearby hills to look for steam rising from the animals' lairs among the trees. They would form a circle around the area from which the most steam was rising and begin to attack the young boar. This was a dangerous undertaking because the older animals would fiercely defend their young.[4]

The *Blaenau* were said to be 'well woodid' in the 1530s when John Leland described the forest of Llwydcoed, in the area where Edward Evan would be born two hundred years later.[5] In the 1570s it was still reported:

There be … parcels of wood within the said lordship called forests, that is to say Llowyd Koyd [and] Glyn Kynon … and that Lowyd Koed is replenished most with oaks, Glyn Kynon most with beach [sic] and some with oaks.[6]

In *The Mountain Shepherd*, Iolo Morganwg describes the Garth mountain above the gorge which the river Taff has cut through the long ridge dividing the uplands from the Vale.

The sides of this mountain are cover'd with wood
Hanging over old Tave with his turbulent flood;
A green velvet plain o'er the summit extends
And here a blithe shepherd his flock daily tends.

The mountain slopes around the base of the Garth bear scars of early industry and conifers were planted in the coal waste seventy years ago, but native trees have visibly spread higher up its southern flank over the last thirty years. Here, on the edge of the coalfield, where the seams crop out near the surface, some of the earliest coal pits were dug to provide fuel for an iron works on the riverbank in the late eighteenth century. The Pentyrch works had first been established in Elizabethan times, when trees were cut down to make charcoal. This was the fuel used before the discovery of accessible coal reserves, and the Garth woods supplied charcoal for the re-established works until the 1790s, when the blast furnace was converted to burn coking coal.[7]

As early as 1578, Rhys Merrick was reporting that 'many fforests and Woodes' had been spoiled and consumed in the areas where 'Iron Milles' were operating.[8] Following the Acts of Union, English ironmasters moved their operations from the Sussex Weald into south Wales, to take advantage of the ready availability of wood for charcoal, running water to power blast furnaces and reserves of iron ore and limestone. It was the ensuing devastation of the woods of Glyn Cynon in Edward Evan's valley that provoked a poet in the time of Elizabeth I, to compose a bitter attack on the 'Saxons', referred to as 'the sons of Alice'.[9]

Os am dorri a dwyn y bar,	*If they break and steal the branch,*
Llety'r adar gwylltion,	*The wild birds' only dwelling,*
Boed yr anras yn eu plith,	*May a foul plague infest the lot*
Holl blant Alys ffeilsion.	*Of Alice's false children.*
Gwell y dylasai'r Saeson fod	*Better that the English should*
Ynghrôg yng ngwaelod eigion,	*Hang in the deepest dungeon,*
Uffern boen, yn cadw eu plas	*And make their home in hellish pain*
Na thorri glas Glyn Cynon. [10]	*Than cut the green of Cynon.*

Almost all of Wales was affected by charcoal burning for iron smelting on an industrial scale between the sixteenth and nineteenth centuries.[11] By the end of the sixteenth century woodland covered only ten percent of the land in much of the country. Water-driven blast furnaces, burning charcoal, had transformed the early, small-scale iron works. It is estimated that it took forty to fifty tons of wood to make one ton of clean iron.

It was not only the 'sons of Alice' who were involved in the early iron industry. Edward Evan was reputed to be descended, at seven generations, from Hywel Gwyn of Pantygerdinen, the blacksmith and owner of the first iron foundry in the Aberdare area – Tawdd-dŷ y Dyffryn.[12] This Hywel must have lived in the late sixteenth century, the very time when the lament for Glyn Cynon's woods was composed. Another of the poet's forefathers was said to have been directly involved in the deforestation so bitterly lamented by his anonymous poetic predecessor. A version of that story appeared in *Gardd Aberdâr* in 1853.

> There was a great wood of mightly oaks on Craig-y-Bwlch; the grandfather of the reverend Edward Evan dragged them away using his animals.[13]

When the ironworks switched from charcoal to coal, demand for wood as fuel reduced but environmental destruction increased, along with the emission of carbon dioxide which made an early and significant contribution to the modern climate crisis. Between 1844 and 1988 the collieries in the Cynon Valley exported approximately 400 million tons of coal which produced, when burned, almost 1,000 million tons of carbon dioxide – the equivalent of 120 years' emissions from every home in modern Wales.[14] The Welsh industrial revolution had an impact on the whole planet. At the time of writing, coal mining came to an end at the massive opencast site above Merthyr Tydfil, whose name, Ffos-y-frân, belonged to a farm which Edward Evan would have known. At Margam (Port Talbot), where he wooed Ann Henry, the history of iron-making with coal in Wales was ending after three hundred years. Worldwide, though, the burning of fossil fuels continues, with devastating consequences.

The iron and coal industries of the past did not transform only the landscape of Edward Evan's *Blaenau*. Over time they also radically changed the the society, the language and the culture of the land he knew. The former Archdruid Christine James has recounted how the anonymous bard who mourned the devastation of Glyn Cynon's woods was followed in later centuries by other poets who echoed their predecessor's concern with ecological and cultural destruction. One was Idris Davies, who left school aged fourteen and worked underground as a miner for seven years before training to become a teacher.

> In Gwalia, in my Gwalia,
> The vandals out of Hell
> Ransacked and marred for ever
> The wooded hill and dell.[15]

In a deliberate echo of the style and sentiments of the sixteenth century poem, Pennar Davies, who was born not far from Ton Coch and the site of Hywel Gwyn's Dyffryn forge,[16] lamented the loss of nature, the Welsh language and a way of life in the Cynon Valley – the life of the *gwerin*, Edward Evan's people. His poem is as bitter in its way as the original and like his mediaeval predecessor Davies blames the foreigner – or in this case his language and values.

Trist wyf innau am a fu	*Sad am I for what's become*
I'r coed oddeutu'r afon,	*Of the woods beside the river,*
Ac nid i'r coed un unig 'chwaith:	*And not just for the woods, I mourn*
Fe faeddwyd iaith Glyn Cynon –	*The language of Glyn Cynon –*

Iaith a gwerin erbyn hyn: *The language and the people,*
Daeth chwyn diwylliant estron, *Weeds of a foreign culture,*
Castiau gwasaidd, moesau crach *Servile behaviour, morals mean*
A sothach yn yr afon. [17]   *And rubbish in the river.*

It's a striking fact that as long ago as 1767, Edward Evan, whose poems often reflected on moral questions, was also concerned about the fate of the Welsh language and its poetry. In his introduction to the verse translation of Ecclesiastes (*Llyfr y Pregethwr*), he made this plea to the readers.

> Receive this piece of Welsh poetry, in its last age – and before it is buried and completely forgotten among the people of Wales.[18]

His twentieth century successor, the poet Harri Webb, was a librarian in Merthyr and Mountain Ash who learned Welsh as an adult. He felt the loss of the Welsh language as acutely as he did the 'plundering to exhaustion' of the land.

> They called us, shyly at first, those words
> That were and were not ours.
> They whispered in names whose meaning
> We did not know, a strange murmur
> Like leaves in a light wind you hardly feel
> Stirring the autumn wood of memories
> That were and were not ours.[19]

In the Dyffryn Woods below Ton Coch stands the circle of stones where Princess Elizabeth, the future queen, was inaugurated into republican Iolo Morganwg's Gorsedd during the National Eisteddfod of 1946.[20] Despite the irony of that event, it's an atmospheric place which might serve as a fitting memorial to Iolo's mentor.[21] In 1790 Edward Evan reported on the state of the woods to his master, Thomas Bruce in Bath. Two hundred years later, as the coal mines closed in the wake of the great strike of 1984, Edward's bardic successor Harri Webb described the Dyffryn trees standing 'in perfect equipoise' about 'the mean and straggling town'.

> Last of the spreading woods of Cynon
> Our nameless poet loved and sung,
> Calling a curse on their despoilers,
> The men of iron heart and tongue,

In stillness at the end of autumn
They wait to see the doom fulfilled,
The final winter of the townships
When the last pithead wheels are stilled.[22]

In the years since the collieries closed, woods have recolonised the Cynon valley, but Harri Webb's poem remains a moving reflection on history and place. Ned Thomas wrote of remembering, not in an 'antiquarian' way, but 'remembering who you are, where you come from, what has happened to you and your people'. And geography is the root of this process. 'The landscape takes on a different quality if you are one of those who remembers. The scenery is then never separate from the history of the place, from the feeling for the lives that have been lived there'.[23]

Eighty years ago, the only memento of Edward Evan that R. T. Jenkins could find in Aberdare was in the old St John's churchyard.

> In the lovely graveyard of the old church, surrounded by trees, with daffodils shining in the grass, lies the gravestone of Edward Evan and his family. But should not something else be set up somewhere to remind the people of Aberdare of the good man who was such an 'ornament' of the town?[24]

The gravestone, moved many years ago, can no longer be found, but the Dyffryn woods, the stones from his cottage on the golf course, the Garth Mountain, these remain as lasting reminders in the landscape of the world of Edward Evan. And in 2024 a Blue Plaque was unveiled on the Clubhouse at Mountain Ash golf course thanks to the efforts of the Cynon Valley History Society. It reads (in Welsh and English), 'Edward Evan, 1716-1798, Author, Bard and Dissenting Minister lived here at Ton Coch Farm'.

Tra'm calon yn ergydio,	*As long as my heart's beating,*
A'r cof mewn hwyl i gofio,	*And memory is working,*
Nis gallaf byth tra phery'm gwa'd	*While life still courses in my veins,*
Rhoi tŷ fy nhad yn angho'.[25]	*Ton Coch won't be forgotten.*

§

164

[1] Anon. 'Coed Glyn Cynon' ('The woods of Glyn Cynon'), C16, quoted by Christine James, 'Coed Glyn Cynon', in *Cwm Cynon*, ed. Hywel Teifi Edwards (1997). I have drawn heavily on this chapter here.

[2] Nigel Jenkins, 'The Lie of the Land', *Wales Arts Review* (30 January 2014). https://www.walesartsreview.org/the-lie-of-the-land-by-nigel-jenkins/

[3] The same opinion was expressed by my grandfather (born in 1889, writing in 1972).

[4] Jenkin Howell, 'Dyffryn Cynon', in *Y Geninen* (1903), pp. 286-7.

[5] Christine James, 'Coed Glyn Cynon', p.36.

[6] Survey of the Manor of Miskin (1570), in Davies, D. L. & Evans, G. (eds.), *The Land Your Fathers Possessed* (2011), p.20. 'Llowyd Koyd' is Llwydcoed, the forest which covered 700 acres in the area where Edward Evan was born.

[7] J. Barry Davies & John G. Owen, 'The Pentyrch Iron Works', Llantrisant & District Local History Society (2002).

[8] Christine James, 'Coed Glyn Cynon', p.36.

[9] See ditto, note 20, p.59.

[10] Anon. 'Coed Glyn Cynon' (C16). In his English translation, the poet Gwyn Williams translates *Saeson* as 'Saxons', which is the root of the Welsh word. But it gives an archaic feel to the poet's anger, which is directed not against a Germanic tribe who arrived in Britain in the sixth century, but to the English inhabitants of the country by which Wales had been annexed under the Acts of Union. The poet Harri Webb, in his translation, uses the same word for the English – a.k.a. 'the sons of Alice'.

[11] William Linnard, *Welsh Woods and Forests* (1982), p.53ff.

[12] Obituary of Rees (Rhys) Evans, Toncoch, *Y Gwladgarwr* (14 September 1867).

[13] 'Gardd Aberdâr', trans. D. L. Davies, in *Old Aberdare*, vol. 2 (1997), p.40. According to the biography of Rhys Evans, (*Afalau'r Awen* (1874) p.167), it was Edward Evan's great grandfather, Rhys who cut the oaks in the time of Cromwell.

[14] Calculations based on coal production figures in Cynon Valley History Society, *Cynon Coal* (2001), p.273.

[15] Idris Davies, *Gwalia Deserta*, quoted by Christine James in 'Coed Glyn Cynon', p.45.

[16] Jeremy Morgan (note to the author): 'Pennar Davies attended Mountain Ash Grammar School in the old Dyffryn House, undoubtedly the site of the early ironworks.'

[17] Pennar Davies, 'Yr Efrydd o Lyn Cynon', quoted by Christine James in 'Coed Glyn Cynon', p.46.

[18] '*Derbyn hyn o Brydyddiaeth Gymraeg, ar ei hoes ddiweddaf; a chyn ei chladdu mewn Cwbl angof o blith y Cymru.*'

[19] Harri Webb, 'The Old Language', *Collected Poems* (1995), p.60. Webb also translated 'Coed Glyn Cynon', see *ditto*, p.210.

[20] 'Druids raise the ancient and sacred sword above their heads for the ceremony at the National Eisteddfod of Wales at Dyffryn Park. High angle shots of the ceremony in progress. Princess Elizabeth (later Queen Elizabeth II), dressed in ancient robes, is led to the Arch Druid to become a bard, everyone applauds her. M/S [mid-shot]

as the Arch Druid drinks from the "Horn of Plenty". C/U [close-up] individual shots of various druids in the ancient white costume of the calling. C/U of Princess Elizabeth dressed in the robes of a novitiate. Various shots of the ceremony. M/S as a lady-in-waiting adjusts the ancient head-dress for Princess Elizabeth. She walks from the ceremony.' https://www.britishpathe.com/asset/166545

[21] Jeremy Morgan (note to the author): 'The unusual gorsedd circle in Dyffryn Woods was constructed by the second Lord Aberdare for the 1905 Mountain Ash Eisteddfod and is another link to Edward Evan through the Bruce family.'

[22] Harri Webb, 'Dyffryn Woods', *Collected Poems*, p.83.

[23] Ned Thomas, *The Welsh Extremist*, p.64

[24] R. T. Jenkins, *Bardd a'i Gefndir*, Trans. Hon. Soc. Cymmrodorion (1948), p.144.

[25] Rhys Evans, 'The Leaving of Ton Coch' (c.1871), *Afalau'r Awen* p.164.

APPENDIX 1

Some of the owners of Edward Evan's Poetry

Copies of Edward Evan's work in a number of libraries give an indication of the extent of interest in his poetry.

1767 *Llyfr y Pregethwr* (Ecclesiastes)
> The copy inscribed by Evan Evans[1] and later owned by Peter Bailey Williams[2], in the National Library: *NLW: XAC909 (JHD 437/3)*

1804 *Caniadau Moesol a Duwiol* (First Edition)
> The copy presented to Tomos Glyn Cothi[3] by Rhys Evans, in the National Library: *NLW: XAC909 (471/1)*
> The copy in the Salisbury Collection at Cardiff University is incomplete, missing the first six poems. On the last page is written 'Jenkin Jenkin Jenkins His Book'. *Salisbury Collection: 994805623402420*

1816 *Afalau'r Awen* (Second Edition)
> Jane Owens, Minffordd, Llangefni, Anglesey. Author's private collection.
>
> Salisbury Collection, Cardiff University: *Afalau'r Awen* bound with several Welsh theological works of the early nineteenth century, variously printed in Aberystwyth, Swansea, Trefriw and Merthyr. They include two treatises on baptism which suggests that the owner who wrote his name on the flyleaf in 1824, was Enoch Williams, the father of the poet William Williams ('Creuddynfab'). Enoch was a stone mason and a baptist deacon from Creuddyn near Llandudno. His son became the first paid secretary of the National Eisteddfod.[4] On one of the first pages is also written 'John Davies 1828'. *Salisbury Collection: 160969527X*
>
> A copy of *Afalau'r Awen* which belonged to Rev. John Jenkins of Ker-

ry[5] in Montgomeryshire, who added the names of fitting harp tunes to many of the poems (see Chapter 10). Bound with other material, including five poems submitted to the first of the revived National Eisteddfodau, held in Carmarthen in 1819 and organised by Jenkins. These include an elegy for General Thomas Picton, whose memorial dominates the skyline of the town, and whose violent involvement in slavery and torture has recently eclipsed his reputation as a hero of the battle of Waterloo.[6] It was at Carmarthen that Iolo Morganwg succeeded in making his 'druidic' bardic Gorsedd an integral element of the National Eisteddfod. John Kerry's copy of *Afalau'r Awen* was later part of the extensive collection of Sir John Williams (1840-1926), first president of the National Library of Wales.[7] *NLW: XAC909 (530)/W.b.4270*

Another copy in the National Library came into the possession of R. T. Jenkins[8], whose 1947 account of Edward Evan and his background is the best source for the poet's life and work. It was given to him by David Rowland Hughes[9] at the National Eisteddfod at Cardigan in 1942. *NLW: XAC909 (1149).*

1837 *Afalau'r Awen* (Third Edition)
One of several copies of the 1837 edition in the National Library is bound with Y Fêl Gafod and several other works. It belonged to the poet Jonathan Reynolds (Nathan Dyfed). Born in Carmarthenshire, he trained as a wheelwright and worked from 1835 at Merthyr Tydfil, where he was later secretary of the Cymreigyddion Society which met at the White Lion Inn. He won more than a hundred prizes for his poetry and edited a Welsh column for the Merthyr Express. The book was presented to the National Library by his son, the Celtic scholar Llywarch Owain Reynolds of Merthyr Tydfil.[10] *NLW: XPB2245.A5(16)*

Another copy of this edition belonged to the editor and 'litterateur', David Owen (Brutus).[11] It came into the possession of the National Library as part of the Castell Gorfod Collection, started by Joseph Joseph of Brecon and expanded by his grandson, Capt James Buckley of Buckley's Brewery, Llanelli and Castell Gorfod, St Clears. *NLW: Castell Gorfod Amryw –16.*

Copy in Cardiff City Library – Thomas Gething (1804-1889), of Ystradgynlais.

1874 *Afalau'r Awen* (Fourth Edition)
  Meyrick Meyrick [coalminer, b. 1848], Eglwysilan. *Author's private collection.*

  British Library: Llew Owain *(scanned copy available online).*

  Harvard University Library: Purchased from the Fund of Frederick Athearn Lane *(scanned copy available online).*

  Bodleian Library, Oxford: Bob Owen, ('historian, bookworm & genealogist'), Croesor.[12] 'He collected an enormous library which spread to almost every corner of his home'. *601904036*

  Bodleian Library: Rev. Lewis Simons, Curate of Pontypridd, presented in 1917 by Elizabeth Evans of Pen y Graig, Cilfynydd, great granddaughter of Edward Evan. *601904078*

  National Library of Wales: William Jones (1817-c.1901) solicitor of Ty'n-yr-heol, Tonna, Neath. *NLW: Dyb 2009 A 430*

APPENDIX 2

Subscribers to the 1837 edition of Afalau'r Awen, as printed
(See Chapter 19)[1]

Austin, Mr. John, (Lamb)
Arnold, Mr. David, (Gwryd)
Brown, Mr. Henry, Plantation
Charles, Mr. Howell
Davies, Mr. Rhys, Post Office, 2 copies
Davies, Mr. Thomas, Harper
Davies, Mr. Richard, Shopkeeper, Aberdare
David, Mr. William, Abernantygroes
Davies, Mr. Thomas, Carpenter, Dowlais
Davies, Mr. David, Ynysglwyd, 3 copies
Davies,Mr. Evan, Surgeon, Ystrad
Evans, Mr. Evan, Hendre Rees, Llanwonno
Edwards, Mr. Herbert, Shoemaker
Edwards, Mr. Edward, Shoemaker
Evan, Mr. John, (Cymmar) Ystrad
Evans, Mr. Evan, Timber Merchant
Edwards, Mr. Thomas, Graig Cottage
Edwards, Mr. Edward
Evans, Mr. Thomas
Evans, Mr. Lancelot, Shopkeeper
Evans, Mr. Samuel, Clerk, 4 copies
Edward, Mr. Evan, Machine, Dowlais
Evan, Mr. Thomas, Shopkeeper
Evans, Mr. Evan, Garthfach
Evans, Mr. Evan, Caerphilly
Evans, Rev. Owen, Cefncoedycymmar
Francis, Mr. Richard, Aber
Felton, Mr. John

Fothergill, Rowland, Esq. 2 copies
Gilbert, Mr. John, Shopkeeper
Griffith, Mr. Titus,
Gunter, Mr. Samuel, Smith
Griffiths, Mr. David, Merthyr
Griffiths, Mr. Evan, Shopkeeper, Aberdare
Gibbs, Mr. John
Harries, Mr. Rees, Cefnygynnen
Howell, Mr. William, Patriot, Merthyr
Hezekiah, Mr. ----
Hawkins, Mrs. Dinah, White Lion
James, Mr. John Thomas
Jones, Mr. Thomas, Tailor
James, Mr. Christopher
Jones, Mr. Williams, Storehouse, Aberdare
Jones, Mr. George, Carpenter, Aberdare
Jones, Mr. Robert, Do.
Jenkins, Mr. John, Cefnglas
James, Mr. Thomas, Mason
Jenkins, Mr. Jenkin, Penyrheol
John, Mr. Griffith, Miner, Hirwaun
Jones, Mr. William, High Street, Merthyr
Jones, Mr. John, Druggist, Aberdare
Jones, Rev. John, Hirwaun[2]
John, Mr. David, Mountain Ash
Jones, Mr. Walter, Carnycrochan
Jenkins, Mr. John
Jones, Mr. Richard, Rising Sun
Jones, Mr. Richard, Smith
Jones, Mr. William, Britannia
Jenkins, Mr. Daniel, White Hart
James, Mr. David
Jones, Mr. William, Gardener
Jones, Mr. James, Dowlais
Jones, Mr. John, Rolling Mill
Jones, Mr. Lewellyn, Ystrad
James, Mr. William, Tai'r Heol
Jones, Mr. Thomas, Glynmaesmafan
Jones, Mr. William, Eglwysfabon
Jones, Mr. Thomas, Miller, Aber

Jones, Mr. William, Bedwas
Jenkins, Mr. Thomas, Parrot, Caerphilly
Jones, Mr. William, Ynyscymmar
James, Rev. John, Gellionen
Jones, Mr. Jenkin, Glyncastell
Jenkin, Mr. John
John, Rev. David, Merthyr[3]
Lewellyn, Mr. David, Hirwaun
Lewis, Mr. Lewellyn, Glyncoli
Lewis, Mr. John, Gethin
Lewis, Mr. James
Lewellyn, Mr. John, Pencelli, Ystrad
Loyd, Mr. Charles, Bedwas
Loyd, Mr. Richard, Passit
Miles, Mr. Rees, Smith
Miles, Mr. William, Do.
Morgan, Mr. Thomas, Shopkeeper, Aberdare
Maybery, Rev. C. Penderin
Morgan, Mr. William, Pontprenllwyd
Morgan, Mr. Morgan, Abercwmboy-isaf
Morgan, Mr. William, Llanharen
Morgan, Mr. Lewis, Havod
Morgan, Rev. T. Lann
Morgan, Mr. Walter, Butcher
Morgan, Mr. Lewis, Graig
Miller, Mr. Thomas, Troedyrhiw
Mason, Mr. Richard
Newell, Mr. Adam, Shopkeeper
Pryce, J. B. and W. B. Knight, Esqrs, 5 copies
Prosser, Mr. John, Star Inn, Aberdare
Price, Mr. Rees, Llwydcoed
Phillip, Mr. Gwylim, Storehouse
Phillip, Mr. Daniel, Nantgarw
Perod, Mrs. Mary Ann, Gelligaer
Perod, Mr. George, Gelligaer
Richards, Mrs. Margaret, Crown, 2 copies
Rosser, Mr. David, Shopkeeper, Merthyr
Rees, Mr. Edmund, Innkeeper
Rees, Mr. John *(Ab Evan)*
Rosser, Mr. David, Merthyr

Richard, Mr. William David, Carpenter
Rees, Mr. John, Cefndon
Rees, Mr. Thomas, Miner, Llwydcoed
Richards, Mr. Eustace, Glazier
Richards, Mr. David, Britannia
Rees, Mr. Evan
Richards, Mr. Thomas, Machine
Richards, Mr. John
Rees, Mr. John
Roberts, Mr. Robert, Canal Warehouse
Rees, Mr. Thomas, Collier, Dowlais
Rees, Rev. Thomas, Blaengwrach
Rees, R. Esqr. Gelligron
Rees, Mr. Morgan, Penderin
Rees, Mrs. Mary, Do.
Rees, Mr. Leyson, D.
Scale, Henry, Esqr.
Thomas, William, Esqr. Court
Thomas, Mr. Thomas, Dowlais
Thomas, Mrs. Court
Thomas, Miss Elizabeth, Do.
Thomas, Mr. Samuel R. Do.
Thomas, Mr. Richard R. Do.
Treharne, Mrs. Ann, Boot Inn, Merthyr
Thomas, Rev. E. P., Curate, Aberdare
Thomas, Mr. Evan Robert, Ystrad
Thomas, Mr. Thomas, Cefnpennar
Thomas, Mr. Thomas, Shoemaker
Thomas, Mr. Nicholas, Serjeant
Thomas, Mr. William, Tŷ'r Arlwydd
Thomas, Mr. John *(Ieuan Ddu)* 5 copies
Thomas, Mr. Edward, Pontyrun
Thomas, Mr. Robert, Harp
Thomas, Mr. Thomas, Agent, Dowlais
Thomas, Mrs. Anne, Aber
Vaughan, Mr. Benjamin
Williams, Mr. Morgan, Penyrheol
Williams, Mr. Thomas, Storehouse, Merthyr
Williams, Mr. William, Watchmaker, Merthyr
Williams, Mr. David, Shoemaker

Williams, Mr. William, Iron Bridge
Williams, Mr. Rees, Mountain Ash
Williams, Mr. William, Do.
William, Mr. David, Pedrhiwgwibir[4]
Williams, Mr. Morgan, Hirwaun
Watkins, Mr. John, Do.
Williams, Mr. William, Ironmonger
Williams, Mr. Morgan, Wellington
Williams, Mr. William, Cyfarthfa
Watkin, Mr. David, Caerphilly
Wayne, Mather, Esqr. Pontypandy
Williams, Mr. William, Miner[5]
Williams, Mr. Robert
Williams, Mr. William, Agent, Dowlais
Williams, Mr. David, Ynysgou[6]
Williams, Rev. Richard, Henfig[7]
Williams, Mr. Thomas, Penheolfawr
Williams, Mr. Roger, Nantgarw
Williams, E. M. Esqr. Garth Hall
Williams, Mr. Lewis, Gellionen
Williams, Mr. Edward, Swan, Merthyr, 30 copies
Williams, Thomas, Esqr. Ysgyborfawr

---

[1] The addresses show how far across south Wales the book was distributed
[2] Rev. John Jones, Old Meeting House, Trecynon, Aberdare (also known as 'the Old Meeting House on Hirwaun')
[3] Father of David John, Chartist
[4] Penrhiwgwibir - Penrhiwceiber?
[5] William Williams ('Carw Coch')
[6] Ynysgau?
[7] Kenfig?

ACKNOWLEDGEMENTS

I am indebted to my aunt Mary Green (born Mary Kingsbury), whose family research into the descendants of Edward Evan laid much of the groundwork for my own exploration of the earlier history. She also gave me many useful and valuable books, including her copy of *Afalau'r Awen*.

I am very grateful to Prof. Mary-Ann Constantine for her constant ecouragement, support and guidance.

My thanks go to the Cynon Valley History Society for agreeing to publish the book. Its secretary Jeremy Morgan in particular supported and encouraged me, and gave valuable feedback on the text. Thanks also to David L. Davies for his encouragement.

Ann Grove-White prepared the book for the printers. I could not have managed without her help.

Elinor Bennett and Rhodri Davies shared with me their expertise and knowledge of the harp.

Dewi Jones, weaver at the National Museum, St Fagans, patiently demonstrated the use of the type of handloom on which Edward Evan worked as a boy.

Geoff Matthews, former chairman of Mountain Ash Golf Club helped me research the history of Ton Coch farm. Hywel Davies helped me find the site of Edward Evan's home.

Eric Jones shared his experience as last minister at the Hen Dŷ Cwrdd, Aberdare. I would also like to thank Christine Moore of Addoldai Cymru, custodians of the Old Meeting House, for permission to use the cover illustration by Grace Payne and Lexi Richards, Ysgol Gyfun Gymraeg Rhydywaun.

Thanks to the following for sharing their knowledge and expertise: Prof. E. Wyn James of Cardiff University; Dr Gruffudd Antur of the Centre for Advanced Welsh & Celtic Studies; Roy Saer, formerly of the National

175

Museum, St Fagans; Andrew Hawke, Geiriadur Prifysgol Cymru.

Hywel Matthews of Aberdare Library was always helpful. I am also grateful to the staff of the following: Bodleian Library; British Library; Cambridge University Library; Cardiff Central Library; Cardiff University Library, Special Collections; Ceredigion Archives; Glamorgan Archives; Merthyr Tydfil Library; National Library of Wales. Thanks also to Blaenau Gwent Heritage Forum and Llantrisant and District Local History Society.

Christine Willison and Mike Joseph kept me going during long weeks of writing in the west.

Finally, thanks to Gail for supporting me throughout the research and writing.

INDEX

Cae'rlan (farm, a.k.a. Cae'r Lan; 63, 85-6, 89
Calvinism 96-100
Canwyll y Cymry (See Prichard, Rhys)
Carmarthen Dissenting Academy 98-100
Cefnpennar 4, 30, 38, 52
Cefnpennar Isaf (farm, home of Edward Evan) 74, 77-8, 81
Celticism 108, 118
Charles I 113-114
Charles, Rev. Philip (Cefncoed y Cymmer) 89
Charles, Thomas (Bala) 37
Chartism & Chartists 1-2, 5, 11-12, 19, 95, 106, 130-6
Coed Glyn Cynon (poem) 158-162
Collieries (Cynon valley) 152, 162
Cuckoo 128
Cwm-y-glo (Dissenting meeting house) 94-5
Davies, Evan ('Myfyr Morganwg') 120
Davies, Rev. Henry 51, 63,
Davies, Idris (poet) 162
Davies, Pennar (poet) 162-3
Davies, Rhodri (harpist) 40
Davies, Rev. Samuel 99
Dociar, Gwenllian 5, 11
Druids & Druidism 2, 5-12, 69, 107-112, 125, 136
Dyffryn Estate (a.k.a. Duffryn, Mountain Ash) 5, 29, 52, 77-8, 80-2, 90 (note), 136, 147, 149, 152, 154-6
Ecclesiastes ('Llyfr y Pregethwr') 14, 63, 67-8, 71 (note), 85, 98, 102 (note)
Eisteddfod (Mountain Ash, 1946) 12 (note), 163
Elizabeth, Princess (Elizabeth II) 12 (note), 163
Evans, Edward ('Cynfab', son of Edward Evan) 72, 150-1
Evans, Evan ('Brydydd Hir') 140
Evans, Evan ('Ieuan Fardd') 119
Evans, Mary (granddaughter of Edward Evan), see Kingsbury, Mary
Evans, Rev. Owen (Unitarian minister, Cefncoed) 134
Evans, Rhys (Ton Coch, a.k.a. Rees, son of Edward Evan) 8, 31, 70 (note), 72, 91 (note), 106, 109, 116 (note), 120, 133, 136, 138-9, 142, 145, 147-52
Evans, Rhys (Penygraig, Llanfabon, grandson of Edward Evan) 145, 158
Evans, Theophilus 51, 54 (notes), 95
Evans, Rev. Thomas ('Tomos Glyn Cothi', Unitarian minister, Aberdare) 106, 109, 134, 142
Evans, Thomas (Cyfarthfa) 132
Fêl Gafod, Y (Lewis Hopkin) 53 (notes), 59 (note), 66-7, 70 (note), 143
Fforchaman (farm) 17, 24, 154-7
Finch, Catrin (harpist) 33
Fothergill, Rowland (ironmaster) 80
Freak shows 57

Garth Mountain, Pentyrch 7-8, 11, 28-9, 33, 108-111, 160

Gentleman's Magazine, The 9, 21, 24, 30, 41, 58

George III 57, 86, 87, 108

Gibbon, Thomas Jenkin (Fforchaman) 17, 32, 155

Glorious Revolution (1688) 94, 112-3

Gododdin, Y 5, 10-11, 90 (note), 117-122

Gorsedd of Bards 5, 8-9, 11, 28, 104, 107-12

Grammarians, Glamorgan (poets) 62-70, 118

Griffith, Robert (historian of harp) 33, 40,

Gwladgarwr, Y (newspaper) 6 (note), 13 (note), 42, 44 (note)

Hardy, Thomas (London Corresponding Society) 105, 115 (note)

Harp 33-44, 63, 65, 74

Harp, horsehair ('telyn rawn') 39-40

Heaney, Seamus 118

Hen Dŷ Cwrdd Trecynon (see Old Meeting House, Aberdare)

Hendre Ifan Goch (Cymmer) 21, 25 (note), 47, 53 (note), 56, 61-3, 77, 85, 89

Hengwrt (Dolgellau) 121, 125

Hirwaun (ironworks) 121, 135

Hopcyn, Dafydd (poet) 62

Hopcyn, Wil (poet) 47

Hopkin, Hopkin ('Hopcyn Bach', son of Lewis Hopkin) 56-9,

Hopkin, Lewis (poet) 14, 21, 45-7, 52, 56-9, 61-9, 74, 77, 85-6, 89, 95, 98, 101

Horsley, Samuel (Bishop of St Davids) 101

Howell, William (Patriot Inn, Merthyr) 133

Hywel Gwyn y Gôf' (Pantygerdinen) 5, 77, 161-2

Ibbetson, J.C. (painter) 24, 31

Iolo Morganwg (See Williams, Edward)

James, Christopher (Chartist, Merthyr) 133

Jenkins, Rev. Jenkin (Carmarthen Academy) 99

Jenkins, Rev. John (Kerry) 41

John, David (Merthyr Chartist; son of Rev. David John) 130-1, 134

John, Rev. David (Unitarian minister, Twynyrodyn) 134

Jones a'i mab (printers, Aberdare) 145

Jones, Edmund ('The Old Prophet') 99-100, 104

Jones, Edward (harpist, 'The King's Bard') 37

Jones, Rev. Eric (Hen Dŷ Cwrdd, Aberdare) 92-4, 98

Jones, Rev. John (Chartist; Unitarian minister, Aberdare) 134, 151

Jones, John (Dyffryn Estate) 81 (and note)

Jones, Rev. Morgan (Cymmer) 100

Jones, Owen ('Owain Myfyr') 119

Jones, Theophilus 116 (note), 119-121, 125

Kingsbury, Jenkin (Fforchaman, husband of Mary Evans), 18, 154

Kingsbury, Mary (Fforchaman, granddaughter of Edward Evan) 18, 145, 156

Knight, Rev. William ('Gwilym o Fargam', Dean of Llandaff) 149

Leland, John 160

Lewis, John (Gethin) 132
Lewis, William (Cae'rlan) (brother of Lewis Hopkin) 86
London Corresponding Society 105
Lord, Colonel Arthur (land owner) 155
Lord, Major Hugh (land owner) 155
Llantrisant 46, 64, 79
Llewelyn, Mary (wife of Edward Evan) 51-2, 68, 72
Llwydcoed 17-18, 28, 45, 61
Llyfr y Pregethwr, see Ecclesiastes
Mabsant (festival) 32, 63
Matthews family (Aberaman) 121, 155
Maybery, Rev. Charles (magistrate, Penderyn) 135
Meistersinger, Die (opera, Richard Wagner) 64-6
Merrick, Rhys 28, 160
Methodism 30, 36-8, 97, 100
Mills 18-19, 30, 45, 61, 62, 79
Mining deaths (Mountain Ash) 152
Montgomery, James (Sheffield) 105-6,
Morgan, Rhys (poet) 31, 34, 47, 49, 62, 63, 69, 74
Morgan, Siencyn (poet) 64,
Morgan, Rev. Thomas (Blaengwrach) 99
Morris, Lewis 119
Morus (Morys), Huw ('Eos Ceiriog', poet) 48, 67
Mountain Ash Golf Course 3, 164
Mountain Ash Inn 148
Nicolas, Dafydd (poet) 34, 38, 43 (note), 47, 53 (note), 62-9
Normanby, Marquis (Home Secretary) 131
Old Meeting House, Trecynon, Aberdare 76, 83, 89, 90, 92-101
'Old Vicar' ('yr Hen Ficer'), see Prichard, Rhys
Owen family (Minffordd, Anglesey) 143
Pantygerdinen (farm) 5, 77
Paradise Lost (Coll Gwynfa) 150
Penderyn 37, 51-2, 72
Penygraig (farm, Llanfabon) 158
Penyrallt (a.k.a. Tir Ifan Siôn Rhys, farm, Llwydcoed) 17, 22, 24
Picton, General Thomas 43 (note)
Pont y tŷ pridd (bridge) 31-2, 67, 79
Powell, Evan (printer, Carmarthen) 140
Powell, Thomas (coal owner) 154
Presbyterians 96-7, 100, 102 (note)
Presbyterian Fund Board 99
Price, Griffith (Penllergaer) 87-8, 122
Price, Rees (Ty'n Ton, Bettws; father of Richard Price) 61, 63
Price, Dr. Richard (Son of Rees; Unitarian & Radical), 62, 88, 101, 112, 122
Price, Rev. Thomas ('Carnhuanawc') 34-6, 40

William, Thomas (Cae'rlan; uncle of Lewis Hopkin) 85-6, 89
Williams, Rev. David 99
Williams, Edward (Pont-y-Tŷ Pridd) 31
Williams, Edward ('Iolo Morganwg') 5, 6 (note), 7-12, 30, 33-4, 38-40, 45-6, 51, 57, 63-4, 67-70, 74, 80, 90, 100-101, 105-106, 107-112, 115-116 (notes), 120, 123-5, 126 (note), 150
Williams, E. M., Garth Hall (magistrate, Merthyr) 135
Williams, Margaret (Sychbant) 88
Williams, Maria Jane (*Ancient Airs of Gwent & Glamorgan*) 41-2, 43 (note)
Williams, Mary (wife of Rhys Evans, Ton Coch) 150
Williams, Morgan (Chartist, Merthyr) 1, 130-6
Williams, Morgan (grandfather of Morgan Williams, Chartist) 19, 132
Williams, Pegi (Blaenau Gwent) 88
Williams, Rev. Peter Bailey (Llanrug) 140
Williams, William ('Y Carw Coch') 133
Williams, William (Cyfarthfa, father of Morgan) 132
Williams, William (Pantycelyn) 139-141
Williams, William (printer, Merthyr Tydfil) 142-4
Winter, Rev. Charles (Hengoed) 100
Woods (Cynon Valley) 29-30, 81-2, 158-164